BEYOND THE
DISEASE MODEL
OF MENTAL DISORDERS

BEYOND THE DISEASE MODEL OF MENTAL DISORDERS

Donald J. Kiesler

PRAEGER

Westport, Connecticut
London

Library of Congress Cataloging-in-Publication Data

Kiesler, Donald J.
    Beyond the disease model of mental disorders / Donald J. Kiesler.
       p.   cm.
    Includes bibliographical references and indexes.
    ISBN 0–275–96570–8 (alk. paper)
    1. Mental illness—Etiology.   I. Title.
  RC454.4.K52   1999
  616.89'071—dc21   98–47765

British Library Cataloguing in Publication Data is available.

Library of Congress Catalog Card Number: 98–47765
ISBN: 0–275–96570–8

First published in 1999

Praeger Publishers, 88 Post Road West, Westport, CT 06881
An imprint of Greenwood Publishing Group, Inc.

Printed in the United States of America

The paper used in this book complies with the
Permanent Paper Standard issued by the National
Information Standards Organization (Z39.48–1984).

10   9   8   7   6   5   4   3   2   1

Copyright Acknowledgments

The author and publisher gratefully acknowledge permission for the use of the following material:

P. J. Mrazek and R. J. Haggerty, eds. 1994. *Reducing Risks for Mental Disorders: Frontiers
for Preventive Intervention Research*, pp. 127–313. Used by permission of National Academy Press.

Contents

Preface

I am a clinical psychologist. The guiding training model for clinical psychology is called "scientist–practitioner" which demands that any Ph.D. clinical psychologist must be trained both as a scientist and practitioner. Since receiving my Ph.D., I have anchored myself in university departments of psychology where I have taught mostly graduate level psychology courses; conducted a long-range program of empirical research in personality, psychopathology, and psychotherapy; supervised the diagnostic and clinical work of clinical psychology graduate student trainees; and conducted my own part-time practice of psychotherapy. On two separate occasions I directed a doctoral training program in clinical psychology.

For several decades I have taught two graduate level courses that are required of most clinical psychology graduate students: psychopathology (the science of mental disorders) and personality (theory and research). Somewhere near the mid-1980s, in the process of teaching these two courses, it became increasingly apparent that some remarkable new discoveries and perspectives were making an appearance, although initially their appearance was quite subtle and gradual. First, within both personality and psychopathology, behavioral genetic findings were establishing robustly and incontrovertibly that both personality traits and mental disorders were to a substantial degree inherited. Second, personality, social, and general psychological research was establishing that radical environmentalism, which glorified the power of external situations, was no longer tenable. Instead, a person's perception of situations was the crucial determinant of behavior, and behavior could be best explained from an "interactionist" framework that assigned important influence to both person and situation factors. Third, research within psychology, including my own long-standing research into interpersonal personality, psychopathology, and psychotherapy (Kiesler, 1996), was moving steadily to the conclusion that the interaction of which we speak was a very dynamic one; namely, that people interpret, choose, and transact to change their situations and relationships with other people. Fourth, personality research was establishing the validity and importance of five (to seven) stable "higher-order" human traits that promised to integrate not only empirical research in personality, but also empirical efforts to understand the relationship between personality and mental disorders. Fifth, behavioral genetics had fairly robustly resolved the long-standing "nature–nurture" controversy with its compelling evidence that each contributes approximately equivalently to human personality and to various mental disorders.

Also during the 1980s, a new area of "risk research" (developmental psychopathology) had begun to identify important vulnerability and protective factors associated with development of various mental disorders. Gradually, seminal new theories (explanatory models) of mental disorders began to appear, advocating that mental disorders result from an interaction between predisposing genetic and/or environmental factors (diatheses) and precipitating stressful life events. Other similarly multicausal theories directly included biological, psychological, and sociocultural vulnerability and protective factors in their attempts to understand and explain particular mental disorders. A revolutionary shift was occurring: Multicausal biopsychosocial theories had begun to arrive.

In line with these developments, I revised both my psychopathology and personality courses, increasingly organizing my coverage around a multicausal biopsychosocial perspective. Subsequently I began to notice that isolated undergraduate and graduate textbooks started to pay lip service to biopsychosocial factors and that research chapters began to report some biopsychosocial research and findings. For the most part, however, psychopathology texts in psychiatry, psychology, sociology, psychiatric nursing, and the like continued their respective traditional monocausal emphases and perspectives.

It is time for a radical change. For the first time, it is possible for the mental health field and its respective scientific disciplines to converge and integrate their efforts under an identical theoretical umbrella. This multicausal biopsychosocial perspective demands that any valid theory of a mental disorder include a matrix of (hereditarily transmitted) biological as well as psychological and sociocultural causal factors.

This multicausal biopsychosocial perspective also demands that the respective mental health sciences increase the number of collaborative attempts that permit concurrent measurements of this wide matrix of multicausal factors. While these newly formulated multidisciplinary research efforts are vital, it nevertheless remains important for the disciplines to continue research efforts guided by their respective disciplines. In fact, the field of psychopathology arrived at the multicausal biopsychosocial perspective only through the competitive efforts and findings of researchers within the separate disciplines. Future optimal progress requires development of both separate and multidisciplinary research projects.

It gradually became apparent to me that opposing forces found within psychiatry, and reflected prominently in the popular media, were making it difficult for the mental health field and the public at large to grasp and embrace this new direction and emphasis. Biological psychiatry recently has enjoyed some of its greatest successes. Genetic researchers have clearly established that mental disorders are inherited; that some mental disorders seem to be associated with identifiable and measurable biochemical and neuroanatomical abnormalities; and that many could be treated effectively with medications that target specific biochemical imbalances found at neuronal synapses in the brain. Another success was that the psychiatric classification of mental disorders was revised substantially in more scientific directions that emphasized the importance of reliable diagnostic decisions.

As a field, psychiatry was rediscovering the scientific method and its roots in medical science. In understandable overreaction, psychiatry departments throughout the county purged previously predominant psychoanalytic, psychosocial, and cultural psychiatrists from their training programs. As a discipline, psychiatry returned with a vengeance to its earlier biomedical model of mental disorders. This model, far from including or emphasizing multiple causal factors, asserts that the primary determinants of mental disorder are inherited biological abnormalities. Its war cry is that mental disorders are diseases just like medical diseases (Andreasen, 1984; Torrey, 1997).

The major task of this book is a detailed examination of the evidence for this currently heralded biomedical or disease model of mental disorders. In pursuing this task, the intent is not to malign biological–medical approaches, but to help bring them up to state-of-the-science form, in which they can be expanded to include powerful psychological and sociocultural factors.

Other psychopathology disciplines, psychology and sociology in particular, have been similarly negligent in highlighting and emphasizing the multicausal biopsychosocial perspective. This book also examines the evidence that invalidates the monocausal environmental and cultural models so prominent within these disciplines.

My major focus, however, is on refutation of the biomedical (disease) model. This model permeates much of present-day psychiatry
and present-day American society. Unquestionably, the "brain disease"
bias permeates newspaper, magazine, and TV coverage and analysis
of mental disorders. The biomedical bias also feeds the economic interests of American drug conglomerates that advocate, support, and
fund biomedical perspectives and research (Breggin, 1991; Peele, 1989).

In contrast, the scientific evidence is clear. Biomedical explanations
alone are inadequate. Indisputable findings from modern behavioral
genetics demonstrate that most complex human behaviors have a substantial genetic component. Accordingly, most, if not all, mental disorders have a substantial genetic component. However, the same
genetic findings demonstrate that most complex human behaviors,
including mental disorders, have substantial environmental components. The unavoidable conclusion is that most, if not all, mental disorders have multiple causes: an array of hereditarily transmitted
biological excesses or deficiencies and environmentally transacted
cognitive and emotional experiences.

If this is the case (and the scientific evidence is overwhelming that it is),
then *mental disorders are not diseases caused predominantly by biological brain
abnormalities*, as the biomedical model asserts. Biological may be contributing (in some cases even necessary) causes to most, if not all, mental
disorders. Yet they are far from being the predominant or only cause.

Multicausal theories, necessitated by current scientific evidence,
postulate a set of biological, psychological, and sociocultural causal
factors to explain particular mental disorders. The fundamental question for the new millennium is the following: *Which set of biological,
psychological, and sociological factors combine to what degree and in interaction with which stressful and protective events, to explain eventual development of particular mental disorders?* Nature does not easily reveal its
secrets. Optimal scientific explanation seeks maximum simplicity, but
without distorting the real complexity of actual human events.

I will show that overwhelming evidence demands this paradigm
shift within psychopathology. The challenges offered by the new
multicausal biopsychosocial perspective are considerable. What is required of us as scientists and as humans is that we first shift our ways
of thinking and talking, and then get on with the task. Before we can
move vigorously in this new direction, we must abandon our old
ways—namely, any approach that exclusively concentrates on a single
domain of causal factors for mental disorders. But first and foremost,
we must quit parroting the deceptively simple and soothing slogans
of the disease model.

I have written this book for interested lay persons and media specialists as well as for mental health scientists, researchers, and practitioners. I hope that my book speeds along the newly developing conceptual currents. My fervent desire is that each of you will be convinced that any valid explanation of mental disorder has to include *bio*logical, *psycho*logical, and *socio*cultural multicausal roots.

REFERENCES

Andreasen, N. C. (1984). *The broken brain: The biological revolution in psychiatry.* New York: Harper & Row.

Breggin, P. (1991). *Toxic psychiatry: Psychiatry's assault on the brain with drugs, electroshock, biochemical diagnoses, and genetic theories.* New York: St. Martin's Press.

Kiesler, D. J. (1996). *Contemporary interpersonal theory and research: Personality, psychopathology, and psychotherapy.* New York: Wiley.

Peele, S. (1989). *Diseasing of America: Addiction treatment out of control.* Lexington, MA: Lexington Books.

Torrey, E. F. (1997). *Out of the shadows: Confronting America's mental illness crisis.* New York: Wiley.

Part I

What Causes Mental Disorders? The Biomedical Answer

Chapter 1

Understanding Mental Disorders: Definitions and Causes

In contemporary society it's difficult not to run into at least some examples of "strange," sometimes "weird," or otherwise noticeable deviant human behaviors—patterns of human activity most frequently referred to as "mental disorders." One historically unique outcome of pervasive modern media and communication is that these behaviors, even the very extreme versions, are becoming more and more commonplace and familiar, and perhaps, less noticeable.

Increasingly, prominent members of our society who have experienced various mental disorders are courageously stepping forward with their personal revelations. Country music singer Naomi Judd, Heisman trophy winner Earl Campbell, and television series actor Vince Van Patten have admitted to bouts with panic disorder. Individuals as varied as actor Rod Steiger, author William Styron, army general's wife Alma Powell, and politicians Thomas Eagleton and Lawton Chiles have declared their backgrounds of unipolar depression. Media mogul Ted Turner, psychologist Kay Jamison, politician's wife Kitty Dukakis, and actress Patty Duke have disclosed their experiences of bipolar mood disorder. TV and radio host Howard Stern and TV actress Roseanne have admitted to episodes of obsessive–compulsive disorder. These are but a few of the valiant individuals who are breaking down barriers and refuting stereotypes.

WHAT IS MENTAL DISORDER?

In the United States, the authoritative source for description and classification of mental disorders—such as panic disorder, unipolar depression, bipolar mood disorder, and obsessive–compulsive disorder—is the *Diagnostic and Statistical Manual of Mental Disorders, Fourth Edition (DSM-IV)*, assembled and published by the American Psychiatric Association (1994). In much of the remainder of the world, the second authoritative source is the *International Classification of Diseases, 10th Revision (ICD-10)* assembled and published by the World Health Organization (1992).

Over the years various attempts from divergent viewpoints have pursued an universally accepted definition of "mental disorder" or "abnormal behavior." It has been suggested that mental disorders are no more nor less than medical diseases, resulting from physiological abnormalities in the brain. Also suggested is the notion that abnormal behaviors represent faulty or inadequate learnings, deriving from unfortunate reinforcements by family and other societal members or reflecting problems in the way an individual processes information. Or abnormal behaviors are those that occur very infrequently within the population and fall statistically at one or the other (or both) extremes of a normal "bell-shaped" distribution. Or mental disorders are merely labels assigned by society to behaviors that it considers undesirable and to actions that violate a society's cultural values and norms. Or mental disorders are the result of cumulative societal oppression in the forms of poverty, discrimination, lack of family cohesion, and other deprivations experienced by the unlucky members found at the bottom of societal organization. Each definition has its staunch advocates. Hot and sometimes bitter debates occur over which definition is correct and "true." Indeed, controversies about the concept of mental disorder produce some of the most heated disputes in the mental health field.

These definitional controversies are not likely to be resolved in the near future. Definitions do not arise randomly, but from one's particular theory or perspective on mental disorders. Physiological, biochemical, psychoanalytic, behavioral, and other theories attempt to explain the causes and specify the underlying mechanisms of various mental disorders. Any serious movement toward definitional resolution would require preliminary progress toward integration of these various theoretical explanations.

Whatever DSM mental disorders are, they can produce dramatic effects on every area of human functioning. *Thoughts* (beliefs, attitudes, and expectations) can be distorted, irrational, and unreal, in extreme instances occurring in the form of bizarre delusions (e.g., of grandeur or persecution). *Perceptions* may become clouded during an episode of delirium or may represent fantasized auditory and other hallucinations (e.g., voices that converse with one another and condemn one's whole existence). Maladaptive *overt behavior* can assume many different patterns, including extreme catatonic immobility or posturing, grossly inappropriate activity (e.g., public masturbation or physical dishevelment), or simply a rigidity in personality style or interpersonal behavior. *Emotions* can assume painful outcomes such as severe depression and a hopeless mood, recurring unexpected panic attacks, or a continuous preoccupation with impending doom. At the opposite pole, periodic episodes of extreme euphoria, grandiosity, and expansiveness may lead the person to engage in fanciful but financially and interpersonally disastrous behaviors.

My purposes with this volume can be adequately served by arbitrary adoption of the definition of mental disorder that is provided in the DSM-IV (1994, p. xxi). A mental disorder is a significant psychological syndrome or behavioral pattern that occurs within a person and that is accompanied by (a) distress (as reported by the person), (b) disability in an important area of functioning, or (c) considerable risk of death, pain, disability, or loss of freedom—any one or all are considered to be an expression of a behavioral, psychological, or biological dysfunction in the person.

Besides absence of agreement on the definition of mental disorder, another important limitation of the available science of psychopathology is that the classification system used to diagnose mental disorders is relatively primitive. Although significant scientific improvements have been incorporated since the advent of DSM-I (1952), DSM-II (1968), DSM-III (1980), and DSM-III-R (1987), the present DSM-IV (1994) is far from being a scientifically validated classification system.

For example, despite decades of research and debate, few if any of the DSM-IV psychiatric disorders have been conclusively demonstrated to be a discrete, independently existing diagnostic entity. To illustrate, considerable difficulty still remains in reliably and validly differentiating schizophrenia from major mood disorder, chronic unipolar depressions from various anxiety disorders, or sundry personality disorders from each other. In the absence of validated knowledge concerning the etiology of mental disorders, classification schemes (as well as models of psychopathology) remain to a substantial degree matters of taste and pragmatics. Diagnoses that assign a specific DSM mental disorder to an individual patient possess wide-ranging degrees of scientific and clinical usefulness.

THE CAUSES OF MENTAL DISORDER

It is one thing to describe abnormal behavior. It is quite another to explain how abnormal behavior arises and why it occurs in some people but not in others.
—Willerman & Cohen, 1990, p. 118.

Whenever we observe or contemplate tragic instances of human maladjustment, the questions that leap into consciousness seem invariably to be, What brings about these various abnormal human conditions? What causes people to behave maladaptively? How can we understand these occurrences in a way that we might explain mental disorders to someone else? Have I experienced any of them? Am I likely to in the future? Is there anything one can discover about human lives, mine or someone else's, that might shed some light on development of these disorders?

To a substantial degree *the search for causes is the essence of science*. To know something scientifically is to know things through their immediate mechanisms and their distal causes. For our purposes this book will use the term *psychopathology* to refer to this science of mental disorders: the multidisciplinary field and activity that pursues knowledge about the mechanisms and causes of mental disorders. A continuing frustration of the field is that "for most psychiatric conditions there *are* no explanations. 'Etiology unknown' is the hallmark of psychiatry as well as its bane. . . . People continue to speculate about etiology, of course, and this is good if it produces testable hypotheses, and bad if speculation is mistaken for truth" (Goodwin & Guze, 1989, p. xiii).

In its most general sense, a *cause* is an act or event or a state of nature (X) which initiates a sequence of events resulting in an effect (Y) (Rothman, 1976, p. 588). It refers to "that which produces an effect, result, or consequence; the person, event, or condition responsible for an action or result" (Mirowsky & Ross, 1989, p. 57). In scientific language the effect is referred to as a *dependent variable*, and denotes the event or outcome we seek to explain or account for. A cause is referred to as the *independent variable*, and denotes a factor that determines or contributes to occurrence of the dependent variable. In psychopathology, the central goal is to identify relationships between particular mental disorders (dependent variables) and their causes (independent variables).

Two basic properties have to be present in the relationship between X (an independent variable; e.g., a suspected causal factor) and Y (a dependent variable; e.g., a particular mental disorder) in order for the relationship to be causal (Susser, 1973, pp. 64–65). First, the relationship must have a single direction, in that X (the causal factor) produces effects in Y (the particular disorder)—not the reverse. Second, X (e.g., extreme child abuse) must precede Y (e.g., dissociative amnesia) in time.

The former Surgeon General's report on smoking (Koop & Luoto, 1982) expanded the number of criteria necessary for establishing a causal relationship to six. (1) The association between X and Y needs to be *consistent* (i.e., observed repeatedly by multiple investigators, in different locations and situations, at different times, using different methods of study). (2) As listed also by Susser, the association needs to show a *temporal relationship* (i.e., exposure to suspected causal factor must precede onset of the disorder). (3) The association must demonstrate a *strong relationship* (i.e., a substantial number of persons experiencing, for example, child abuse must show later onset of, for example, dissociative amnesia). (4) The association should be *specific* (i.e., the presumed causative factor, such as extreme child abuse, must be present for one, and only one, disorder, such as for dissociative amnesia, but not for others such as unipolar depression or generalized anxiety disorder). (5) The association must evince *coherence* (i.e., must mesh with other known facts about the particular disorder). (6) Finally, *preventive clinical trial studies* need to demonstrate, if possible, that a reduction in exposure to the suspected causal agent leads subsequently to a reduction in the incidence and severity of the disorder.

Maximal confusion can easily occur in thinking about mental disorders if we substitute the notion of the cause for the notion of a cause. To speak of the cause is to suggest that there is only one; this has been called the doctrine of "monocausation" (King, 1982, p. 204). In practice, causal investigation rarely yields the unique or perfectly predictable connection between two phenomena. If this book aims to accomplish anything, it is the unqualified rejection of this monocausal doctrine. Mental disorders are caused by multiple factors. Sophisticated present-day study and treatment of mental disorders can validly be guided only by the "doctrine of multiple causality" (Lipowski, 1975, 1980).

HOW MANY DIFFERENT "CAUSES" DO WE NEED?

Confusion easily arises from a poor understanding of the various alternative meanings of the term "cause." When we ask, "What causes a person to behave maladaptively?" we are in effect asking which and how many of various possible types of causes are involved in any resulting explanation. Traditionally, scientists differentiate several crucial, different possible meanings or types of causes: sufficient, necessary, or contributory (Carson, Butcher, & Mineka, 1996; Susser, 1973).

Sufficient, Necessary, and Contributory Causes

A *sufficient cause* is a condition that, if present, guarantees occurrence of a particular mental disorder—a factor that inevitably produces the effect. Whenever the condition, X, is present, it will always be the case that the mental disorder, Y, will occur. No other co-occurring conditions are necessary to produce the disorder; monocausation has been demonstrated; a single factor or cause is sufficient. For example, whenever a human cortex is invaded by the syphilitic spirochete and remains untreated, the host person inevitably suffers damaged cortical tissue and, over time, develops the psychotic dementia known as general paresis. The only condition necessary for the occurrence of general paresis (Y) is presence in the human cortex of the syphilitic spirochete (X)—if X, then Y. To take another example, the death of a parent is not a sufficient condition for developing adult unipolar depression. Even if 100 percent of adult depressive patients experienced loss of a parent during their childhoods, it could also be the case that 20 percent of the general population suffer parental death but as adults do not develop unipolar depression. Based on these percentages, clearly something else has to be present besides parental death in order for unipolar disorder to eventuate.

A *necessary cause* is a condition that must be present in order for a particular mental disorder to occur. The condition, X, must always be present whenever the mental disorder, Y, is present. For example, a certain cortical neurotransmitter imbalance in the caudate nucleus and frontal areas of the cortex is a necessary cause for a form of dementia called Huntington's Chorea (HC Dementia). Whenever HC Dementia (Y) is present, this cortical neurotransmitter imbalance (X) will also be found. As another example, the death of a parent is not a necessary condition for development of adult unipolar depression if only 40 percent (rather than 100%) of depressed patients had experienced a parent's death during their childhood. Since, in this example, a person can develop unipolar depression even though neither parent died during childhood, parental death is not a necessary condition.

A condition that is necessary may or may not be sufficient. In the example of HC Dementia, the necessary cause turns out also to be sufficient. That is, if the neurotransmitter imbalance in the caudate nucleus and frontal areas of the cortex is present, the outcome inevitably will be HC Dementia. Nothing else, in addition to the specific neurotransmitter imbalance, needs to be present. Hence, neurotransmitter imbalance in the caudate nucleus and frontal areas of the cortex is both necessary and sufficient to cause HC Dementia. A physical medicine example involves the distinctive genes that, when present, invariably produce phenylketonuria (PKU) or sickle-cell anemia.

On the other hand, a condition that is necessary may not be sufficient. Let us say, for example, that a necessary condition for occurrence of schizophrenia (Y) is presence of a subtle neurotransmitter (dopamine) imbalance (X) that disrupts the neural transmission underlying perceptual and attentional cognitive processes. Asserting that this necessary cause (neurotransmitter imbalance) is not sufficient means that its presence in the cortex, by itself, does not guarantee onset of a schizophrenic episode. Indeed, scientific evidence supports that whatever biological brain abnormality may be present in the case of schizophrenia is probably necessary, but certainly not sufficient. "We take it as a given that there are necessary but not sufficient genetic components to schizophrenia" (Hanson, Gottesman, & Heston, 1990, p. 425). Instead, occurrence of schizophrenia (Y) requires the presence of at least another factor or cause (Z)—perhaps, presence of severe familial and peer stressors during the early adolescent years. In this case, for Y to occur, both X and Z must be present. It could also be the case that each is necessary, but neither is sufficient.

An excellent physical medicine example of a necessary but not sufficient cause is the case of tuberculosis. Exposure of an individual to the tubercle bacillus is a necessary but not sufficient cause to guarantee onset of the disease. Expression of the dormant bacillus requires presence of one or more other mediating factors such as malnutrition, alcoholism, and/or stressors usually associated with lower socioeconomic status.

A *contributory cause* is a condition whose presence makes it more probable that a mental disorder will occur, but that is neither necessary nor sufficient for its occurrence. The experience of severe physical and sexual abuse as a child may increase the likelihood that, as an adult, a person will develop some form of dissociative disorder (such as amnesia, fugue, depersonalization, or identity disorder). Nevertheless, since it is a contributory cause, occurrence of severe physical and sexual abuse as a child often may not have been present with adult dissociative disorder. Onset of the latter mental disorder would require instead simultaneous presence of a set of other factors or causes.

A controversial physical medicine example involves the relationship of cigarette smoking to lung cancer. A history of smoking cigarettes is neither necessary nor sufficient for an individual to develop the disease. Most smokers do not develop lung cancer, and some cases of lung cancer show no history of cigarette smoking. The fact is that smoking has been shown to be associated with increased risk for lung cancer, but is not required.

Contributory causes are frequently referred to also as *risk factors* (see Chapter 7) for mental disorder: Their presence increases the likelihood of occurrence of a particular disorder; but, unless some combination of other risk factors co-occur, the mental disorder will not eventuate. Key meanings, then, of contributory causes are increased risk, increased probability, and the like. "In modern human sciences, the effect is viewed as an alteration of probabilities, rather than a determination of outcomes. . . . Statements about social causes are statements of probability" (Mirowsky & Ross, 1989, pp. 57, 59). They are also statements involving contributory causes.

Proximal and Distal Causes

Before leaving the various notions of cause, we need to address an important distinction that differentiates the action of causes at various stages of human development. Particularly when one is searching for environmental causes of mental disorders, one looks at events or happenings that may occur in utero, in infancy, in early or late childhood, and in early or late adolescence—indeed, at any developmental stage throughout the life span. As a general way of distinguishing these temporally arranged factors, one can talk about "distal" versus "proximal" causes.

A *distal cause* is a condition or factor occurring in utero or relatively early in life (or more precisely, a long time before the onset of the disorder) that contributes to eventual development of a particular mental disorder. Some examples of distal causes are maternal drug abuse during pregnancy, malnutrition in infancy, sexual abuse as a young child, parental neglect or rejection, and death of a parent when a child is young. If a distal cause operating from early life increases a person's vulnerability to causes acting closer to the onset of a disorder, it can be referred to also as a *predisposing cause*.

A *proximal cause* is a condition or factor occurring during some period closer in time to the actual onset of a particular mental disorder. An example might be the initiation of college work that occurred several years before the onset of an episode of schizophrenia; or divorce from one's spouse with accompanying separation from one's young children several months before the onset of a first panic attack; or being a witness to acts of terrorism or mutilation during combat, ten years before the onset of post-traumatic stress disorder.

The closer the proximal event to the actual onset of a particular disorder, the more likely we are to call the proximal factor a *precipitating cause* (namely, the "last straw" stressor or causal factor). If, after the onset of a disorder, a proximal factor is discovered to prolong the course of a disorder, it can be referred to also as a *perpetuating factor*.

Thus, when we speak of the set of causes of a particular mental disorder, one of the important distinctions to make is between causes that are more distal and those that are more proximal. Some causes operate in a distal manner, setting up vulnerability for disorder later in life. Other causes have a more proximal relationship to the onset of a disorder. Still others may contribute to the maintenance of a disorder.

CONCLUSION

Valid understanding of mental disorders requires that we keep these causal meanings sharply separate. What I hope to demonstrate with this volume is that, with the exception of a few rare disorders, virtually all mental disorders involve the action of causal factors that are never singularly "sufficient," and that often individually are not even "necessary." "For many forms of psychopathology we do not yet have a clear understanding of whether there are necessary or sufficient causes, although this remains the goal of much current research. However, we do have a good understanding of many of the contributory causes for most forms of psychopathology" (Carson, Butcher, & Mineka, 1996, p. 64).

I will argue that the doctrine of monocausation needs desperately to be abandoned. Within the field of mental disorder, "nothing is simple and straightforward unless we omit and thereby falsify. . . . We must not confuse a simplistic account with reality. . . . Any simple formulation is incomplete and, in its ultimate sense, wrong" (King, 1982, p. 318). As humans, and as scientists, ideally we prefer simple explanations—that our causes be singular, and simultaneously both necessary and sufficient.

However, available evidence makes it clear that most of the major psychiatric disorders are etiologically heterogenous—each has a set of different causes (Akiskal & McKinney, 1975; Cloninger, Sigvardsson, Gilligan, von Knorring, Reich, & Bohman, 1989; Baron, Endicott, & Ott, 1990). No one explanation is correct for all mental disorders. As a science we must come to understand "which explanations are best for which disorders" (Holmes, 1997, p. 20). In addition, for virtually all mental disorders, more than one cause is involved. For example, anxiety disorders may be caused by stress, but may also be learned, and may also include biochemical abnormalities. In the case of mental disorders, complex causal chains are often involved, and it's not always clear which processes should be regarded as the primary causal factor (Meehl, 1977; Whitbeck, 1977).

To complicate the picture even further, it is possible for a single set of causal factors to produce different psychopathological symptoms depending on the severity of the causal agent, accompanying environmental circumstances, or other mediating variables. For example, it may be that chronic depression and some anxiety disorders are expressions of the same genetic predispositions, but get triggered by distinctly different environmental experiences (Kendler, Heath, Martin, & Eaves, 1987; Kendler, Neale, Kessler, Heath, & Eaves, 1992). In similar fashion, antisocial personality disorder and somatization disorder (also known as hysteria or Briquet's syndrome) may represent expressions of similar genetic predispositions, but in persons of male versus female gender respectively (Cloninger, 1978). According to Eley, more recent evidence leads to a broader hypothesis: "Perhaps genes are not specific to the development of any one behavior problem; perhaps their influence is more general" (1997, p. 95).

Unfortunately, a prevailing paradox is that, although mental disorders do not seem to have even necessary causes, a substantial portion of mental health research is dominated by a search for singular necessary causes. The various mental health sciences have been appropriately guided by their respective theoretical and methodological viewpoints. Psychiatry has been dominated by a search for biological necessary causes; psychology by cognitive and behavioral necessary causes; and sociology by cultural and subcultural necessary causes. The situation fulfills the old adage: If the only tool one has is a hammer, everything begins to resemble a nail.

With this book I hope to demonstrate that in virtually all cases of mental disorder, causal factors are multiple, interactive, and at best contributory.

At all times we need to keep in mind that it is invariably difficult and complex to understand, explain, or predict mental disorder through knowledge about causal factors. First, the sheer number of possible causes, distal and proximal, that may need to be taken into account is often overwhelming. Even the possible combinations of only a few factors quickly result in unwieldy lists. Second, unknown critical events (e.g., involving an unlucky random sequence of aversive events on a particular day) can occur that may never be isolated. Third, situational influences unique to the individual (that are not shared with other family members) seem to play a crucial role in mental disorders; this, in turn, makes it much more difficult to isolate causal environmental factors that may be central for a particular disorder.

"In short, the difficulty with theorizing about causality is that events insignificant in themselves may collectively lead to disorder, and no convincing causal sequence can be reconstructed. Although theories may identify the 'big' causal factors that occur with sufficient frequency or potency, we may never be able to devise any theory that can handle individual human beings in all their uniqueness, and this may be true for both abnormal and normal variations in human behavior" (Willerman & Cohen, 1990, pp. 142–143).

REFERENCES

Akiskal, H. S., & McKinney, W. T. (1975). Overview of recent research in depression: Integration of ten conceptual models into a comprehensive clinical frame. *Archives of General Psychiatry, 32,* 285–305.

American Psychiatric Association. (1952). *Diagnostic and statistical manual of mental disorders.* Washington, DC: Author.

American Psychiatric Association. (1968). *Diagnostic and statistical manual of mental disorders* (2d ed.). Washington, DC: Author.

American Psychiatric Association. (1980). *Diagnostic and statistical manual of mental disorders* (3d ed.). Washington, DC: Author.

American Psychiatric Association. (1987). *Diagnostic and statistical manual of mental disorders* (3d ed., rev.). Washington, DC: Author.

American Psychiatric Association. (1994). *Diagnostic and statistical manual of mental disorders* (4th ed.). Washington, DC: Author.

Baron, M., Endicott, J., & Ott, J. (1990). Genetic linkage in mental illness: Limitations and prospects. *British Journal of Psychiatry, 157,* 645–655.

Carson, R. C., Butcher, J. N., & Mineka, S. (1996). *Abnormal psychology and modern life* (10th ed.). New York: HarperCollins.

Cloninger, C. R. (1978). The antisocial personality. *Hospital Practice, 13,* 97–106.

Cloninger, C. R., Sigvardsson, S., Gilligan, S. B., von Knorring, A. F., Reich, T., & Bohman, M. (1989). Genetic heterogeneity and the classification of alcoholism. In E. Gordis, B. Tabakoff, & M. Linnoila (Eds.), *Alcohol research from bench to bedside* (pp. 3–16). New York: Haworth.

Eley, T. C. (1977). General genes: A new theme in developmental psychopathology. *Current Directions in Psychological Science, 6,* 90–95.

Goodwin, D. W., & Guze, S. B. (1989). *Psychiatric diagnosis* (4th ed.). New York: Oxford University Press.

Hanson, D. R., Gottesman, I. I., & Heston, L. L. (1990). Long range schizophrenia forcasting: Many a slip twixt cup and lip. In J. Rolf, A. S. Masten, D. Cicchetti, K. H. Nuechterlein, & S. Weintraub (Eds.), *Risk and protective factors in the development of psychopathology* (pp. 424–444). New York: Cambridge University Press.

Holmes, D. S. (1997). *Abnormal psychology* (3d ed.). New York: Addison Wesley Longman.

Kendler, K. S., Heath, A. C., Martin, N., & Eaves, L. J. (1987). Symptoms of anxiety and symptoms of depression. *Archives of General Psychiatry, 122,* 451–457.

Kendler, K. S., Neale, M. C., Kessler, R. C., Heath, A. C., & Eaves, L. J. (1992). Major depression and generalized anxiety disorder: Same genes, (partly) different environments? *Archives of General Psychiatry, 49,* 716–722.

King, L. S. (1982). *Medical thinking: A historical preface.* Princeton, NJ: Princeton University Press.

Koop, C. E., & Luoto, J. (1982). The health consequences of smoking: Cancer; Overview of a report of the Surgeon General. *Public Health Reports, 97,* 318–324.

Lipowski, Z. J. (1975). Psychiatry of somatic diseases: Epidemiology, pathogenesis, classification. *Comprehensive Psychiatry, 16,* 105–124.

Lipowski, Z. J. (1980). Organic mental disorders: Introduction and review of syndromes. In H. I. Kaplan, A. M. Freeman, & B. J. Saddock (Eds.), *Comprehensive textbook of psychiatry III* (Vol. 2). Baltimore: Williams & Wilkins.

Meehl, P. E. (1977). Specific etiology and other forms of strong influence: Some quantitative meanings. *Journal of Medicine and Philosophy, 2,* 33–53.

Mirowsky, J., & Ross, C. E. (1989). *Social causes of psychological distress.* New York: Aldine de Gruyter.

Rothman, K. (1976). Causes. *American Journal of Epidemiology, 104,* 587–592.

Susser, M. (1973). *Causal thinking in the health sciences.* New York: Oxford University Press.

Whitbeck, C. (1977). Causation in medicine: The disease entity model. *Philosophy of Science, 44,* 619–637.

Willerman, L., & Cohen, D. B. (1990). *Psychopathology.* New York: McGraw-Hill.

World Health Organization. (1992). *International Classification of Disease (ICD-10) classification of mental and behavioral disorders: Clinical descriptions and diagnostic guidelines* (10th ed.). Geneva, Switzerland: Author.

Chapter 2

The "American Way" of Understanding Mental Disorders: The Biomedical Model

> Are mental disorders biological or psychological? Are they "no one's fault" or "caused" by parents, spouse, or patients or by social disadvantage?
>
> —Eisenberg, 1995, p. 1563.

Credible scientific voices have offered distinctive perspectives on the nature of mental disorders. Various scientists of psychopathology have asserted that maladjusted human behavior is the result of abnormal brain physiology; of painful life events (stressors); of faulty behavioral conditioning; of problems in cognition and information processing; of cycles of self-defeating interpersonal behaviors; of societal oppression; of societal labeling and self-fulfilling prophecy; and so on.

In general, mental disorders have been studied at either of two poles:

From the standpoint of knowledge about how the brain works, or from knowledge about how man behaves as a social animal. The former approach uses powerful new methods of enquiry deriving from molecular biology, neuropharmacology and immunochemistry, while the latter uses methods derived from epidemiology and the social sciences. Recent technical advances in molecular biology have led to an increased emphasis on the former, so that some psychiatrists approach the subject as though they need to know little more than the way in which cerebral functions can become disorganized during episodes of mental illness. At the other end of the spectrum are those psychotherapists and social workers who believe that abnormal behavior can be wholly explained in social and psychological terms, and who take little account of accumulating knowledge about disordered cerebral function. (Goldberg & Huxley, 1992, p. 1)

The study of mental disorders encompasses many disciplines, including psychiatry, psychology, social work, public health, nursing, anthropology, and sociology. Absent compelling reasons to the contrary, traditional mental health disciplines have approached the study of mental disorders almost exclusively from their respective historical and methodological perspectives. Research psychiatrists predominantly search for biochemical, physiological, and/or structural abnormalities, and prefer medication as the major form of treatment. Sociological and social work researchers seek explanations of mental disorders that reflect the cultural and subcultural norms, mores, and differences to which individuals have been exposed, and prefer interventions that bring about changes in social orders or environments. Psychological researchers seek answers in the developmental histories and experiences of individuals and resulting reinforcement and cognitive abnormalities, and prefer treatments that target these maladaptive learnings and thought processes. Ironically, these separate pursuits have provided much of the available evidence as to why it no longer makes sense to continue these isolated and distinct traditions.

This chapter concentrates on only one of these mental health traditions. It provides a critique of the biological psychiatry tradition, since its perspectives and beliefs permeate American culture, dominate the mental health establishment, and mesh so neatly with the basic American bias toward providing answers to human problems in the form of easy-to-administer medications. "Americans rely more on medical technology for solutions to both sickness and ordinary life problems than any other society. Americans invariably seek more medical treatment, and American doctors and other professionals seek to provide this treatment, whereas Europeans more often allow healing to take its course and recognize that every medical intervention has its own risks. . . . The American credo . . . is that medicine can ultimately fix everything that is wrong with us. This reliance on medicine extends to our attacks on our largest, most complex social problems [such as alcoholism and other mental disorders]" (Peele, 1989, pp. 256–257).

Within psychiatry, the predominant framework for studying mental disorder is known variously as the "biomedical," "medical," or "disease" model. Its most general notion is that psychiatric illnesses are equivalent in all important respects to illnesses treated in general medicine. Its bottom-line position is that any mental disorder is the result of biological abnormalities (primarily in the brain, central nervous system, autonomic nervous system, and/or endocrine system).

The history of science teaches that entrenched ideas are seldom replaced until (a) the counter-evidence is consistently overwhelming and (b) persuasive counter-arguments that integrate and crystallize more valid emerging trends and paradigms are advanced both to the field and to the public at large.

Fortunately, all mental health disciplines, including psychiatry, are today publicly committed to a scientific decision-making stance. If we are to revise our DSM classification system, for example, or if we are to accept new learnings about psychopathology, we will do so based on the available empirical evidence. As two prominent research psychiatrists assert, "Without evidence, we do not believe pills are better than words. Without evidence, we do not believe chemistry is more important than upbringing. Without evidence, we withhold judgment" (Goodwin & Guze, 1989, pp. xiii–xiv).

This chapter argues that perpetuation of the biomedical model (or for that matter, any other monocausal model) can only deflect the field of psychopathology away from valid understandings of mental disorders. It will remain for subsequent chapters to review the scientific evidence promoting the multicausal biopsychosocial perspective that needs to dominate and guide the next century of activity within the science of psychopathology.

If a new, more valid scientific paradigm is ever to replace this biomedical model, it seems expeditious and pivotal that the biomedical model's inadequacies and shortcomings be exposed. In fairness we need to add that other monocausal disciplinary models for understanding mental disorders—psychological or sociological—are similarly inadequate, misleading, and invalid.

POPULAR ADOPTION OF THE BIOMEDICAL MODEL

Unless challenged, contemporary culture will progressively regard *homo sapiens* as *homo biologicus*—something on the order of a highly evolved, intricately wired, and socially verbose fruit fly.
—Pam, 1995, p. 2.

The biomedical model understandably has been promulgated by physicians and psychiatrists as well as by the health-care industry, especially by pharmaceutical companies. Its perspective has become the prevailing lay-person view of disease and medical treatment in Western society (Fabrega, 1974). One of its major tenets is that mental disorders are biologically based brain diseases (Andreason, 1984; Torrey, 1997).

The mass media, including our most respected mass circulation periodicals, offers an inordinate amount of coverage to genetic, biochemical, and neurologic research on human behavior, often reflecting the biomedical theme that the study of human behavior has been revolutionized (Breggin, 1991; Peele, 1981, 1989). A recent pharmaceutical advertisement claims, "Scientists now know that the causes of schizophrenia and psychosis are often rooted in powerful chemicals in the brain called neurotransmitters." Another magazine ad echoes, "Today, scientists know that many people suffering from mental illnesses have imbalances in the way their brains metabolize certain chemicals called neurotransmitters. Too much or too little of these chemicals may result in depression, anxiety, or other emotional or physical disorders." Still another advertisement says, "A chemical that triggers mental illness is now being used to stop it. . . . By developing vital drug treatments that alter various chemicals in the brain, pharmaceutical company researchers are offering real hope for the mentally ill." A recent newspaper column concludes, "A few decades ago, breakdowns were seen as mental freaks of personality. Since then, advances in neuroscience—the study of the nervous system—have shown that many stem from chemical imbalances in the brain. In this sense, they don't differ much from many physical diseases." These universal popular messages are dramatic. Chemicals trigger mental illness. Chemical brain imbalances cause mental disorder.

The influential National Alliance for the Mentally Ill (NAMI) is the largest national organization of individuals (and their families) who have personally experienced mental illness. NAMI unyieldingly and passionately asserts that "severe mental illnesses, such as schizophrenia and bipolar disorder, are at their root brain disorders." Its leaders add, "And yes, there is some relief for parents in the knowledge that they did not cause their child's disabling illness, a concern with which many parents of children with serious diseases struggle." NAMI "looks to and actively supports biomedical research on severe mental illnesses to promote the discovery of better treatments and, ultimately cures . . . for these brain disorders" (Hall & Flynn, 1996, pp. 1373–1374). The message of NAMI is that modern genetics offers scientific data that provides people suffering from mental illness a biological causal understanding for their experience, thereby destigmatizing their condition (Hall, 1996). Also, as a brain disorder, mental illness is ipso facto not the result of parental abuse or incompetence.

Paradoxically, several of the scientific chapters presented in Hall's (1996) volume highlight that the emergent paradigm in the field is one in which joint effects of genes and life experiences underlie as liabilities to mental disorder. According to this new viewpoint, what is inherited is not disease, but disease susceptibility; genes confer a predisposition or diathesis, not a disease. We return to this theme in some detail in Chapter 4.

Throughout these present-day popular messages, the theme being advanced is that all mental illness is a biologically based disease of the brain, or that mental disorder is brain dysfunction. Any mental disorder is a physical illness; the brain just isn't "wired" right. Recent brain technologies, such as CAT scans and magnetic resonance imaging, reveal precise, vivid images of the physical differences between normal brains and "brains with disorders." Mental or brain disorders are matters of genetics and biochemistry—not of child rearing, societal malaise, or personal willpower.

A closely related biomedical theme asserts that mental disease is a genetic disease, and that mental disorders are genetically transmitted. Without qualification or elaboration, these statements suggest that the ultimate culprit in the case of mental disorders is faulty genes transmitted from parents to their children. The assertion is that scientific evidence from familial, twin, and adoption studies leads to the inescapable conclusion that most, if not all, mental disorders are inherited. These faulty genes, in turn, produce biological brain abnormalities that lead to the abnormal behaviors that characterize mental disorder.

These contemporary biomedical themes are pervasive. These and similar pronouncements authoritatively assert or imply a clear-cut monocausal explanation of mental disorder. What inevitably gets conveyed in these passionate assertions is that *mental disorders are caused predominantly or solely by biological conditions*. All by themselves (as "necessary and sufficient" causes), biological abnormalities produce mental disorders. Most, perhaps all, mental disorders are caused predominantly, if not exclusively, by biological factors—faulty genes that produce abnormal neurotransmitter activity at cortical synapses, structural anomalies of the CNS, or abnormal hormonal activity. As a result, mental disorders are not the result of aversive parental behaviors, of societal deprivations or discriminations, and certainly are not the result of personal choice. To suffer from schizophrenia or major depression is no more a character flaw (of patients or their parents) than to be a victim of Alzheimer's or Parkinson's disease.

These prevalent popular biomedical assertions about mental disorder seem to reflect what a recent writer described as the "biologizing of American culture": "Everything from criminality to addictive disorders to sexual orientation is seen today less as a matter of choice than of genetic destiny" (Herbert, 1997, p. 72). If it is in our genes or biology, it's something that "happens to us," and we're not accountable; rather than being in control of our mental destinies, we are helpless victims of our biology. By restricting all "correct" searches for causes to biological deficits, it becomes easy "to 'blame the body' for disturbed behavior, rather than the family or society" (Pam, 1995, p. 3). The upshot is that biomedical beliefs can easily be offered up as no-fault rationalizations.

PSYCHIATRIC ENDORSEMENTS OF THE BIOMEDICAL MODEL

> Just at the moment when the rest of medicine is being pressed to expand its horizons to include psycho–social determinants of illness, findings from therapeutic and basic research are sweeping psychiatry into the biomedical mainstream.
>
> —Eisenberg, 1986, p. 499.

The father of medicine, Hippocrates, provided the first biological theory of mental disease in the form of a humoral theory. Hippocrates believed that brain pathology (body–fluid imbalance) was the major cause of mentally disordered behavior. The disease of melancholia (similar to current unipolar mood disorder) resulted from an excess of phlegm; mania (current bipolar mood disorder) from too much bile; and phrenitis (current schizophrenia) resulted from an excess of blood.

Among the mental health fields, psychiatry legitimately has taken the lead in application of the biomedical (biological) model to the understanding of mental disorders. In dealing with clinical phenomena, psychiatry has been heavily influenced by medicine. The pioneers of psychiatry, such as Griesinger, Kraepelin, and Bleuler, all were convinced that the major mental disorders eventually would be explained as brain diseases. These nineteenth century psychiatrists concluded that madness took the form of a finite number of disease entities, each with its own distinct cause and cerebral pathology, together with distinctive psychological symptoms and outcome.

Near the beginning of the twentieth century, the popularity of the biomedical model received a substantial boost as the result of its unequivocally successful application to the then popular mental disorder of *general paresis*. The distinctive general paresis syndrome had previously been identified: delusions of grandeur, dementia, and progressive paralysis accompanied by defective speech. The syndrome was found to be stable over time. Its course and outcome were invariable: untreated patients deteriorated, then died. Morphological changes had been identified in the form of damaged brain tissue accompanied by a growth of foreign connective tissue.

Just before the turn of the twentieth century, new medical discoveries dramatically clarified the etiological picture. Case and laboratory studies first empirically established that patients with general paresis had a high prevalence of syphilitic infection. Next, all doubt that the disorder was biomedical was removed when the exact etiologic infectious biological agent—the syphilitic spirochete (treponema pallidum)—was isolated in the brain tissue of general paretics. Finally, when treatment designed to destroy the spirochete was applied early enough in the stages of syphilitic infection, onset of general paresis was forestalled.

The upshot of this historical episode was that the biomedical model once again had borne fruit. The biological etiology of a serious mental disorder was exposed, isolated, and rendered amenable to successful biological treatment, resulting in virtual elimination of the disorder.

Despite this remarkable demonstration, in the first half of the twentieth century the biomedical model gradually was eclipsed by other developments, especially by Adolph Meyer's biosocial theory and by the onslaught of Freudian psychoanalysis. During the 1960s and 1970s, the model received serious challenges from several directions. Psychiatric diagnosis was described as a politically and socially motivated judgment, not a valid designation of true mental disorder. Mental illness was said to be either a myth with no biological substrate (Szasz, 1960, 1974), an unlucky breach of society's "residual rules" resulting in psychiatric labeling and self-fulfilling prophecy (Scheff, 1966), or an adaptive and creative response to parental invalidation of one's basic identity (Laing, 1964, 1967; Laing & Esterson, 1964). Szasz, for example, took the position that "mental illness is a myth whose function is to disguise and thus render more palatable the bitter pill of moral conflicts in human relations" (1970, p. 53).

In the 1980s, with the emergence of the biologically oriented neo-Kraepelinian school of psychiatrists (Blashfield, 1984; Guze, 1978; Klerman, 1978) and the advent of the DSM-III revision of the diagnostic manual for mental disorders (American Psychiatric Association, 1980), the biomedical model returned with a vengeance to psychiatric training and research, demonstrating once again its continuing vitality and attractiveness to members of the medical profession. Bolstered especially by recent new laboratory techniques and biochemical discoveries, many psychiatrists view the discipline as entering a new era, one in which psychiatry attains at least equivalent scientific respectability to that enjoyed by other medical specialties. Weiner, a psychiatrist, characterizes this development more sarcastically: "For reasons that resist explanation, psychiatry has once again asked for admittance into medicine" (Weiner, 1978, p. 27).

A prominent psychiatrist forcefully described the shift as follows: "Psychiatry is in the process of undergoing a revolutionary change and realigning itself with the mainstream biological traditions of medicine.

During the past ten to twenty years, the neurosciences have produced an explosion of knowledge about how the brain works, and this has taught us that many forms of mental illness are due to abnormalities in brain structure or chemistry. Psychiatry is moving from the study of the 'troubled mind' to the 'broken brain'" (Andreasen, 1984, p. viii).

All mental disorders included in DSM-III were defined as "organismic dysfunctions which are relatively distinct with regard to clinical features, aetiology and course" (Spitzer, Sheehy, & Endicott, 1977). This attribution directly reflected contemporary psychopharmacologic and psychobiologic discoveries in psychiatry. As a result, "psychiatrists are now donning white coats and spending greater periods of time in consultation and liaison work within general hospitals. In many departments across the nation, there has been a strong backlash and disapproval of psychodynamic and social understanding of mental illness" (Foulks, 1979, p. 238). Present-day departments of psychiatry faculty, especially those with neo-Kraepelinian emphasis, tend to "excommunicate" matters psychological or social from psychiatric textbooks and training curricula. The authors of one classic psychiatric text, for example, declared rather blatantly: "Our definition of what constitutes a psychiatric illness is simply a medical illness with major emotional and behavioral aspects. . . . We are not interested in the 'psyche.' We are interested in specific psychiatric illnesses" (Winokur & Clayton, 1986, pp. ix–x).

Recent applications of the biomedical model take the form of various biological hypotheses about mental disorders, currently those favoring neurotransmitter dysfunction and/or structural abnormalities in the brain. A contemporary biomedical analysis of schizophrenia, for example, might emphasize that schizophrenia is a distinct disease syndrome that can be reliably diagnosed through the presence of delusions, hallucinations, and other deviant behaviors or symptoms described in DSM-IV. Untreated, the disorder has a characteristic progressive and deteriorating course that culminates in, at best, marginal societal adjustment (e.g., requiring periodic hospitalization or resulting in chronic "street people" existence). Morphological studies have identified structural abnormality in the form of subtle cortical atrophies (especially in the left-frontal cortex) in the brains of schizophrenic patients. Excessive dopamine neurotransmitter activity has been isolated as a key etiologic biological agent. Treatment with antipsychotic medications, which target dopamine transmission (block dopamine receptors at the synapse thereby improving neural transmission), results in significant reduction of schizophrenic patients' symptoms and substantial improvement in their life adjustment.

Throughout the psychiatric literature, the reader runs across equivalent unqualified or unelaborated analyses. Schizophrenia is a genetically transmitted disorder of brain development. Repetitive movements that are so prominent in obsessive–compulsive disorder are a function of abnormal activity in multiple neural circuits between the frontal cortex and the striatum of the basal ganglia. Attention-deficit and hyperactivity disorder involves abnormal functioning of the dopamine-mediated neural pathways of the frontal lobes. In all substance-use disorders, addictive behavior is the result of a common, long-term effect in the reward circuitry of the brain that involves the mesolimbic dopamine system. In panic disorder patients, one finds abnormalities of brain function in the structures surrounding the hippocampus and areas of the brain stem, including the locus coeruleus and raphe nucleus. In short, present-day, biologically dominated psychiatry has become devoted almost exclusively to the investigation of constitutional biological determinants of mental disorders.

Refreshingly, some contemporary medical and psychiatric visionaries argue the need for a contrasting and much-broadened perspective than that provided by the biomedical perspective. Discontent with the restrictive nature of the medical model surfaced within physical medicine itself (Engel, 1977). "While psychiatry is being 'biologized,' general medicine is being 'psychologized'. . . . Just as the psychodynamic approach is perceived as having failed to live up to the hopes of its advocates in the mental health field, the biomedical approach is now perceived as failing to live up to expectations in general medicine" (Bloom 1986, p. 5). Ironically, in contrast to psychiatry, the medical community itself increasingly recognized the importance of psychological factors in the natural history of physical disease, prevention of disability and illness, and promotion of recovery.

Within psychiatry, Weiner advocated for a "broad biological model" in which "disease can be viewed as a failure of adaptation, that may occur in one of many systems; it is a biological phenomenon. Because it is a biological phenomenon, it deals with organisms in interaction with their natural, social, and cultural environments. . . . A modern biological model of disease . . . is broad enough to accommodate diverse points of view from the molecular to the evolutionary level" (1978, p. 32). Reiser (1988) warned that the focus of psychiatry residency programs has increasingly shifted away from the patient as person and toward disease. In Chapter 3, we review in more detail these contrasting views within psychiatry and medicine.

Much more commonly, one can find present-day psychiatrists of some prominence making claims that the biomedical model enjoys unqualified confirmation from the available scientific evidence. Television presentations often strongly reflect biopsychiatric theory. Interviewed psychiatrists often make statements of these forms: "We know that schizophrenia is a brain disease; it's like multiple sclerosis or

Alzheimer's disease," or "Depression literally flows out of the brain and into the body; the endocrine system provides the channel."

A major consultant and supporter of NAMI, E. Fuller Torrey, in a volume concentrating on schizophrenia, concluded that "Based on studies of gross pathology, microscopic pathology, neurochemistry, cerebral blood flow, and metabolism as well as electrical, neurological, and neurophysiological measures, schizophrenia has been clearly established to be a brain disease, as sure as multiple sclerosis, Parkinson's disease, and Alzheimer's disease are established as brain diseases" (1988, pp. 137–138). In his most recent book, Torrey promulgates the more general theme that all serious mental illnesses are now known to be diseases of the brain. People with severe mental diseases, such as schizophrenia and bipolar mood disorder (manic–depressive psychosis) have "neurobiological disorders of their brains that affect their thinking and moods and that can be measured by changes in both brain structure and function" (1997, p. 4). He advocates that, within the United States, all state departments of mental health should be abolished and all medical departments of psychiatry should be combined with neurology.

The September 8, 1997, cover story for the *U.S. News and World Report*, entitled "What AA Won't Tell You," carefully observed that "science has yet to come up with enough information to resolve the disease versus behavior argument. Odds are that alcohol abuse will prove to be a combination of both the behavioral factors dominating in problem drinkers and biological factors weighing more heavily in the physically addicted" (pp. 60–61). In a subsequent issue (September 29, 1997), in separate rejoinders to the editor, two prominent psychiatrists were quick to challenge this rather innocuous (but valid) assertion. The first letter, from the director of the National Institute on Alcohol Abuse and Alcoholism, pointed out that "current evidence supports abstinence as the appropriate goal for persons with the medical disorder 'alcohol dependence' (alcoholism)" (Gordis, 1997, p. 5). The second letter, from the President of the American Society of Addiction Medicine, complained that "your article did not explain the critical difference between the problem drinker (the abuser) and alcoholics (those with the disease of addiction). . . . It is the genetic condition of compulsion . . . that causes the diseased alcoholic to lose control and continue to consume alcohol despite any legal or lethal consequences. . . . Americans have a difficult time accepting the medically established fact that alcoholism is a primary, biogenetic disease, principally because they don't understand the differences between self-imposed abuse versus alcoholism, with its compulsive disorder that causes loss of control. Genetic neurological brain research, brain imagery, and effective treatment programs have clearly established the medical model of alcoholism" (Talbott, 1997, p. 5).

It seems obvious that the effect of both letters is much more than an assertion that biological factors serve as "contributory" causes for alcoholism. Instead, the messages imply, at the very least, "necessary," and likely "necessary and sufficient" causation for these biological events. Breggin warns that "psychiatry and psychiatrists must not be allowed to make false claims about the genetic and biological origins of so-called mental illness. Such claims are unethical, if not fraudulent, and serve only to perpetuate the influence of the profession and individual practitioners" (1991, pp. 408–409).

Consider what the scientific evidence actually shows. Searles (1988) emphasized that alcohol use and abuse seems to be an area in which acceptance of genetic influence may have outstripped the data. Indeed, available scientific evidence supports the conclusion that alcoholism is not a genetic disease (Caddy, 1978; Fingarette, 1988a, 1988b; Mello, 1975; Pattison, 1976). Genetic influences on alcoholism and substance abuse are moderate at best and contribute only to susceptibility to these syndromes (Dinwiddie, 1992; George, 1993; Hill, 1992; Searles, 1988, 1991; Zucker & Lisansky-Gomberg, 1986).

Peele (1981) refuted several theories that emphasize that a complete answer to substance abuse cannot be found through analysis of genetic or biochemical factors alone. He demonstrated that these approaches completely ignored other data convincingly demonstrating the importance of environmental and psychosocial factors. In a more recent book on addiction, Peele (1989; see also Fingarette, 1988b) documented convincingly that "alcoholism involves a host of personal and environmental considerations aside from how alcohol affects the bodies of drinkers. . . . Biology is not behavior even in these areas where a drug or alcohol is taken into the body" (pp. 26–27). In a similar vein, the authors of prominent theories of alcoholism and substance abuse (Cox & Klinger, 1990; Newcomb & Earleywine, 1996; see also Begleiter & Kissin, 1995; Galizio & Maisto, 1985; and Levin, 1989) go out of their way to point out that genetic–biological factors do not guarantee that an individual will or will not use drugs. The weight contributed by biochemical reactivity is only a fraction of the entire causal network; biochemical reactivity can be nullified by contributions from sociocultural and psychological factors.

The present-day scientific consensus is that alcoholism is a genetically influenced disorder in which biological conditions serve primarily as "contributory" causal antecedents. "Even the most 'dyed in the wool' geneticist must accept that environmental factors are crucial to the development of alcoholism. . . . Rather than conceive of the genetic predisposition to alcoholism as a single-gene effect, or even as several, simple, major loci . . . it is more appropriate to consider a model based on many interacting components, each contributing only a small percentage of the overall risk" (Hodgkinson, Mullan, & Murray, 1991, p. 193). Similarly, in their summary chapter, the editors of a recent authoritative volume in alcoholism research emphasize that there is ample evidence that each of several levels of analysis—biological, psychological, and social—separately are needed to explain substance use (Galizio & Maisto, 1985, p. 428). We examine the genetic evidence for mental disorders in considerable detail in Chapter 4.

THE BIOMEDICAL MODEL: DEFINITION

Psychiatry is moving from the study of the "troubled mind" to the "broken brain."

—Andreasen, 1984, p. viii.

The biomedical viewpoint dictates that in essence mental disorders are medical diseases. Both types of illnesses result from biological and physiological malfunctions that lead to the person's distress and disability. Instead of the primary symptoms being physiological or anatomical, as in physical disease, the primary symptoms of mental disorder appear as psychological and behavioral problems. In mental disorder the human activity that is disturbed is behavior governed by the body's brain and nervous system. Accordingly, the symptoms of mental disorder involve our inner perceptions, thoughts, and emotions as well as our overt behaviors.

Mental disorders thus take the specific form of diseases of the central nervous system, the autonomic nervous system, or the endocrine system—any or all of which are inherited and/or caused by some pathological process. As a result, neither psychological factors nor a person's social–cultural environment are believed to play a causal role in the mental disorder—the percentage of their combined contribution to development of any mental disorder is quite low to nonexistent. As Andreasen observed, "The psychological or social terms used to describe ["breaks" in the brain], such as *loss of ego boundaries* or *lack of self-esteem*, are metaphors used to describe biological processes that we are just beginning to understand" (1984, p. 222).

A medical "disease" traditionally is defined as a harmful deviation from the normal structural or functional state of an organism, its abnormal state reflected in a distinctive pattern of signs or symptoms. It is an inability to perform functions in a natural fashion (King, 1982). Signs and symptoms are produced by the disease; the patient, in turn, is subjected to the signs and symptoms. Diseases disturb the typical efficiency of bodily structures and functions. A disease is a harmful deviation from the normal structural or functional state of an organism; health, in contrast, is the absence of illness (what people have when they are not sick or dying).

The major assumption of the model is that psychological disorders are really physical disorders. "Whenever you see mental illness, look to biology for the significant etiological data" (Bursten, 1979, p. 662). One needs to approach mental disorders in a manner equivalent to the study of physical illness. The biomedical tradition encompasses a well-defined, three-step sequence of investigative method. (1) It is necessary to identify a distinct disorder by grouping different, but co-occurring symptoms, together into a coherent disease entity, a *syndrome*, that can be reliably diagnosed. (2) Researchers need to isolate the *biological etiology* of the identified syndrome (i.e., explore its genetic origins and establish that the cause is a germ, a biochemical imbalance, or a neuroanatomical abnormality). (3) Researchers must discover a way to alleviate the abnormality through a *biological treatment* (most typically a drug) that directly targets the biological deviance. The goals of biological psychiatry, then, are to isolate a particular mental disorder (syndrome), discover its biological cause, and identify an effective biological treatment. Kety noted that a medical model evolves "from symptoms through syndromes to diseases with specific pathology and, ultimately, with definitive etiologies and rational treatment." Syndromes are labeled diseases when a common pathogenesis or underlying biological pathology is discovered. In short, the biomedical model is "an excellent example of the scientific method applied to the alleviation of human suffering" (1974, p. 959).

In sum, within the biomedical model, mental disease syndromes exist, each with a specific etiology, a disease-specific cure, and a disease-specific prevention. In cases where etiology is unknown, as typically is the case, the unshakable belief still remains that the cause ultimately will be found in the biology of the organism.

It is important to note that different versions of the medical model have been offered, and new variations continually appear. Its quintessential version, the infectious disease model, "pervades all of medicine and seeks a full explanation of a disease on the basis of a single cause, whether the cause is bacterial, genetic, viral, enzymatic, immunologic, toxic, nutritional, or physiological. In its most general form it states that most diseases can be explained on the basis of single causes" (Weiner, 1978, p. 27). By taking a circumscribed view of people, the prototypical biomedical model leaves little if any room within its framework for the social, psychological, or behavioral dimensions of human living.

Biomedical Causes of Mental Disease

Medical practitioners refer to diseases as resulting from specific causes (etiology). For example, bacteria are said to cause pneumonia and gonorrhea; common viruses are said to cause measles, mumps, and hepatitis; an accidental fall causes a broken leg. In general, diseases have two major sets of causes, endogenous and exogenous. Endogenous pathological factors arise from the operation of genes (known or unknown) transmitted through heredity. Exogenous pathological factors arise from the environment. Some diseases show significant genetic influences; some are heavily environmental in origin.

Bloom (1988) observed that during the mid-nineteenth century, the great human killers and maimers were the infectious and nutritional physical diseases. Germ theory, developed in major part by Louis Pasteur (1822–1895) and Robert Koch (1834–1910), became the predominant theory of disease. Starting in 1850 and continuing over the next hundred years, one victory after another was attained over the major infectious diseases (smallpox, typhus, cholera, typhoid fever, plague, malaria, diphtheria, tuberculosis, and tetanus), many sexually transmitted diseases, diseases caused by malnutrition (scurvy, beriberi, pellagra, rickets, and epidemic goiter), and diseases such as rubella and polio.

Within the biomedical model, causation of mental disorder similarly is thought to be singular and unilateral. Mental disease reflects the one-way effects of abnormal biological activity on human behavior. If the physiology is affected (e.g., by genes, infection, or trauma), the inevitable result is a corresponding effect on human action itself. Andreasen pulls no punches when she notes, "The various forms of mental illness are due to many different types of brain abnormalities, including the loss of nerve cells and excesses and deficits in chemical transmission between neurons; sometimes the fault may be in the pattern of wiring or the circuitry, sometimes in the command centers, and sometimes in the way messages move along the wires" (1984, p. 221).

Within the biomedical framework, only biological factors are considered. As Engel (1980) emphasized, since social, psychological, and behavioral dimensions fall outside its narrow framework, they are, for all purposes, ignored. Mental disorders are not the result of unfortunate sociocultural, environmental, or other learning experiences, nor the result of violations of societal norms and values that evoke societal retribution and confinement (whether or not in the guise of concerned treatment).

Instead, mental disorders, like other medical diseases, are real diagnostic entities having a specific organic etiology, organic pathology, and natural course and outcome (unless treated). These mental diseases have an existence independent of the patient: "The etiology and manifestations of mental disorders [are] entirely impersonal or alien, not to be found in or relevant to the life history of the patient. The patient's symptoms are seen as the reaction of an organism under siege from without" (Kessler, 1990, p. 142). A noted health psychologist described this feature of the model as mechanistic: "The body is treated like a machine that is fixed by removing or replacing the ailing part or destroying the foreign body that is causing the problem" (McClelland, 1985, p. 452). What is involved is an affliction of the body that is sharply separate from the psychological and social processes of the mind. Psychosocial factors contribute minimally, if at all, to the resulting mental disorder. In short, different mental disorders are the sole expression of different biological disease processes. All mental disorders can be explained as problematic or aberrant physiological processes.

For biomedical adherents, the legitimate role of scientific research into mental disorders is to isolate the aberrant physiological processes, the specific biochemical or structural defects, that characterize particular disorders and to discover treatments that would specifically counteract these biological defects. Scientific study of disease (pathology) concentrates on any disease that can be reliably diagnosed through a distinctive syndrome. Scientific explanation occurs through determination of the disorder's specific biological cause (etiology) and through understanding of (a) the mechanisms of its development (pathogenesis); (b) the structural changes associated with its disease process (morphological changes); and (c) the functional (mental and behavioral) consequences of these changes. The causes are either endogenous (idiopathic, innate, primary, "essential," and found within the organism itself) or exogenous (external or occurring from outside the organism—for example, agents that are toxic or traumatic, communicable or noncommunicable).

A Caution

Present-day psychiatric proponents of the biomedical model may disagree about the validity of any one particular assumption or theme just summarized. One can clearly find conflicting and often arbitrary discussions of the biomedical model. It's likely that more sophisticated present-day advocates would acknowledge, for instance, that the science of psychopathology is far from possessing incontrovertible information about the exact biological causes of the wide range of mental disorders listed in DSM-IV (American Psychiatric Association, 1994). They might be quick to admit, for example, that whatever neurotransmitter abnormality is distinctive to a specific disorder is likely complex, involving multiple (rather than single) transmitters at multiple brain sites.

Present-day biomedical proponents, especially the currently dominant neo-Kraepelinians, validly underscore that (a) "the practice of medicine is based on the application of knowledge concerning human biology to the prevention and treatment of illness" (Guze, 1978, p. 303), and that (b) biology has a vital place in psychiatry. Accompanying these assertions, however, remains a basic conviction that whenever precise scientific information about mental disorders eventually arrives, its basic shape will involve structural and functional abnormalities within identified areas of the human brain and nervous system. Successful treatments, in turn, will be biological in the form of medications or other interventions that remediate the specific biological abnormalities identified. Unfortunately, however, biological psychiatrists often tend to endorse research fads "that momentarily 'explain' in sophisticated terms the physiological etiology and mechanics of various syndromes and diagnoses. Later, such results are not replicated, and specific hypotheses quietly fade away while the general theoretical approach remains" (Ross & Pam, 1995, p. 3).

Guze, a prominent neo-Kraepelinian psychiatrist, offered some up-to-date reformulations of the biomedical model. Unexpectedly he noted that "the medical model does not require ignoring the patient's psychosocial context. On the contrary, the medical model suggests that the social and psychological environments of the individual may be very important, but their role in illness cannot be assessed correctly if the medical model is ignored." He continued, "No comprehensive view of illness can ignore man's psychosocial world; but neither can it ignore man's biological nature." Guze added that "adherents of the medical model generally consider biological processes important in the development of psychiatric disorders, while opponents of the medical model generally minimize the role of biologic processes" (1978, pp. 296, 303). Kety similarly asserted, "Environmental factors have always been an important part of medical models of illness, and, in the case of disorders of thought, mood, and behavior, one recognizes the operation of psychological processes and social influences that cannot be described or examined in physicochemical terms" (1974, pp. 961–962).

Taking these assertions at face value, one easily might conclude that multicausality is entirely compatible with the biomedical model. However, one gradually learns first that biomedical adherents often use the term "environment" in a quite restricted sense. Environment refers primarily to those external environmental onslaughts on an organism or person that produce biological (brain) damage: factors such as viruses, head injuries, or abnormalities resulting from brain malnourishment. In this restricted sense, the term *environment* is not being used to denote interpersonal, familial, social, or cultural factors that are influential in human development and adjustment. At best, the restricted use may include precipitating stressors.

Moreover, as one continues to read these authors, the overwhelming predominance accorded biological factors eventually emerges intact and steadfast. The disarming deception of Guze's earlier ecumenical comments is revealed within the same article in Guze's final summary:

"Biologic processes play important, specific roles in the development of many psychiatric disorders, just as they do in general medical disorders. Medical training provides the best preparation to understand etiology and pathogenesis in psychiatric conditions and for prescribing and supervising treatments" (Guze, 1978, p. 306). In a separate journal article, Guze reveals further inconsistent sentiments when he advocates that biology is the science of psychiatry, and that no other science is relevant: "Biology clearly offers the only comprehensive basis for psychiatry just as it does for the rest of medicine. . . . I believe the continuing debate about the biological base of psychiatry is derived much more from philosophical, ideological, and political concerns than from scientific ones" (1989, pp. 318, 322). Kety echoes similarly inconsistent emphases when he amplifies later, in the same article quoted, that "the psychiatrist is best equipped to carry out these responsibilities toward the mentally ill on the basis of his broad background in medicine, in clinical psychology and psychopathology, and in the scientific method as it is applied to medicine" (1974, p. 962). One frequently encounters similar instances of what seems to be fairly described as "medical imperialism": the insistence that anything remotely connected with health belongs under the supervision of the medical profession (Illich, 1976).

Ross, describing his experiences as a psychiatric resident in training, noted what he calls "the universal disavowal of biological reductionism upon direct challenge. Any direct challenge to the cognitive errors of biomedical reductionism was always met with the response that the biopsychosocial model was accepted throughout biological psychiatry. Once lip service was paid to the biopsychosocial approach, however, and the challenge forgotten, the logical fallacies rose to the conversational surface immediately" (1995, p. 87).

Kleinman offered another interpretation of the lip service so often given by psychiatrists to the biopsychosocial model. He noted that the entrenched biomedical model "offers a stratographic view of disorder in which biology is the foundation, and psychological and social dimensions of sickness are seen as epiphenomenal, superstructural layers to be stripped away to get at the infrastructural, i.e. biological, base" (1988, pp. 143–144). Pam adds that "biological psychiatry has made a travesty of the biopsychosocial paradigm, either by largely omitting psychosocial factors in its clinical formulations or by downplaying them to mere incidental 'triggers'" (1995, p. 4).

Despite earlier protestations by these and other contemporary psychiatric authorities, the enduring message that recurrently emerges is the following: Madness is predominantly a disease of the brain; the psychiatrist is and must remain the primary scientist and guardian of the mentally disturbed. If the central problem in the etiology and treatment of the mental disorders is one of biology, little reason exists for biomedical psychiatrists to be concerned with the phenomenological meanings that a troubled person makes of his or her experience, or with the social and cultural setting in which he or she conducts daily living.

If present-day psychiatrists really believe in multiple causes for mental disorders, (a) they must be ready to repudiate the classic unicausal, biomedical model of mental disorders or substantially redefine the model to include explicitly psychological and sociocultural causal and treatment factors; (b) they must be ready to proclaim that all mental health disciplines have something real and important to offer toward scientific understanding and treatment of mental disorders; and (c) they must, in order to counterbalance continuing misunderstandings, be ready to shout from the roof tops that it is a misleading, partial truth to assert simply that mental disorders are diseases of the brain. One always must simultaneously shout that mental disorders also involve deviant cognitive and behavioral learning processes and are the result of sociocultural influences and stressors.

Unfortunately, one seldom finds careful qualifications anywhere in the psychiatric literature. The result of the continuing imperial reign of the biomedical model, among both psychiatrists and the lay public, is an overwhelming monocausal message: Mental disorders are nothing more than brain diseases. Without qualification or expansion, the traditional biomedical model leaves little, if any, room within its framework to address seriously a person's patterns of thoughts, feelings, overt behaviors, and the social relationships that can play an essential role in mental disorder. As Eisenberg warns, "The peril is that psychiatry may come to focus exclusively on the brain as an organ and to overlook the experience of the patient as a person" (1986, p. 500).

THE BIOMEDICAL MODEL: CRITIQUE ONE

The major argument I will make against the biomedical model is that the scientific evidence from the field of genetics robustly and overwhelmingly contradicts any monocausal theory of psychopathology, hence contradicting the long-standing biomedical model. This evidence is presented in Chapter 4. The remainder of this chapter will offer several logical analyses of the biomedical position.

Chapter 1 clarified that, in contrast to an immediate or efficient cause, a *distal cause* refers to an ultimate factor, remote in time, that initially sets a mental disorder into motion. In general, the distal or ultimate cause of a mental disorder can refer to one or both of two broad groups of factors: genetic or environmental. Valid etiological understanding of mental disorders involves both distal and proximal processes.

No sophisticated scientist of psychopathology would deny that what can be called the *immediate cause* (mechanism) of mental disorder—or, for that matter, of all human behavior—occurs through physiological activity within the brain. Faulty conditioning or learning that occurred during childhood has to be represented presently in some lasting change in brain structure and activity. The same can be said for such conditions as presently found irrational cognitions, deficits in interpersonal relationships, or societal oppressions. The structure and activity patterns of the brain reflect experience, not just the biology one is born with. Our brains are the control mechanisms for the entire range of our physical and mental functioning. Our thoughts, feelings, and memories occur within episodes of cortical neural firings. Whatever new learnings we acquire or arrive at, through maturation or pathogens, invariably are registered in our ongoing cortical processes.

"If the mind exerts rational control over behavior, then it is the nerve cells, in their ceaseless synaptic interactions, that are exerting rational control. If the mind experiences depression, then the nerve cells have fallen into a particular physiological state. If the mind hears voices, real or imagined, it is the nerve cells, in a particular pattern of secretion, that perform the task of hearing. These notions imply that agents that change the state of activity in nerve cells will change the psychological state of the mind. The converse is also true. Agents that change the state of the mind will change the state of the corresponding brain cells" (Lickey & Gordon, 1991, p. 355).

The biomedical model, however, uniquely makes the additional assertion that the distal causes of mental disorder reside in abnormal brain structure and/or activity, either congenitally present through genetic transmission or introduced traumatically from various external sources. The uniquely distinctive biomedical claim is that the sole or major starting point for mental disorder invariably is remotely initiated (often at conception) and is continually active in creating aberrant biology and brain activity.

This distinction between immediate and distal causes is crucial. The *immediate* cause of a mental disorder has been referred to metaphorically in the psychiatric literature as the "final common pathway" of the mental disorder. The assertion is that no matter what remote etiological causes may be operative, the immediate precursor to onset of mental disorder invariably is in the form of a dysfunctional contemporary biological process operating within a particular individual.

For example, in Akiskal and McKinney's (1973, 1975) theory of depression, the biological pathway immediately disrupted in depression is the activity of the diencephalon of the midbrain, which is the brain center of reinforcement and is involved in the modulation of arousal, mood, motivation, and psychomotor functioning. Although a variety of chemical, experiential, and behavioral events can serve as preceding and remote causal factors, the presenting symptoms of all episodes of depression reflect the contemporarily present abnormally functioning diencephalon. If understood correctly as the immediate cause of mental disorder, the final common pathway is a quite powerful and sophisticated notion, although yet to be empirically established.

A neurological psychologist recently demonstrated in detail the same important distinction. In his terms, the inescapable biological nature of the final common pathway in mental disorder reflects the fact that "all mentation and behavior originate from what would commonly be described as biological events. Behavior itself derives from muscular activity controlled by the peripheral nervous system. The peripheral nervous system is controlled, in turn, by central nervous system activity. Thus, all mentation and behavior are entirely traceable to neural—read biological—events." The central nervous system "does not play favorites between biological and psychological causes. Both types of causes are reflected in the structure and function of the central nervous system." This emphasizes that "one important point of unanimity among various schools of thought in psychology [is] that the efficient causes of behavior reside ultimately in neural events" (Gorenstein, 1992, pp. 33, 123, 124).

Holmes noted similarly that mental disorders "can be due to any one of a number of different causes, but it is essential to recognize that ultimately *all disorders are caused by physiological processes in the nervous system.*" The essential mechanism underlying a mental disorder will always be expressed through some physiological substrate: "There are different starting points for abnormal behavior, but ultimately they are all funneled through physiology" (1997, p. 20).

Human activity always occurs through the vehicle of the central nervous system. "Ultimately, the distinction between biological and psychological processes may be artifactual. All behavior rests on a biological substrate, but one which is responsive to and facilitates interaction with the external environment" (Shelton, Hollon, Purdon, & Loosen, 1991, p. 214).

The conceptualization of brain physiology as constituting the final common pathway, as the proximate cause of all mental disorder, has both theoretical and practical implications (Holmes, 1997, p. 20). By forcing our explanations to specify, whenever possible, precise underlying biological abnormalities for specific mental disorders, it expands our understanding of how etiological factors actually produce their effects. If a series of stressors lead to depression, for example, an important understanding occurs if we know precisely what effects the sequence of aversive events has on which specific brain and central nervous system physiology, whose altered activity produces the symptoms of clinical depression.

The distinctive claim of the biomedical model is not that the immediate cause of mental disorder is in the form of aberrant brain activity. Instead, the unique claim of the biomedical model is that there is only one distal or starting point for abnormal behavior: genetic transmission of, or environmental insult-producing, aberrant brain biology. The biomedical model places an exclusive priority on distal biological causes of mental disorder. It is this biological distal-cause bias that so vividly separates the biomedical model from other perspectives on psychopathology.

The implication seems to be that only organic, biological distal causes can be responsible for an organic immediate cause (e.g., the final common pathway). This notion, however, is contradicted by a recent large scale task force that reviewed the available evidence regarding psychological stressors and mental disorders (American Psychological Society, 1996). The task force concluded that extensive research on both animals and humans has demonstrated that repeated exposure to stressful psychological experiences can result in persisting changes in brain structure and biochemistry. Psychological, environmental, and sociocultural factors thus can directly produce abnormal brain biology.

THE BIOMEDICAL MODEL: CRITIQUE TWO

Another logical inadequacy of the biomedical model has been documented. Essentially the counterargument is that mental disorders do not satisfy the conditions necessary for defining a biological disorder.

Heinrichs examined in detail the three central conditions of the biomedical model that need to be satisfied before one can identify a mental disorder as a biologically based brain disease. (1) A particular mental disorder must have a set of symptoms that cohere as a clinical entity, an entity that is distinct from other disorders. (2) A disorder must be linked, through empirical research, with nervous system dysfunction—it must have evidence of a clearly discovered biological abnormality. (3) Brain systems thought to exhibit the established abnormality must be known to control behavior functions that fit the psychological characteristics actually seen in the given mental disorder; "the behavioral consequences must be understandable in terms of functional properties of affected brain areas or systems" (1993, p. 221).

Heinrichs applied the three criteria to schizophrenia, one of the major (i.e., most severe) mental disorders; schizophrenia must fit, if any disorder does, the biomedical model. His analysis of the three necessary conditions led to the unavoidable conclusion that "in each case, the evidence is weak, or equivocal." First, the evidence supports that schizophrenia is a heterogeneous disorder, not a coherent, differen- tiable clinical entity: "Researchers have been unable to decide whether schizophrenia is a single entity with variable forms of expression or a diversity of unrelated and partly related disorders and syndromes." (In an independent authoritative analysis, Boyle [1993] documented the identical conclusion.) Second, little consistent evidence exists that links schizophrenia to a particular brain abnormality; schizophrenia is a neurologically ambiguous disorder, in that the search for neuro- pathology has yielded inconsistent, even contradictory, findings: "Some schizophrenic patients seem to have a dopamine-related illness; some have alterations in brain volumes, chemistry, or metabolism. But neuropathologies that are linked directly to schizophrenia have not been found." Finally, the anatomy and activity of the brains of schizo- phrenia patients often are found to be abnormal, with a kind of rough convergence on certain neural structures; however, "patients with schizophrenia do not behave in ways that closely resemble the behav- ior of patients with frontotemporal brain dysfunction. Conversely, neurological patients with damage to these structures rarely demon- strate schizophrenic behavior" (1993, pp. 221, 229).

Heinrichs's argument can validly be generalized to the entire gamut of mental disorders. Very few disorders found in DSM-IV have strong evidence that they constitute clear-cut, distinct clinical entities. In fact, the same patient very often receives multiple diagnoses; that is, in both community and clinical samples, rates of comorbidity of DSM disor- ders are substantial (Kessler, McGonagle, Zhao, Nelson, Hughes, et al., 1994; Lilienfeld, Waldman, & Israel, 1994; Robins, Locke, & Regier, 1991). Also, although DSM-IV permits generally reliable diagnoses of mental disorders, a major question remains about the validity or ac- tual existence of many of the distinct categories described (Clark, Watson, & Reynolds, 1995; Garfield, 1993).

Also, thus far, only a few DSM-IV disorders have accumulated any evidence for biological "markers"—laboratory tests that might invari- ably document the presence of a particular mental disorder. In the case of the few biological markers that have been suggested (e.g., short latency to REM sleep for depression, elevated blood lactate levels for panic disorder), the evidence indicates the markers are far from uni- versal indicants; in some cases, such as schizophrenia, psychological markers (e.g., deficient smooth-pursuit eye tracking) are equally plau- sible. Hence, even though the biomedical model has led to formula- tion of biological treatments for the mental disorders, it has failed thus far to identify the essential biological cause of particular mental disor- ders. One psychiatrist makes this point quite sarcastically: "The only biochemical imbalances that we can identify with certainty in the brains of psychiatric patients are the ones produced by the psychiatric treatment itself" (Breggin, 1991, p. 12).

Last, though suggestive evidence points to some structural pathology and biochemical imbalance in the brain for some mental disorders, the abnormalities suggested have not been tied to specific, known brain mechanisms that would explain the respective symptoms and behaviors of the various mental disorders involved.

The overall conclusion is that available scientific evidence offers little firm support for the three major conditions required to establish that mental disorders are biological conditions. Hence, one must fall back on an act of faith to justify continued promulgation of the traditional biomedical model.

Postscript

Spitzer and Wilson (1975) similarly concluded that most mental disorders do not meet their four presumed criteria for a psychological dysfunction. That is, most mental disorders (a) do not have an identified specific etiology (e.g., a germ); (b) are not qualitatively different from some aspect of normal functioning; (c) do not show a demonstrable associated physical pathology or marker; and (d) are not internal biological processes that when once initiated proceed somewhat independently of environmental conditions outside the body. They concluded that mental disorders do not fit the requirements of a traditional medical model. Spitzer and Wilson, nevertheless, advocated that the biomedical model should not be abandoned until a more valid model should arise.

The remainder of this book offers the thesis that a more valid model, supported strongly by scientific evidence, has arrived—the multicausal biopsychosocial model. Accordingly, now is the time to abandon the biomedical model. Unfortunately, evidence alone, no matter how robust, may not be sufficient to overcome the status quo. Engel (1977, 1980) emphasized that, within psychiatry, the biomedical model has gone beyond the limits of scientific method. Instead, it has acquired the authority and tradition of dogma—a dogma that distorts or ignores any conflicting data.

PHYSICAL MEDICINE'S EXPANSION OF THE BIOMEDICAL MODEL: CRITIQUE THREE

Unquestionably in physical medicine the biomedical disease model has been enormously successful in the conquest of infectious diseases, such as smallpox, typhoid fever, malaria, cholera, diphtheria, tuberculosis, measles, polio, sexually transmitted diseases, and e-coli infestation. The history of medicine is a story of triumphs of disease control and prevention.

Nevertheless, the biomedical model more recently has been unable to address adequately a number of contemporary physical health problems. It has encountered considerable difficulties with chronic diseases such as cancer, diabetes, and coronary heart disease, which have become the bane and primary challenge of modern medicine. "With the reduction in the number of new cases of infections and nutritional diseases . . . , the extent of illness and number of deaths due to chronic disease became more visible. Along with their increased visibility came the realization that a simple-minded . . . mechanistic biological approach to their prevention and treatment was no longer successful. . . . [An increased interest has risen] in how psychological factors interacted with biomedical factors in the development of illness" (Bloom, 1988, pp. 12–13). Whereas infectious diseases tend to be tied to specific single causal agents, chronic diseases have multiple behavioral and sociocultural as well as biological causes. Chronic diseases, for example, are related significantly to an individual's health habits and ability to adapt to economic, social, and cultural stressors. Promotion or restitution of health often necessitates change in peoples' behaviors.

Though the biomedical model has been most successful in the conquest of infectious diseases, it has encountered considerable difficulties with the more complex and chronic diseases (e.g., cancer, diabetes, and coronary heart disease) that account for most of the deaths in modern society. "These diseases represent chronic and usually slowly developing degenerative processes with markedly heterogeneous etiologies, where the boundaries of the organism must be transcended in the search for causal factors" (Ohman & Magnusson, 1987, p. 8).

As a result, rather than limiting themselves to necessary and sufficient biological causal factors, medical researchers have begun to cope with multiple networks of causal factors where a prominent role must be given to psychological and sociocultural environmental domains. Medical science, then, has adopted a new position: Most medical diseases have multiple causes and most causal factors are merely "contributory"—rather than "necessary" or "sufficient." Physical medicine, in turn, is also discovering the validity of newly developed ancillary disciplines such as health psychology and behavioral medicine.

CONCLUSION

Approaching the millennium, we Americans, and the psychiatric establishment, have become most comfortable thinking about mental disorder through the template of the unicausal biomedical model. Mental disorders are solely medical diseases that are expressed through psychological and behavioral symptoms. A mental disease is a present-day expression of a congenital or traumatic disturbance in the normal structural or functional biological state of an organism. Mental disorder is brain disorder. Mental disorder is genetically transmitted. Mental disorder reflects the one-way effects of abnormal biological activity on human behavior; psychosocial factors contribute minimally, if at all, to development of mental disorder. All mental disorders result from congenital or early problematic or aberrant physiological processes. The only legitimate role of scientific research into mental disorders is to isolate the specific biochemical or structural defects that characterize particular disorders and to discover treatments that specifically reembody these biological defects. Mental disorders result from genetic transmission of biological abnormalities in mental disorder.

Is it valid to assert that, far from being complex or multiple, actual causation of mental disorder is singularly and unilaterally biological? Is it valid that all mental disorders are genetically transmitted? Is it valid that environmental factors play no major role except in the form of invasive pathogens or other biological traumas that produce abnormalities in a person's biology? Our logical analyses above suggest that the initial answer to each question is "No."

It is vital to keep in mind, in light of the discussion in Chapter 1, that rejection of the biomedical model as the "necessary and sufficient" explanation of mental disorders is not to reject its legitimate role in identifying either "necessary" or "contributory" biological causal factors. Instead, the approach to disease must be broadened "to include the psychosocial without sacrificing the enormous advantages of the biomedical approach" (Engel, 1977, p. 130). Similarly, rejection of the biomedical model does not require adoption of Cartesian dualism and requires no position in regard to the unity of brain and mind. Rejection of the biomedical model does not necessitate designation of mental disorders as defects in character or lapses in morality, or as resulting from a parental ineptitude—all of which can signal an occasion for casting blame. Most importantly, rejection of the biomedical model is not a rejection of scientific method and empirical evidence; indeed, the weight of the evidence demands rejection of the biomedical model as a sole explanatory framework for mental disorders.

What is direly needed is that either the scope of the traditional biomedical model be broadened significantly or that a new, more satisfactory multicausal model be formulated. From either perspective, researchers and practitioners of psychopathology, rather than limiting their perspectives to specific biologically defined necessary and sufficient causal factors, can begin to learn to cope with multiple networks of causality in which a prominent role must be given also to environmental and psychological factors. "Any single-factor linear causal model is unrealistic for understanding disease in general, and mental disorder in particular" (Oman & Magnesian, 1987, p. 18).

Chapter 4 will examine in detail additional and crucial scientific evidence that unambiguously invalidates the basic tenets of the monocausal biomedical model.

REFERENCES

Akiskal, H. S., & McKinney, W. T. (1973). Depressive disorders: Toward a unified hypothesis. *Science, 182,* 20–29.

Akiskal, H. S., & McKinney, W. T. (1975). Overview of recent research in depression: Integration of ten conceptual models into a comprehensive clinical frame. *Archives of General Psychiatry, 32,* 285–305.

American Psychiatric Association. (1980). *Diagnostic and statistical manual of mental disorders* (3d ed.). Washington, DC: Author.

American Psychiatric Association. (1994). *Diagnostic and statistical manual of mental disorders* (4th ed.). Washington, DC: Author.

American Psychological Society. (1996, February 1). Human Capital Initiative (HCI) (Report No. 3). *APS Observer* (special issue). Washington, DC: Author.

Andreasen, N. C. (1984). *The broken brain: The biological revolution in psychiatry.* New York: Harper & Row.

Begleiter, H., & Kissin, B. (Eds.). (1995). *The genetics of alcoholism.* New York: Oxford University Press.

Blashfield, R. (1984). *The classification of psychopathology.* New York: Plenum.

Bloom, B. L. (1986). Primary prevention: An overview. In J. T. Barber & S. W. Talbott (Eds.), *Primary prevention in psychiatry: State of the art* (pp. 3–12). Washington, DC: American Psychiatric Press.

Bloom, B. L. (1988). *Health psychology: A psychological perspective.* Englewood Cliffs, NJ: Prentice Hall.

Boyle, M. (1993). *Schizophrenia—A scientific delusion?* New York: Routledge.

Breggin, P. R. (1991). *Toxic psychiatry: Psychiatry's assault on the brain with drugs, electroshock, biochemical diagnoses, and genetic theories.* New York: St. Martin's Press.

Bursten, B. (1979). Psychiatry and the rhetoric of models. *American Journal of Psychiatry, 136,* 661–666.

Caddy, G. R. (1978). Toward a multivariate analysis of alcohol abuse. In P. E. Nathan, G. A. Marlatt, & T. Loberg (Eds.), *Alcoholism: New directions in behavioral research and treatment.* New York: Plenum.

Clark, L. A., Watson, D., & Reynolds, S. (1995). Diagnosis and classification: Challenges to the current system and future directions. *Annual Review of Psychology, 46,* 121–153.

Cox, W. M., & Klinger, E. (1990). Incentive motivation, affective change, and alcohol use: A model. In W. M. Cox & E. Klinger (Eds.), *Why people drink: Parameters of alcohol as a reinforcer.* New York: Gardner.

Dinwiddie, S. H. (1992). Patterns of alcoholism inheritance. *Journal of Substance Abuse, 4,* 155–163.

Eisenberg, L. (1986). Mindlessness and brainlessness in psychiatry. *British Journal of Psychiatry, 148,* 497–508.

Eisenberg, L. (1995). The social construction of the human brain. *American Journal of Psychiatry, 152,* 1563–1575.

Engel, G. L. (1977). The need for a new medical model: A challenge to biomedicine. *Science, 196,* 129–136.

Engel, G. L. (1980). The clinical application of the biopsychosocial model. *American Journal of Psychiatry, 137,* 535–544.

Fabrega, H. (1974). *Disease and social behavior: An interdisciplinary perspective.* Boston: MIT Press.

Fingarette, H. (1988a). Alcoholism: The mythical disease. *The Public Interest, 91,* 3–22.

Fingarette, H. (1988b). *Heavy drinking: The myth of alcoholism as a disease.* Berkeley and Los Angeles: University of California Press.

Foulks, E. F. (1979). Discussion: Relevant generic issues. In A. Gaw (Ed.), *Cross-cultural psychiatry* (pp. 237–246). Boston, MA: John Wright.

Galizio, M., & Maisto, S. A. (1985). Toward a biopsychosocial theory of substance abuse. In M. Galizio & S. A. Maisto (Eds.), *Determinants of substance abuse: Biological, psychological, and environmental factors* (pp. 425–429). New York: Plenum.

Garfield, S. L. (1993). Methodological problems in clinical diagnosis. In P. B. Sutker & H. E. Adams (Eds.), *Comprehensive handbook of psychopathology* (2d ed., pp. 27–46). New York: Plenum.

George, F. R. (1993). Genetic models in the study of alcoholism and substance abuse mechanisms. *Progress in Neuropsychopharmacology and Biological Psychiatry, 17,* 345–361.

Goldberg, D. P., & Huxley, P. (1992). *Common mental disorders: A bio-social model.* London: Tavistock/Routledge.

Goodwin, D. W., & Guze, S. B. (1989). *Psychiatric diagnosis* (4th ed.). New York: Oxford University Press.

Gordis, E. (1997, September 29). Letters: Controlled drinking. *U.S. News & World Report, 123,* 5.

Gorenstein, E. E. (1992). *The science of mental illness.* San Diego, CA: Academic Press.

Guze, S. (1978). Nature of illness: Why psychiatry is a branch of medicine. *Comprehensive Psychiatry, 19,* 295–307.

Guze, S. (1989). Biological psychiatry: Is there any other kind? *Psychological Medicine, 19,* 315–323.

Hall, L. L. (Ed.). (1996). *Genetics and mental illness: Evolving issues for research and society.* New York: Plenum.

Hall, L. L., & Flynn, L. M. (1996). In defense of families of the mentally ill. *American Journal of Psychiatry, 153,* 1373–1374.

Heinrichs, R. W. (1993). Schizophrenia and the brain: Conditions for a neuropsychology of madness. *American Psychologist, 48,* 221–233.

Herbert, W. (1997, April 21). Politics of biology. *U.S. News & World Report, 122,* 72–80.

Hill, S. Y. (1992). Is there a genetic basis of alcoholism? *Biological Psychiatry, 32,* 955–957.

Hodgkinson, S., Mullan, M., & Murray, R. M. (1991). The genetics of vulner-
    ability to alcoholism. In P. McGuffin & R. Murray (Eds.), *The new genetics of
    mental illness* (pp. 182–197). Oxford, England: Butterworth-Heinemann.
Holmes, D. S. (1997). *Abnormal psychology* (3d ed.). New York: Addison Wesley
    Longman.
Illich, I. (1976). *Medical nemesis: The expropriation of health.* New York: Pantheon.
Kessler, R. C., McGonagle, K. A., Zhao, S., Nelson, C. P., Hughes, M., Eshleman,
    S., Wittchen, H-V., & Kendler, K. S. (1994). Lifetime and 12-month preva-
    lence of DSM-III-R psychiatric disorders in the United States: Results from
    the National Comorbidity Study. *Archives of General Psychiatry, 51*, 8–19.
Kessler, R. J. (1990). Models of disease and the diagnosis of schizophrenia.
    Psychiatry, 53, 140–147.
Kety, S. S. (1974). From rationalization to reason. *American Journal of Psychia-
    try, 131*, 957–963.
King, L. S. (1982). *Medical thinking: A historical preface.* Princeton, NJ: Princeton
    University Press.
Kleinman, A. (1988). *Rethinking psychiatry.* London: Free Press.
Klerman, G. (1978). The evolution of a scientific nosology. In J. Shershow (Ed.),
    Schizophrenia, science and practice. Cambridge: Harvard University Press.
Laing, R. D. (1964). Is schizophrenia a disease? *International Journal of Social
    Psychiatry, 10*, 184–193.
Laing, R. D. (1967). *The politics of experience.* London: Pelican Books.
Laing, R. D., & Esterson, A. (1964). *Sanity, madness and the family.* New York:
    Basic Books.
Levin, J. D. (1989). *Alcoholism: A bio-psycho-social approach.* New York: Hemisphere.
Lickey, M. E., & Gordon, B. (1991). *Medicine and mental illness: The use of drugs
    in psychiatry.* New York: Freeman.
Lilienfeld, S. O., Waldman, I. D., & Israel, A. C. (1994). A critical examination
    of the use of the term and concept of comorbidity in psychopathology
    research. *Clinical Psychology: Science and Practice, 1*, 71–83.
McClelland, D. C. (1985). The social mandate of health psychology. *American
    Behavioral Science, 28*, 451–467.
Mello, N. K. (1975). A semantic aspect of alcoholism. In H. D. Cappell & A. E.
    LeBlanc (Eds.), *Biological and behavioral approaches to drug dependence.*
    Toronto, Canada: Addiction Research Foundation.
Newcomb, M., & Earleywine, M. (1996). Intrapersonal contributions to drug
    use: The willing host. *American Behavioral Scientist, 39*, 823–837.
Ohman, A., & Magnusson, D. (1987). An interactional paradigm for research
    in psychopathology. In D. Magnusson & A. Ohman (Eds.), *Psychopathol-
    ogy: An interactional perspective* (pp. 3–21). Orlando, FL: Academic Press.
Pam, A. (1995). Introduction. In C. A. Ross & A. Pam (Eds.), *Pseudoscience in
    biological psychiatry: Blaming the body* (pp. 1–6). New York: Wiley.
Pattison, E. M. (1976). Nonabstinent drinking goals in the treatment of alco-
    holism. In R. J. Gibbons, Y. Israel, H. Kalant, R. E. Popharn, W. Schmidt,
    & R. G. Smart (Eds.), *Research advances in alcohol and drug problems* (Vol.
    3). New York: Wiley.
Peele, S. (1981). Reductionism in the psychology of the eighties: Can biochem-
    istry eliminate addiction, mental illness, and pain? *American Psycholo-
    gist, 36*, 807–818.

Peele, S. (1989). *Diseasing of America: Addiction treatment out of control.* Lexington, MA: Lexington Books.

Reiser, M. (1988). Are psychiatric educators "losing the mind"? *American Journal of Psychiatry, 145,* 148–153.

Robins, L. N., Locke, B. Z., & Regier, D. A. (1991). An overview of psychiatric disorders in America. In L. N. Robins & D. A. Regier (Eds.), *Psychiatric disorders in America* (pp. 328–366). New York: Free Press.

Ross, C. A. (1995). Errors of logic in biological psychiatry. In C. A. Ross & A. Pam (Eds.), *Pseudoscience in biological psychiatry: Blaming the body* (pp. 85–128). New York: Wiley.

Ross, C. A., & Pam, A. (Eds.). (1995). *Pseudoscience in biological psychiatry: Blaming the body.* New York: Wiley.

Scheff, T. J. (1966). *Being mentally ill: A sociological theory.* Chicago, IL: Aldine.

Searles, J. S. (1988). The role of genetics in the pathogenesis of alcoholism. *Journal of Abnormal Behavior, 97,* 153–167.

Searles, J. S. (1991). The genetics of alcoholism: Impact on family and sociological models of addiction. *Family Dynamics of Addiction Quarterly, 1,* 8–21.

Shelton, R. C., Hollon, S. D., Purdon, S. E., & Loosen, P. T. (1991). Biological and psychological aspects of depression. *Behavior Therapy, 22,* 201–228.

Spitzer, R., Sheehy, M., & Endicott, J. (1977). DSM-III: Guiding principles. In V. Rakoff, H. Stancer, & H. Kedward (Eds.), *Psychiatric diagnosis.* London: Macmillan.

Spitzer, R. L., & Wilson, P. T. (1975). Nosology and the official psychiatric nomenclature. In A. Freedman, H. Kaplan, & B. Saddock (Eds.), *Comprehensive textbook of psychiatry* (Vol. 1, pp. 826–845). Baltimore: Williams & Wilkins.

Szasz, T. S. (1960). The myth of mental illness. *American Psychologist, 15,* 113–118.

Szasz, T. S. (1974). *The myth of mental illness* (rev ed.). New York: Harper & Row.

Szasz, T. S. (1970). Repudiation of the medical model. In W. S. Sahakian (Ed.), *Psychopathology today* (pp. 47–53). Itaska, IL: Peacock.

Talbott, G. D. (1997, September 29). Letters: Controlled drinking. *U.S. News & World Report, 123,* 5.

Torrey, E. F. (1988). *Surviving schizophrenia: A manual for families, consumers, and providers* (2d ed.). New York: Harper Perennial.

Torrey, E. F. (1997). *Out of the shadows: Confronting America's mental illness crisis.* New York: Wiley.

U.S. News and World Report. (1997, September 8). What AA won't tell you, *123,* 45–62.

Weiner, H. (1978). The illusion of simplicity: The medical model revisited. *American Journal of Psychiatry, 135* (Suppl.), 27–33.

Winokur, G., & Clayton, P. J. (1986). *The medical basis of psychiatry.* Philadelphia: Saunders.

Zucker, R. A., & Lisansky-Gomberg, E. S. (1986). Etiology of alcoholism reconsidered: The case for a biopsychosocial process. *American Psychologist, 41,* 783–793.

Chapter 3

Dissatisfaction with the Biomedical Model within Medicine and Psychiatry

Those who cannot remember the past are condemned to repeat it.
—George Santayana

Since the early part of this century both physicians and psychiatrists have raised voices of doubt about the biomedical model that guides both disciplines. This chapter will review these concerns primarily to set the stage for the later chapters of this book that present an alternative model for mental disorders. Though the model proposed later, the multicausal, biopsychosocial model, is a valid framework for both disciplines, I will concentrate my focus on psychiatry and psychopathology.

In reviewing dissatisfactions with the biomedical model, my goal is not to be historically exhaustive. Rather I intend simply to provide background coverage of the distinctive reactionary ideas and movements that set the stage for present-day multicausal developments.

A PSYCHOBIOLOGICAL LIFE HISTORY ALTERNATIVE

A practicing psychiatrist, Adolph Meyer (1866–1950), for three decades was the Director of the Henry Phipps Psychiatric Clinic at Johns Hopkins Medical School in Baltimore, Maryland. Meyer became dissatisfied with the solely materialistic approach of the biomedical model. He took the model to task for attempting to eliminate any notion of mind while directing attention entirely to biological events (Meyer, 1919/1948, 1957).

Meyer felt that, in their shared conception of disease, psychiatry and medicine exclusively concentrated on an organism's "part reaction" (e.g., maladaptive responses of stomachs, hearts, or glands). What unfortunately got lost was consideration of the responses (especially mental reactions) of the organism as a whole. In contrast to reactions of stomachs or hearts, these mental reactions were conscious and interrelated at their own level; together with physiological events, they reflected the functioning of a whole organism.

Meyer believed that the disease model was incomplete since it ignored the psychosocial context. Rejecting the biomedical idea that an underlying biological dysfunction was the sole precipitant to psychiatric illness, Meyer emphasized the importance of psychosocial stressors in determining the onset and course of mental disorders. He felt that mental disorder was the expression of a person's attempts to adapt to the ever-changing psychosocial environment. These attempts directly reflect the person's childhood and interpersonal experiences, especially those within the family.

Meyer viewed psychiatric illnesses as basically failures to adapt to stressors. He sought to understand why wide differences existed in individuals' reaction to life experiences—generally, why life stressors sometimes led only to transient problems, while at other times they led to lasting mental disorder. Meyer recognized that individuals seldom are mere passive recipients of external forces. Rather, throughout life, individuals engage in dynamic interactions with these important environments, interpreting life events and learning to cope.

Meyer believed that the only way to gain a valid perspective on patients' current situations was in terms of their *life history*. The psychiatrist must examine all the details of patients' histories in order to uncover potential clues to their illnesses, even though the task was often time-consuming and unwieldy. Life experiences that Meyer specifically identified included previous illnesses, "changes of habitat, of school entrance, graduations . . . or failures; the various jobs; the dates of possibly important births and deaths in the family, and other fundamentally important environmental influences" (Meyer, 1919/1948, pp. 420, 422). Meyer (1957) concluded that adequate understanding of mental disorders requires consideration of a multitude of biological, psychological, and sociocultural factors and their interactions.

Meyer (1957) offered, for adoption by psychiatry, what came to be called a *psychobiological life history* approach to mental disorder. His approach emphasized the interdependence of biology, psychology, and the social environment in shaping mental disorder. His key tenet was that somatic and mental factors, far from being separate and mutually exclusive entities, are components of the same underlying abnormal process. Both the familial environment and the extrafamilial sociocultural context are central to human development.

In summary, Meyer taught that the individual patient is unique and could neither be broken down into separate aspects nor classified into diagnostic categories. He insisted on the unity of body and mind, and the necessary interaction of psychological and biological aspects in determining mental disorder. He stressed the importance of using knowledge from both psychology and biology in order to understand how individuals respond to life events. Under his influence a whole generation of psychiatrists learned to take painstaking histories of their patients and to pay special attention to past habits of adjustment, social influences, and precipitating stressful events.

Despite Meyer's revolutionary suggestions, most psychiatrists have continued to hold to the biomedical model's assertions that mental disorders are produced by discrete biological abnormalities. A minority, however, have attempted in various ways to continue Meyer's tradition that mental disorders are reactions of a dynamically active whole person to its total environmental context.

PSYCHOSOMATIC MEDICINE

Another psychiatrist, Franz Alexander, emphasized the unity of mind and body and their dynamic interaction. Through his writings (Alexander, 1939, 1950; Alexander & French, 1946), Alexander commandeered a new group of psychiatric conditions that came to be called first "psychosomatic disorders" and later "psychobiological disorders." The latest DSM version (DSM-IV) (American Psychiatric Association, 1994) uses the awkward but etiologically more precise name of "Psychological Factors Affecting Physical Condition."

Alexander believed that psychological factors are important in the development of all physical disease. He emphasized how emotions and personality difficulties affect physiological functions in ways that can lead to physical disorder. Psychological factors play their primary role either in constituting a predisposition to a particular disease, or in determining the initiation, progression, or aggravation of a disease.

Alexander concentrated on diseases of the autonomic nervous system such as bronchial asthma, ulcerative colitis, peptic ulcer, essential hypertension, rheumatoid arthritis, neurodermatitis, and thyrotoxicosis. For each of these medical diseases he postulated the following essential process: an onset situation that takes the form of a current threat or stressor, which reactivates a specific "old" unconscious psychological conflict and which, in turn, (through recurrent autonomic, neural, or humoral arousal) produces disregulation in the functioning of a particular physiological tissue, organ, or system. The specific tissue, organ or system that came to be targeted represented a constitutional vulnerability for a given person.

For example, bronchial asthma in an adolescent boy might be precipitated by the situational threat of having to leave home and go to college. This onset situation reactivates the young man's unconscious childhood fear of separation from his mother. Since his childhood this specific conflict may have led to multiple instances of physiological arousal during which functioning of the targeted organ, the lungs, was recurrently disrupted. Besides the fact that the lungs represent the specific constitutional vulnerability for this individual, existing physiological symptoms such as "wheezing" express a symbolic connection (e.g., a cry for mother to help) to the specific underlying psychological conflict.

Through his publications Alexander quickly established the new psychiatric discipline of *psychosomatic medicine*. For each of the diseases he analyzed, he offered clearly monocausal psychodynamic formulations. Hypothesizing specific unconscious psychological conflicts, Alexander relied almost exclusively on psychoanalytic concepts and virtually ignored the possible importance of other psychological or sociocultural influences. Alexander also gave inordinate emphasis to very early childhood experiences and conflicts, deemphasizing the importance of later developmental periods. His concentration on unconscious conflicts also led him to underplay almost entirely causal input from conscious cognitive and personality processes.

All in all, however, Alexander's study of psychosomatic disorders established within medicine, psychiatry, and the culture at large universal acceptance of the notion that not only can abnormal biology affect mental functioning, but abnormal psychological processes can affect physical functioning. This constituted an emphasis on the unity of mind and body different from that of Meyer. It also led to further questioning of the validity both of the biomedical model as well as of the very distinction itself between mental and physical disorders— between psychiatry and medicine.

Currently there is increasing agreement that the term, psychosomatic, is inadequate and misleading. In fact, all physical diseases are psychosomatic (Weiner, 1979). The World Health Organization highlighted the point as follows: "When we speak of psychological processes and physiological processes, we are speaking of different ways of approaching one phenomenon. The phenomenon itself is not so divided. In this sense, then, there is neither psychogenic nor somatogenic disease, but only disease" (1964, p. 6).

THE BIOPSYCHOLOGICAL PERSPECTIVE

The heavily psychoanalytic bias of psychosomatic medicine assured its gradual decline within psychiatry over the subsequent years as the neo-Kraepelinian emphasis picked up speed and influence. Vestiges of the psychosomatic tradition are retained in recent versions of DSM, which now classify these disorders as "Psychological Factors Affecting Physical Condition." Also, in contrast to earlier DSM versions that classified them among the mental disorders, DSM-IV (American Psychiatric Association, 1994) lists these conditions under the general category of "Other Conditions That May Be a Focus of Clinical Attention"—which includes numerous conditions that lead individuals to seek help from medical and mental health practitioners, but that are *not* mental disorders.

The essential feature of these Psychological Factors Affecting Physical Condition is the "presence of one or more specific psychological or behavioral factors that adversely affect a general medical condition" (American Psychiatric Association, 1994, p. 675). These factors can influence a medical disorder by affecting its course, interfering with its treatment, constituting an additional health risk for the individual, or by precipitating or exacerbating its symptoms through elicitation of stress-related physiological responses. They also can take a wide range of forms: (a) a specific mental disorder, (b) psychological symptoms, (c) personality traits or coping style, (d) maladaptive health behaviors, or (e) stress-related physiological responses.

Though clinical and other psychologists have had a long-standing interest in mental disorders and personal adjustment, only recently have they also become excited about medical disorders and physical health. During the same period in which retrenchment and redefinition was occurring within psychiatry, the field of psychology was experiencing gradual development of three new areas of study that concentrated on physical disorders and physical health.

Behavioral medicine (Ferguson & Taylor, 1980, 1981, 1982; Gentry, 1984; Miller, 1983; West & Stein, 1982) emerged as an interdisciplinary field that sought to integrate behavioral and biomedical knowledge for the treatment of physical disease, the promotion of physical health, and the understanding of both, including also prevention, diagnosis, and rehabilitation (Schwartz & Weiss, 1978a, 1978b). Behavioral and physiological psychologists, together with neuroscientists and other medical researchers, epidemiologists, social workers, and nurses, began to combine their efforts toward identification and application of effective and enduring psychological treatment procedures.

Establishment of the field of behavioral medicine resulted from a series of important developments (Blanchard, 1982). Earlier research in psychosomatic medicine had clearly linked psychological factors to a number of medical illnesses. Behavioral treatments, originally developed for mental disorders, increasingly were applied to patients with medical problems such as obesity and smoking. The technique of biofeedback, in particular, was uniquely able to effect reliable changes in internal bodily functioning itself (e.g., in heart rate and blood pressure). Increasing attention was brought to bear on how behavior change could serve an ancillary role in both treatment and prevention of the medical diseases that were major killers among adults (e.g., cancer and cardiovascular diseases). Further, many of the most serious medical problems—such as why patients fail to adhere to medical treatment, or why people engage in lifestyles that markedly increase the risk of illness and death—could be solved only by changing human behavior. As a result of all these factors, it became evident that psychology and behavior play central roles in the maintenance of physical health and in the development of physical illness.

This new field of behavioral medicine studied how psychological principles of behavior change might apply to treatment, control, and prevention of medical disorders. Medical diseases no longer were the exclusive province of physical medicine. Medical researchers and practitioners now began to include as collaborators and partners psychologists and others who came to represent this new discipline of behavioral medicine.

Health (medical) psychology (Ahmed, Kolker, & Coelho, 1979; Asken, 1979; Bloom, 1988; Matarazzo, Weiss, Herd, & Miller, 1984; Prokop & Bradley, 1981; Stone, Cohen, & Adler, 1979), the second new discipline that concentrates its study on medical problems and diseases, overlapped historically with behavioral medicine. Health psychology is a specialized subfield within psychology itself (and within behavioral medicine). It was formally recognized in 1979 when the American Psychological Association approved formation of the Division of Health Psychology (Division 38).

Health psychology develops and applies psychological knowledge relevant to the diagnosis, treatment, and prevention of psychological factors that affect medical diseases and problems. Health psychology is "broader" than behavioral medicine in that the latter concentrates on methods of intervention, while health psychology considers diagnosis and prevention as well; health psychology also is "narrower" than behavioral medicine in that the latter is a multidisciplinary activity, while health psychology has been conducted by psychologists.

Health psychology parallels developments within medicine itself as part of a new way of thinking comprehensively about health and illness (Lalonde, 1974; Robbins, 1984; Terris, 1984). Lalonde argued that, in order to understand and influence patterns of health and illness, it is necessary to understand more than biology. He introduced the concept of the *health field*, which included four components. The first was human genetics and biology. The second was the environment or those matters outside the body that can affect health (e.g., food and water purity, air pollution, sewage disposal practices, noise control, and road and vehicular safety)—matters over which the individual has little control. The third important factor is lifestyle or a person's behaviors that can affect his or her health (e.g., overeating, smoking, abuse of alcohol and other drugs, insufficient exercise, or careless driving)—matters over which the individual has considerable control. Finally, Lalonde thought that it is necessary to understand the health-care organization—that is, the quality, quantity, and distribution of health-related services in any particular community. Lalonde's health field concept implied that the greatest potential for defeating illness, facilitating health, and prolonging life was to develop intervention programs that focus on the psychology and sociology of illness, rather than on biology alone. Findings in health psychology that behaviors, attitudes, and life events indeed influence health have substantially weakened the validity and predominance of the biomedical model within medical science.

Behavioral health, a third related discipline, is part of the development of the area of holistic medicine and health. Behavior health refers to "a new interdisciplinary subspecialty within behavioral medicine specifically concerned with maintenance of health and the prevention of illness and dysfunction in currently healthy persons" (Matarazzo, 1980, p. 7). In contrast to both behavioral medicine and health psychology, the focus of behavioral health is on illness prevention and health enhancement within the population at large.

What is apparent is that the range of study of these three biopsychological subdisciplines—and of more recent emerging ones (e.g., "health care psychology," American Psychological Association, 1976)—is both widening and overlapping. Underlying all the developments is the theme that psychological factors play "contributory" causal roles in medical disorders, in healthy physical functioning, and in utilization of health care services. Substantial evidence supports that behavior is a major factor in promoting health and in preventing and treating disease (Rodin & Salovey, 1989; Taylor, 1990). This evidence demands basic revision of the mental health biomedical model.

It is now scientifically indisputable that psychological and environmental factors are important for the promotion and maintenance of physical health and in the prevention, diagnosis, and treatment of physical disorder. Even more so, then, it must be the case that psychological and environmental factors are important for the promotion and maintenance of mental health and in the prevention, diagnosis, and treatment of mental disorder.

HOLISTIC HEALTH AND MEDICINE

Another movement that challenged any rigid separation of mental and physical disorders developed within the field of physical medicine itself. The basic premise of *holistic medicine* is that, although a disorder may present as primarily physical or as primarily mental, it always constitutes a disorder of the whole person. The affliction is not just of the body, not just of mental processes, but of the dynamic whole system.

Holistic proponents admit that some of the great advances in medicine derived from the biological perspective that considers illness to result from an affected bodily organ. They add, however, that this exclusive biomedical emphasis can easily derail our understanding of disease, especially of the more complex modern physical diseases. A basic problem resides with the biomedical definition that health is the absence of disease; health is what people have when they are not sick or dying.

A holistic viewpoint redefines health by replacing essential "negative" (absence of disease) notions with essential "positive" reformulations. Health is redefined as "a sense of optimum well-being that all people can attain by reducing their exposure to health risks and by living in harmony with themselves and their environment as much as possible" (Edlin & Golanty, 1992, p. 3). This new holistic emphasis has been endorsed by the World Health Organization, which now explicitly defines health as "a state of complete physical, mental, and social well-being, and not merely the absence of disease or infirmity."

Holistic emphasis on "positive wellness" focuses attention on the ongoing living process rather than on categories of disease. The ongoing state involves an interrelatedness of physical, psychological, social, spiritual, and environmental factors; no part of the complex is truly separate and independent. "Fatigue or a bad cold may lower tolerance for psychological stress; an emotional upset may lower resistance to physical disease; maladaptive behavior, such as excessive alcohol use, may contribute to the impairment of various organs, like the brain and liver. Furthermore, a person's overall life situation has much to do with the onset of a disorder, its nature, duration, and prognosis" (Carson, Butcher, & Mineka, 1996, p. 279).

"Illness" represents then, not solely a malfunction of a particular part of the body, but some imbalance in the harmonious interaction of a person's mind, body, and interacting environment.

Textbooks on holistic health emphasize several distinct themes. First, among society's efforts directed at disease, highest priority should be given to *prevention* of illness. Second, all persons need to accept responsibility for their own health; we all need to gather relevant information and initiate appropriate changes in our lifestyles. Third, we all must reduce the use of medications and medical care for illness conditions that are better served by exercise, stress reduction, and improved nutrition. Holistic advocates contend that our present health-care system is, in effect, a "sickness care system" that provides little attention to either illness prevention or to health promotion.

It is not surprising that some health professions have been critical of those who advocate holistic health practices and holistic medicine countering by saying, for example, that the concepts and methods are antiscientific and hence harmful. Unquestionably, holistic health concepts threaten well-established and powerful economic interests represented by hospitals, pharmaceutical companies and commercial providers of medical equipment, supplies, and services. Holistic health easily can challenge the entire medical–pharmaceutical complex. Nevertheless, by encouraging individuals to take personal command of their health, including how they utilize medical services, holistic health practices may be less harmful than various traditional medical practices, such as unnecessary surgery and frequent unintended but harmful pharmacological side effects.

ENGEL'S BIOPSYCHOSOCIAL MODEL

George Engel began his career as a physician working in medical settings that offered considerable interdisciplinary collaboration. He subsequently held joint appointments in the Departments of Psychiatry and Medicine at the University of Rochester. He came to see health and illness in a very broad context, coined the term "biopsychosocial" to describe his new orientation, and promulgated his message within both medicine and psychiatry.

Engel (1977, 1978, 1980, 1982, 1987, 1990, 1992a, 1992b, 1997a, 1997b) claimed that the biomedical model considers disease to be solely a deviation from the norm of one or more biological (somatic) variables. The medical model "leaves no room within its framework for the social, psychological, and behavioral dimensions of illness" (Engel, 1980, p. 130). While recognizing its significant contributions to medicine, Engel objected to the dogmatic stance the biomedical model had assumed. In his mind its two serious flaws were that it is reductionistic in advocating that all behavioral phenomena (e.g., personality acts or mental disorders) essentially are physiochemical; and that it is exclusionist in its belief that whatever cannot be explained biologically must be excluded or ignored.

In contrast, Engel felt it was vital to recognize the role of behavior in the maintenance of physical health and in the development of physical illness. He developed a systems model in which biological, psychological, and social factors represent different levels of organization that interact, to varying degrees, to determine instances of physical dysfunction. A complete view of health and illness must take into account not only the biology of the person but the psychology and sociology of the person as well. The three domains must be studied in their natural interactions.

For example, in both schizophrenia and diabetes, any active biochemical defect may define a necessary but not a sufficient condition for occurrence of the disorder; on its own, the biological defect cannot account for the disorder. In each instance, indispensable psychological and social factors also interact to determine the course of the illness, such as whether the person considers himself or herself to be "ill," and which treatments might be offered.

To understand a particular mental disorder, then, it is necessary to identify the systemic interaction of biological, psychological, and social factors. For example, chronic pain is a clinical condition usually considered to be multifactorial in origin. There is a physiological basis for the pain, which is followed by a psychological reaction that can develop into a chronic pain syndrome. Similarly, "marital discord (a social problem) may result in anxiety or depression (psychological symptoms) and a worsening of back pain or GI symptoms (biological phenomena). Alternatively, a flare-up of multiple sclerosis (a biological phenomenon) may impact on mood (through psychological or biological mechanisms), or on employment status (a social phenomenon). Moreover, a change in any one of these domains may alter the subjective experience in any of the other domains" (Robbins, 1997, p. 222). Treatments also need to be multidisciplinary in that they operate on the person within a particular environmental context. Basically, it is essential to understand how the triad of biological, psychological, and social factors predispose an individual to a disorder, precipitate disorder in those who are vulnerable, and perpetuate disorder once it occurs.

Engel offered his new model as a plea that formulations about human disease and mental disorder should include social and psychological as well as biological factors. It was offered to the medical and psychiatric communities to stimulate a new era of integrated research, teaching, and clinical action. More recently, Jasnoski and colleagues (Jasnoski & Schwartz, 1985; Jasnoski & Warner, 1991) proposed a modified "synchronous" systems model designed explicitly to interconnect physical, physiological, psychological, and social systems.

In reaction to Engel's writings, other physicians and psychiatrists began to see the necessity of a biopsychosocial model for understanding both mental and physical disorders (Fink, 1988; McKeown, 1976; Panel on the General Professional Education of the Physician and College Preparation for Medicine, 1984). Psychologists also began to consider the biopsychosocial approach as basic to their developing fields of behavioral medicine and health psychology. For example, Schwartz argued that the ultimate challenge facing behavioral medicine is the empirical test of Engel's biopsychosocial model—testing the view that biological, psychological, and social "variables interact and that health and illness can best be understood by considering interactions of variables that cut across multiple levels" (1982, p. 1043).

Unfortunately, though often cited in the literature, until recently Engel's proposed model has had limited influence on the actual research and practice of psychiatry (Sadler & Hulgus, 1990). As a model for medical education and practice, it has been criticized as being too time consuming (Joynt, 1980) and often not very practical (Sadler & Hulgus, 1990). Goldberg and Huxley suggest that Engel's argument is stronger "as an attack on a view of disease in a rigid bio-medical framework than as a positive statement of a testable theory" (1992, p. 3). Fink (1988), in his address as incoming president of the American Psychiatric Association, sounded a challenge to "integrate the many factions of contemporary psychiatry" through revitalizing applications of the biopsychosocial model. As a correction for the tendency to take one of the three constricted, unidimensional paths (biological, psychological, or social), Fink argued that the more comprehensive biopsychosocial model urgently needs to be firmly incorporated into clinical practice, education, and research—*not* continue to be used merely as a password or slogan. Davidson and Strauss noted that "what remains difficult to achieve is a unitary framework that appreciates the constant interweaving of all these elements throughout the person's ongoing life, providing a context for the transformations of health, illness, and recovery" (1995, p. 49).

What remains clear is that Engel's biopsychosocial theorizing expressed a growing dissatisfaction within both medicine and psychiatry with a rigid biomedical model. In its place was offered a triad of concepts and factors that scientists and clinicians found more and more difficult to ignore. Though the model has had increasingly significant influence on the teaching and practice of psychiatry and medicine (Leigh, 1997), it has been minimally adopted as the predominant, most valid *etiological* model that should guide theory and research into mental disorders. In subsequent chapters, we will see how Engel's basic framework is being rediscovered in other contexts and is leading to initial offerings of quite powerful and testable multicausal etiological theories of mental disorders.

DIATHESIS–STRESS AND VULNERABILITY–STRESS MODELS OF MENTAL DISORDER

A clinical psychologist (Meehl, 1962), followed shortly by a psychiatrist (Zubin, 1976; Zubin & Spring, 1977), elaborated similar and overlapping diathesis–stress models for schizophrenia. The Meehl and

Zubin models subsequently came to serve as useful models for understanding mental disorders in general. Both models were based on the then-emerging (but still valid) evidence that genetic influence in schizophrenia is strong, yet not sufficient in itself to explain occurrence of an episode of schizophrenia. The evidence also showed that environmental stressors played a role both in the onset of initial, as well as in precipitation of subsequent, schizophrenic episodes.

These and other researchers began to conclude that what is inherited is not the disorder of schizophrenia, but rather a "diathesis" (a predisposition or vulnerability) for contracting the disorder. A diathesis is a constitutional predisposition or tendency. Individuals inherit and/or acquire enduring deviations or vulnerabilities that increase their risk for eventual onset of a particular mental disorder. After conception, the transmitted genetic vulnerability is amplified (or modulated) throughout subsequent development. An episode of disorder becomes manifest only in reaction to the impact of precipitating psychosocial stressors.

The diathesis or vulnerability lowers the individual's *threshold* of susceptibility to environmental stressors that may precipitate a breakdown in the person's adaptive behavior and trigger onset of psychopathology. Falconer (1965) hypothesized a normal distribution of risk or liability to various mental disorders; if the threshold for a particular individual is met or exceeded, an episode of mental disorder results. The *stress–vulnerability model* assigned a dual role to stress: *formative* influence, in which childhood environmental stressors increase a person's vulnerability to future disorder; and *precipitating* influence, in which present-day environmental stressors trigger the actual onset of disorder when a person's threshold is exceeded.

In short, neither genetic vulnerability, development, nor precipitating stressors singly are sufficient for onset of disorder; disorder requires interactive influence from them all. Neither nature alone nor environment alone can explain the onset of even our most serious and extreme mental disorders.

Meehl's Diathesis–Stress Model

Meehl's original (1962) theory of schizophrenia, together with his later revision (1989, 1990), had an escalating impact on the entire field of psychopathology. I will confine my description to his revised theory.

In Meehl's theory, schizophrenia at its root consists of an inherited single dominant gene, diathesis (called *schizotaxia*), which takes the form of a neural cortical defect preventing integration of signals arriving at synapses connecting brain neurons. This inherited predisposition in and of itself will not guarantee later onset of schizophrenia. A virtually certain result of this inherited neural defect, instead, is that the affected child's transactions with the environment and people are subtly undermined, leading to formation of a *schizotypic* personality organization. This anomalous organization shows up in signs of abnormal cognitive activity (e.g., slippage, autism, or ambivalence), alienation of people, and unusual emotional expression.

The large majority (perhaps 90%) of these schizotypic children and adolescents never experience an episode of schizophrenia. Instead, they show a range of lesser mental disorders or a more permanent nonclinical pattern of unusual and eccentric thought and interpersonal ineptitude. For an episode of schizophrenia to actually occur requires the presence of two misfortunes built on top of schizotaxia and schizotypy: (a) Through inheritance of other multiple genes, certain other trait patterns (e.g., extreme social introversion, submissiveness, and an inability to experience pleasure) potentiate the person's entire maladaptive drift and further compromise his or her ability to cope; and (b) the person also has "bad luck" in the form of sequences of life experiences that are adverse or stressful to the individual.

In sum, in Meehl's revised theory, onset of schizophrenia is the cumulative interactive effect of (1) an inherited neural defect (schizotaxia), (2) that produces a pattern of deficit in cognitive and interpersonal functioning (schizotypy), together with (3) multigenic inheritance of maladaptive traits that put the person at additional risk for coping and adjustment, and (4) encounter of unlucky stressful experiences. The overall effect was that the field was offered an elegantly creative model, based on the latest scientific evidence, that went clearly beyond either a pure biomedical or a pure environmental–behavioral explanation.

Zubin and Colleagues' Vulnerability–Stress Model

Zubin and his colleagues (Day, Zubin, & Steinhauer, 1987; Zubin, 1976, 1986; Zubin, Magaziner, & Steinhauer, 1983; Zubin & Spring, 1977; Zubin & Steinhauer, 1981; Zubin, Steinhauer, Day, & van Kamman, 1985) similarly argued that a certain proportion of the general population is endowed with a level of vulnerability that, under suitable circumstances, will express itself in an episode of schizophrenia. The description below includes their latest expansions.

Zubin and colleagues felt that schizophrenia does not imply a chronic mental disorder, but rather a permanent vulnerability to develop the disorder. The basic vulnerability is an enduring, more permanent trait. In contrast, an episode of schizophrenia is a waxing and waning state. It is usually time limited, arising in response to an encounter with life stress and abating with the process of gradual recovery.

An individual's vulnerability to schizophrenia is determined by a convergence of biological, psychological, and sociological influences.

A vulnerable person is one with sufficient causal input from these factors to be left with an enduring potential for a schizophrenic episode. A host of very different factors, biological and environmental, interact together to determined a person's "overall etiological loading." This overall vulnerability to illness is not a uniform threshold, but varies widely from one individual to another.

Possession of this vulnerability does not of itself guarantee an episode of schizophrenia. Zubin and Steinhauer (1981) suggest that as many as 75 percent of vulnerable individuals never experience a clinical episode of schizophrenia. Whether a vulnerable individual will experience onset of an actual episode of schizophrenia depends on three additional variables. The first is the individual's level of etiological loading (the severity of his or her predisposition). Highly vulnerable persons can succumb to schizophrenia after only minimal life stress; invulnerable persons need to be exposed to very intense and prolonged stress before a psychotic episode ensues. The second variable consists of the strengths within an individual's premorbid personality, especially possession of competence and learned coping skills. With adaptive coping skills, a person can often counteract the incapacitating effects of stress. The third crucial variable is the level of stress present in the person's immediate (precipitating) environment. Vulnerability theory suggests that a certain critical level of life stress must be present in order to provoke appearance of actual schizophrenic symptoms such as psychotic delusions and hallucinations.

In contrast to Meehl's model, which posits a hereditarily transmitted, biological (neural defect) diathesis, Zubin and colleagues' vulnerability can derive from any one or a combination of biopsychosocial influences. For Zubin and colleagues, further, psychosocial factors play multiple etiological roles, both affecting a person's core vulnerability to disorder as well as influencing, as stressors, the onset, clinical characteristics, course, and outcome of an episode of disorder. Further, schizophrenia is not the result of a single universal (invariable) pattern of causal factors; rather, it can result from multiple combinations of biological, psychological, and sociological influences.

A major impact of the appearance of Zubin and colleagues' vulnerability–stress theory was that a group of prestigious contemporary research psychiatrists had offered, for one of the most biologically loaded, major mental disorders, a conceptualization that rejected any monocausal explanatory framework, either biomedical or behavioral. They offered instead a multifactorial causal model that included interactions of biological, psychological, and sociological influences.

More recent examples of diathesis–stress models of psychopathology have been offered for schizophrenia (Eaton, 1980; Eaton, Day, & Kramer, 1986; Freeman, 1989; Gottesman, 1991; Nuechterlein &

Dawson, 1984) and for depressive disorders (Abramson, Metalsky, & Alloy, 1989; Beck, 1987; Dalgleish & Watts, 1990).

A fortunate result of both Meehl's and Zubin and colleagues' formulations was that explanations of psychopathology could never remain as simple as they had been. Subsequent theoretical shifts were at first subtle, but eventually took on the form of explicit multicausal, biopsychosocial theories of the various mental disorders. These revolutionary formulations are described in detail in Chapters 8 and 9.

CONCLUSION

Various mental health researchers and clinicians have become dissatisfied with monocausal models that purport to explain mental disorder. Perhaps loudest has been the disappointment within psychiatry and medicine with the historically prominent and enduring biomedical model of disease.

Prominent themes of protest are found in Adolph Meyer's writings on psychobiology, Franz Alexander's formulations of psychosomatic medicine, the emergence of holistic health and medicine, and Engel's advocacy of a biopsychosocial medicine and psychiatry. These themes coalesced most powerfully in emergence of the diathesis–stress and vulnerability–stress models of schizophrenia, models built primarily on empirical evidence of genetic influence of the disorder. Multifactorial causal models increasingly were demanded, and the new theories of schizophrenia constituted highly creative first attempts.

Clearly a substantial aspect of the developments charted in this chapter is what might the called the "psychologizing" of medicine itself. *Within medicine itself, the biomedical (biological) view of disease is gradually giving way to a more complex model*—first, in the form of the biopsychological model adopted by behavioral medicine and health psychology; then, in the form of Engel's biopsychosocial model and the diathesis–stress models that force scientific attention to the interactions among biological, psychological, and sociocultural factors in the etiology, course, and treatment of both medical and mental disorders. Unfortunately, the existence, application, and revolutionary implications of this badly needed new paradigm still remain lost on many within the mental health disciplines.

Another evolving theme is that *it is increasingly difficult to differentiate physical and mental disorder*. In its report on psychosomatic disorders, the World Health Organization concluded that "when we speak of psychological processes and physiological processes, we are speaking of different ways of approaching one phenomenon. The phenomenon itself is not so divided. In this sense, then, there is neither psychogenic nor somatogenic disease but only disease" (1964, p. 6).

Finally, in light of the themes developed in Chapter 2, it should be clear that *none of the revisionary notions offered by the historical developments summarized in this chapter have found their way into popular media reports and discussions regarding mental disorder.* One seldom finds mention, much less emphasis, on either psychobiological or biopsychological viewpoints, and certainly not on vulnerability–stress or multicausal biopsychosocial theories. Instead, what continues to permeate magazine and newspaper accounts and TV presentations are biochemical, neuroanatomical, genetic, pharmacological, and other brain disease formulations—all direct offshoots of the relentless biomedical model.

Chapter 2 presented initial logical critiques of the biomedical model. The present chapter reviewed dissenting voices calling for its expansion or abandonment. Unfortunately, only a presentation of overwhelming scientific evidence that contradicts the validity of the biomedical model has any hope of reversing this chronic and stagnating state of affairs. Chapter 4 responds to that intimidating challenge.

REFERENCES

Abramson, L. Y., Metalsky, G. I., & Alloy, L. B. (1989). Hopelessness depression: A theory-based subtype of depression. *Psychological Review, 96,* 358–372.

Ahmed, P. I., Kolker, A., & Coelho, G. V. (1979). Toward a new definition of health: An overview. In P. I. Ahmed & G. V. Coelho (Eds.), *Toward a new definition of health: Psychosocial dimensions* (pp. 7–22). New York: Plenum.

Alexander, F. (1939). Psychoanalytic study of a case of essential hypertension. *Psychosomatic Medicine, 1,* 139–154.

Alexander, F. (1950). *Psychosomatic medicine: Its principles and applications.* New York: Norton.

Alexander, F., & French, T. M. (1946). *Psychoanalytic therapy.* New York: Ronald.

American Psychiatric Association. (1994). *Diagnostic and statistical manual of mental disorders* (4th ed.). Washington, DC: Author.

American Psychological Association. (1976). Task force on health research. Contributions of psychology to health research: Patterns, problems, and potentials. *American Psychologist, 31,* 263–274.

Asken, M. J. (1979). Medical psychology: Toward definition, clarification, and organization. *Professional Psychology, 10,* 66–73.

Beck, A. T. (1987). Cognitive models of depression. *Journal of Cognitive Psychotherapy: An International Quarterly, 1,* 5–37.

Blanchard, E. B. (1982). Behavior medicine: Past, present, and future. *Journal of Consulting and Clinical Psychology, 50,* 859–879.

Bloom, B. L. (1988). *Health psychology: A psychosocial perspective.* Englewood Cliffs, NJ: Prentice Hall.

Carson, R. C., Butcher, J. N., & Mineka, S. (1996). *Abnormal psychology and modern life* (10th ed.). New York: HarperCollins.

Dalgleish, T., & Watts, F. M. (1990). Biases of attention and memory in disorders of anxiety and depression. *Clinical Psychology Review, 10*, 589–604.

Davidson, L., & Strauss, J. S. (1995). Beyond the biopsychosocial model: Integrating disorder, health, and recovery. *Psychiatry, 58*, 44–55.

Day, R., Zubin, J., & Steinhauer, S. R. (1987). Psychosocial factors in schizophrenia in light of vulnerability theory. In D. Magnusson & A. Ohman (Eds.), *Psychopathology: An interactional perspective* (pp. 25–39). Orlando, FL: Academic Press.

Eaton, W. W. (1980). A formal theory of selection for schizophrenia. *American Journal of Sociology, 86*, 149–157.

Eaton, W. W., Day, R., & Kramer, M. (1986). A formal theory of selection for schizophrenia. In M. Tsuang & J. Simpson (Eds.), *Handbook of schizophrenia* (Vol. 4). Amsterdam: Elsevier.

Edlin, G., & Golanty, E. (1992). *Health and wellness: A holistic approach* (4th ed.). Boston, MA: Jones & Bartlett.

Engel, G. L. (1977). The need for a new medical model: A challenge to biomedicine. *Science, 196*, 129–136.

Engel, G. L. (1978). The biopsychosocial model and the education of health professionals. *Annals of the New York Academy of Science, 310*, 169–181.

Engel, G. L. (1980). The clinical application of the biopsychosocial model. *American Journal of Psychiatry, 137*, 535–544.

Engel, G. L. (1982). The biopsychosocial model and medical education. *New England Journal of Medicine, 306*, 802–805.

Engel, G. L. (1987). Physician–scientists and scientific–physicians: Resolving the humanism–science dichotomy. *Medicine, Science, and Society, 82*, 107–111.

Engel, G. L. (1990). On looking inward and being scientific: A tribute to Arthur H. Schmale, M.D. *Psychotherapy and Psychosomatics, 54*, 63–69.

Engel, G. L. (1992a). How much longer must medicine's science be bound by a seventeenth century world view? *Family Systems Medicine, 10*, 333–346.

Engel, G. L. (1992b). The need for a new medical model: A challenge for biomedicine. *Family Systems Medicine, 10*, 317–331.

Engel, G. L. (1997a). From biomedical to biopsychosocial: Being scientific in the human domain. *Psychosomatics, 38*, 521–528.

Engel, G. L. (1997b). From biomedical to biopsychosocial: I. Being scientific in the human domain. *Psychotherapy and Psychosomatics, 66*, 57–62.

Falconer, D. S. (1965). The inheritance of liability to certain diseases, estimated from the incidence among relatives. *Annals of Human Genetics, 29*, 51–76.

Ferguson, J. M., & Taylor, C. B. (Eds.). (1980). *The comprehensive handbook of behavioral medicine: Vol. 1, Systems interventions.* New York: SP Medical & Scientific Books.

Ferguson, J. M., & Taylor, C. B. (Eds.). (1981). *The comprehensive handbook of behavioral medicine: Vol. 2, Syndromes and special areas.* New York: SP Medical & Scientific Books.

Ferguson, J. M., & Taylor, C. B. (Eds.). (1982). *The comprehensive handbook of behavioral medicine: Vol. 3, Extended applications and issues.* New York: SP Medical & Scientific Books.

Fink, P. J. (1988). Response to the presidential address: Is "biopsychosocial" the psychiatric shibboleth? *American Journal of Psychiatry, 145*, 1061–1067.

Freeman, H. (1989). Relationship of schizophrenia to the environment. *British Journal of Psychiatry, 155* (Supplement 5), 90–99.

Gentry, W. D. (Ed.). (1984). *Handbook of behavioral medicine.* New York: Guilford.

Goldberg, D. P., & Huxley, P. (1992). *Common mental disorders: A bio-social model.* London: Tavistock/Routledge.

Gottesman, I. I. (1991). *Schizophrenia genesis: The origins of madness.* New York: Freeman.

Jasnoski, M., & Schwartz, G. (1985). A synchronous systems model for health. *American Behavioral Scientist, 28,* 468–485.

Jasnoski, M., & Warner, R. (1991). Graduate and post-graduate medical education with the synchronous systems model. *Behavioral Science, 36,* 253–273.

Joynt, R. J. (1980). Introduction to the challenge of the biopsychosocial model. *Psychosomatic Medicine, 42* (Supplement 77).

Lalonde, M. (1974). *A new perspective on the health of Canadians.* Ottowa: Canadian Government Printing Office.

Leigh, H. (Ed.). (1997). *Biopsychosocial approaches in primary care: State of the art and challenge for the 21st century.* New York: Plenum.

Matarazzo, J. D. (1980). Behavioral health and behavioral medicine: Frontiers for a new health psychology. *American Psychologist, 37,* 1–14.

Matarazzo, J. D., Weiss, S. M., Herd, J. A., & Miller, N. E. (Eds.). (1984). *Behavioral health: A handbook of health enhancement and disease prevention.* New York: Wiley.

McKeown, T. (1976). *The role of medicine: Dream, mirage, or nemesis?* London: Nuffield Provincial Hospitals Trust.

Meehl, P. E. (1962). Schizotaxia, schizotypy, schizophrenia. *American Psychologist, 17,* 827–838.

Meehl, P. E. (1989). Schizotaxia revisited. *Archives of General Psychiatry, 46,* 935–944.

Meehl, P. E. (1990). Toward an integrated theory of schizotaxia, schizotypy, and schizophrenia. *Journal of Personality Disorders, 4,* 1–99.

Meyer, A. (1919/1948). The life chart. In A. Lief (Ed.), *The commonsense psychiatry of Dr. Adolph Meyer* (pp. 418–422). New York: McGraw-Hill.

Meyer, A. (1957). *Psychobiology: A science of man.* Springfield, IL: Charles C. Thomas.

Miller, N. E. (1983). Behavioral medicine: Symbiosis between laboratory and clinic. *Annual Review of Psychology, 34,* 1–31.

Nuechterlein, K. H., & Dawson, M. E. (1984). A heuristic vulnerability/stress model of schizophrenia episodes. *Schizophrenia Bulletin, 10,* 300–312.

Panel on the General Professional Education of the Physician and College Preparation for Medicine. (1984). *Physicians for the twenty-first century.* Washington, DC: Association of American Medical Colleges.

Prokop, C. K., & Bradley, L. A. (Eds.). (1981). *Medical psychology: Contributions to behavioral medicine.* New York: Academic Press.

Robbins, A. (1984). Creating a progressive health agenda: 1983 presidential address. *American Journal of Public Health, 74,* 775–779.

Robbins, S. W. (1997). A biopsychosocial critique of managed mental health care and its relation to primary care. In H. Leigh (Ed.), *Biopsychosocial approaches in primary care: State of the art and challenges for the 21st century* (pp. 217–233). New York: Plenum.

Rodin, J., & Salovey, P. (1989). Health psychology. *Annual Review of Psychology, 40*, 533–579.

Sadler, J. Z., & Hulgus, Y. F. (1990). Knowing, valuing, acting: Clues to revising the biopsychosocial model. *Comprehensive Psychiatry, 31*, 185–195.

Schwartz, G. E. (1982). Testing the biopsychosocial model: The ultimate challenge facing behavioral medicine. *Journal of Consulting and Clinical Psychology, 50*, 1040–1053.

Schwartz, G. E., & Weiss, S. M. (1978a). Yale conference on behavioral medicine: A proposed definition and statement of goals. *Journal of Behavioral Medicine, 1*, 3–12.

Schwartz, G. E., & Weiss, S. M. (1978b). Behavioral medicine revisited: An ammended definition. *Journal of Behavioral Medicine, 1*, 249–251.

Stone, G. C., Cohen, F., & Adler, N. E. (Eds.). (1979). *Health psychology: A handbook*. San Francisco: Jossey-Bass.

Taylor, S. E. (1990). Health psychology. *American Psychologist, 45*, 40–50.

Terris, M. (1984). Newer perspectives on the health of Canadians: Beyond the Lalonde report. *Journal of Public Health Policy, 5*, 327–337.

Weiner, H. (1979). Psychobiological markers of disease. *Psychiatric Clinics of North America, 2*, 227–242.

West, L. J., & Stein, M. (Eds.). (1982). *Critical issues in behavioral medicine*. Philadelphia: Lippincott.

World Health Organization. (1964). *Psychosomatic disorders*. Technical Report Series No. 275. Geneva, Switzerland: Author.

Zubin, J. (1976). The role of vulnerability in the etiology of schizophrenic disorders. In L. West & D. Flinn (Eds.), *Treatment of schizophrenia: Progress and prospects*. New York: Grune & Stratton.

Zubin, J. (1986). Models for the aetiology of schizophrenia. In G. D. Burrows, T. R. Norman, & F. Rubinstein (Eds.), *Handbook of studies on schizophrenia, Part 1* (pp. 97–104). Amsterdam: Elsevier.

Zubin, J., Magaziner, J., & Steinhauer, S. (1983). The metamorphosis of schizophrenia: From chronicity to vulnerability. *Psychological Medicine, 13*, 551–571.

Zubin, J., & Spring, B. J. (1977). Vulnerability: A new view of schizophrenia. *Journal of Abnormal Psychology, 86*, 103–126.

Zubin, J., & Steinhauer, S. (1981). How to break the logjam in schizophrenia: A look beyond genetics. *Journal of Nervous and Mental Disease, 169*, 477–492.

Zubin, J., Steinhauer, S., Day, R., & van Kamman, D. P. (1985). Schizophrenia at the crossroads: A blue print for the 80s. *Comprehensive Psychiatry, 26*, 217–240.

Part II

What Causes Mental Disorders? The Scientific Evidence

Chapter 4

Scientific Evidence Invalidates the Biomedical Model: Findings from Behavioral Genetics

> Science is always replacing itself with new knowledge and ideas as its old ideas are tested and found wanting.
> —M. Susser, 1973, p. 11.

After reviewing the reigning biomedical model of mental disorder, Chapter 2 asks whether the causes of the various mental disorders are indeed singularly biological. Are all mental disorders genetically transmitted? Are environmental factors mostly noninstrumental in the etiology of mental disorders, except perhaps as periodic precipitating triggers? It is time to examine the most relevant evidence available from contemporary science.

Central to the analyses offered in this chapter are the findings of one of the newest disciplines studying human behavior, *behavioral genetics* (Loehlin & Nichols, 1976; Mann, 1994; Plomin, Chipuer, & Neiderhiser, 1994; Plomin, DeFries, McClearn, & Rutter, 1997; Scarr, 1992). The field is one of the most active and exciting areas of present-day medical, behavioral, and psychopathological investigation. The accumulated results of behavioral genetic research convincingly demonstrate the role of genetic factors both in normal variations in psychological functioning and in psychopathology.

NATURE VERSUS NURTURE

In line with the biases of their respective disciplines, psychological and social sciences advocate unequivocally for the primacy of the environment in determining human and other animal behavior. John Watson, the famous psychologist and founder of behaviorism, considered hereditary influence crucial only for physical traits—not for behavioral traits (those patterns operative, for example, in personality and maladjustment). Watsonian behaviorism, together with its direct offshoot, Skinnerian radical behaviorism, advocated the importance of environmental events (circumstances external to the individual) for human behavior that could be publicly observed and measured. Explanations of human behavior were to be found in external situations or settings in which individuals' developmental histories and current activities are imbedded. Watson boasted that, if permitted sufficient control of a child's environment, he could train any healthy baby to become a doctor, artist, or thief—regardless of the child's hereditary endowment.

Until very recently, discussions of human personality and maladjustment continued to line up on one side or the other of the nature–nurture question. Prior to the 1980s, psychology, sociology, and even a substantial section of psychiatry adopted more or less extreme environmental positions that denied the importance of inheritance for mental disorders. Beginning in the 1980s, however, prominent psychiatrists began vigorously to reject popular psychoanalytic explanations that emphasized the importance for development of psychopathology of early parental (environmental) behaviors. In their place, new-age psychiatrists began to insist passionately that the abnormalities central to mental disorders are hereditarily transmitted structural and/or biochemical abnormalities. "Fifty years ago, psychoanalysis dominated the academic scene; for the past two decades, reductionist biological determinism has held the fort" (Eisenberg, 1995, p. 1563).

Unfortunately, what gets sidestepped during remaining present-day arguments favoring either nature or nurture explanations of human maladjustment is any appreciation of the actual latest findings of empirical science. Since the 1980s behavioral genetic studies multiplied and produced robust empirical findings. Unfortunately, important basic findings from this field have not found a sustained spotlight within contemporary psychopathology; the findings do not as yet appear prominently in professional, graduate, or undergraduate textbooks and seldom can be found in present-day public discussions. Today's genetic findings, however, are vital to mental disorder science and policy making. The findings are too central to remain blurred and unexamined on the back burner of contemporary psychology and psychiatry.

What are these central scientific conclusions? The most basic is that whether nature or nurture is more important for human behavior—the issue of heredity versus environment—is no longer a matter of opinion or preference. Solid empirical answers are available (Plomin, DeFries, McClearn, & Rutter, 1997). Though the general answer is far from startling, and indeed may seem trite, the fact that the answer reflects scientific consensus means that it must be centrally appreciated and highlighted. The empirical answer, in turn, negates prior prevailing myths about both human personality and psychopathology. These myths need to be exposed and laid to rest. They must not be permitted to continue to obfuscate scientific research, theoretical understanding, and serious popular discussion of these important human issues.

LEARNINGS FROM MODERN BEHAVIORAL GENETICS

The traditional wisdom embodied in the phrase "Nature proposes, environment disposes" is in need of some emendation, for both the proposing and the disposing are jointly determined.
                    —Bronfenbrenner & Ceci, 1994, p. 580.

During the past two decades, behavioral genetics emerged as an authoritative discipline within psychology and psychopathology. Behavioral genetic researchers have demonstrated the importance of both genetic and environmental factors for most forms of psychopathology. "The question no longer is whether nature or nurture shapes human development but rather how complex genetic and environmental influences act together to form specific behavioral outcomes" (Carey & DiLalla, 1994, p. 32).

Recent reviews of the major empirical findings regarding genetic influences in mental disorders can be found in Carey and DiLalla (1994); Lander and Schork (1994); Loehlin (1992); McGuffin, Owen, O'Donovan, Thapar, and Gottesman (1994); Mellon (1997); Plomin, DeFries, McClearn, and Rutter (1997); Plomin and Rende (1991); Rende and Plomin (1995); Rose (1995); Rutter, Macdonald, LeCouteur, Harrington, Bolton, and Bailey (1990); and Vandenberg, Singer, and Pauls (1986). A robust conclusion from these reviews is that most if not all forms of mental disorder have a genetic basis. The evidence is particularly strong in the case of schizophrenia, bipolar mood disorder, major unipolar depression, the anxiety disorders, and antisocial personality disorder.

Robert Plomin, a major authority in the field, stated the central conclusion powerfully and succinctly: "The first message of behavioral genetic research is that genetic influences on individual differences in behavioral development is usually significant and often substantial"

(1989, p. 108). He advises that we ask not what is heritable; instead we need to ask what is not heritable.

Plomin continued, "The second message [of behavioral genetic research] is just as important: These same data provide the best available evidence of the importance of the environment . . . nongenetic factors are responsible for more than half of the variance for most complex behaviors" (1989, p. 108; see also Reiss, Plomin, & Hetherington, 1991). "Complex" behaviors refer to those human behaviors involved in intelligence, personality, and mental disorder. Seymour Kety, a psychiatric geneticist and major author of the classic Danish adoptive studies of schizophrenia, observed similarly, "Evidence that genetic factors are important in etiology does not argue against the existence of significant or essential environmental influences" (1996, pp. 481–482).

Michael Rutter, another authority in behavioral genetics, concluded that in regard to a wide range of human traits and disorders, genetic factors usually account for "some 20% to 60% of the variance. In other words, the effects of genetics on human behavior are relatively strong but far from overwhelming. The genetic evidence has been as important in pointing to environmental influences on behavior as it has been in its demonstration of genetic effects: Environmentality and heritability are both strong" (1997, p. 390).

Various estimates of what is referred to as "heritability" are available from twin, adoption, and familial studies routinely used to study the contribution of heredity to human behaviors. A "heritability index" provides an estimate of the percentage of a particular behavior or trait that can be explained in terms of genetic differences among members of a population. If a particular trait shows a high heritability estimate, genetic influences predominate; if a trait shows a low to zero heritability estimate, environmental influences predominate. It is helpful to keep in mind that, in quantitative genetics, environment refers to any *nonhereditary influence*. This includes, in addition to psychological environmental factors, exogenous biological agents or events such as prenatal traumas, malnutrition, viruses, and/or head traumas.

Findings from behavior genetic studies document the highest heritability indices for the trait of general intelligence (about 50 to 60%), and personality traits (about 50%), with various types of mental disorders ranging from very low heritabilities for some disorders, to about 40 percent for schizophrenia and, representing a likely ceiling effect, about 60 percent for bipolar mood disorder. So far, the only human behavioral domains that exhibit little or no genetic influence are religious and political beliefs as well as the part of human creativity that is independent of general intelligence.

In our evaluation of the reigning biomedical model, we can highlight our first scientific consensus: In the domain of personality and mental disorders, genetic influence is significant, but rarely explains more than half of the variance. Heritability estimates rarely exceed 50 percent, "suggesting that environmental and genetic factors are of similar magnitude" (Rende & Plomin, 1995, p. 300). Hence, no mental disorder comes even close to being a pure genetic disease.

DRAMATIC SINGLE-GENE INSTANCES
OF MENTAL DISORDER

While medical genetics has generally focused on classic, rare, Mendelian disorders where the genetic signal is so powerful that environmental effects are irrelevant, genetic epidemiology examines common familial disorders where an inherited vulnerability interacts with environmental risk factors in often complex and uncertain ways.
—Kendler, 1995, p. 85.

Behavioral geneticists have identified well over a thousand rare genes that may dramatically disrupt normal development. Genetic studies throughout the medical disciplines have shown that more than 3,000 illnesses are *monogenic* (that is, caused by defects in a single gene) and are transmitted according to Mendelian patterns (dominant, recessive, or sex-linked). Approximately 25 percent (about 750) of these illnesses affect mental functioning (McKusick, 1983).

Among physical disorders, hundreds of human diseases and physical defects are caused by gross chromosome abnormalities (e.g., Down's syndrome, Kleinfelter's syndrome) or by X-linked (e.g., hemophilia, Duchenne muscular dystrophy), autosomal recessive (e.g., PKU, Tay Sach's syndrome), or autosomal dominant (e.g., retino blastoma) gene mutations. These "genetic" diseases result from permanent changes in the physical structure of a person's chromosomes, inside which all hereditary (DNA) information is contained.

Genetic evidence indicates that most mental disorders are not governed by deterministic, single genes. It is the case that researchers have isolated a group of rare mental disorders that are determined or caused solely by genetic factors. One example is a dementia named *Huntington's Chorea*, which produces abnormal movements of the face, neck, and arms, and impairments in speech and walking, accompanied by progressive loss of cognitive abilities, depression, impulsiveness, and dramatic changes in personality. The disorder is transmitted in the form of a single autosomal dominant gene. Over time, excessive dopamine and deficient GABA neurotransmitters in the caudate nucleus and frontal areas of the cortex lead to neural atrophy in these areas, with progressive loss of function. Huntington's Chorea, thus, is clearly a genetically determined (single autosomal dominant gene) mental disorder—the heritability index approaches 100 percent. Its deteriorating cortical and behavioral effects will occur regardless of environmental history or experience and independent of other genetic endowment.

Another classic genetic mental disorder is *Parkinson's Disease*, which produces severe muscular tremors, instances of muscular rigidity, and abrupt loss of rhythm in initiating or stopping movement. This motor pattern is accompanied often by mild dementia, depression, expressionless face, small-stepping gait, and impaired balance and speech. Though the precise mechanism of genetic transmission has not been identified, the disorder is known to result from deficient levels of the neurotransmitter dopamine that produce lesions and neuronal atrophy in the substantia nigra nucleus of the brain stem. Once again, then, a specific mental disorder has been found to be the direct result of a hereditarily transmitted (mechanism unknown) biochemical abnormality in the brain—the heritability index approaches 100 percent. Occurrence of the disorder is virtually independent of any other genetic endowment or of environmental history or present context.

It is plausible that American history might have been different if King George III of England (1738–1820) had not suffered from *porphyria*, a genetic disease (autosomal dominant) with variable expression (from mild to severe). Individuals with the disease exhibit symptoms that are both physical (acute pain in the abdomen and back, headaches, nausea, and insomnia) and mental (depression, hallucinations, and delirium). All the symptoms are due to a toxic effect from the overproduction of porphyrins, molecules that are present in most body cells and essential for enzyme functioning. During more than 200 years of British royalty, George and some of his ancestors and descendants were afflicted with the disease. In George's case, his medical records reveal five periods of insanity, the first in 1765 when he was twenty-six years old; at that time severe physical symptoms together with delirium and hallucinations were predominant. The historical upshot is that during the important period before 1776, the year of the American declaration of independence, and during the ensuing revolutionary war, King George was having serious, recurrent health problems that affected his mental state and judgment and reduced his ability to manage colonial affairs. What the historical outcome might have been had George not been so inflicted will remain an unresolved mystery (Clarke, 1972).

PHYSICAL DISEASES AND MENTAL DISORDERS: THE MUCH MORE TYPICAL CASE

Medical genetics has generally focused on "classic, rare, Mendelian disorders where the genetic signal is so powerful that environmental effects are irrelevant" (Kendler, 1995, p. 895). In contrast, prevalent contemporary disorders that are familial have ambiguous hereditary bases and do not obey any of the accepted genetic rules. "Familial risk rates are inconsistent with simple, fully penetrant, Mendelian dominant or recessive transmission" (Carey & DiLalla, 1994, p. 35).

The list of familial disorders includes medical diseases such as allergies, diabetes, rheumatoid arthritis, hypertension, obesity, and some rare forms of cancer—as well as mental disorders such as alcoholism and schizophrenia. A rapidly growing body of evidence indicates that multiple major genes play a contributory role, as part of multifactorial inheritance, in development of the complex medical diseases including diabetes, heart disease, and hypertension (Weatherall, 1992). It is incorrect to regard any of these latter disorders as genetic diseases equivalent to the Mendelian disorders described that result from chromosomal or single-gene abnormalities. In the case of mental disorders, familial patterns also do not conform to the expectations generated by Mendelian (i.e., single-gene) models (Rutter, McDonald, LeCouteur, Harrington, Boton, & Bailey, 1990). Single-gene disorders are atypical and far from representative of the way genes most typically influence complex human behavior and psychopathology (Pardes, Kaufman, Pincus, & West, 1989). In sum, both medical and mental familial disorders are the result of quite complex interactions of multiple genes with environmental factors.

For the majority of mental disorders it is a misconception to assert that genetic influences are singly deterministic. Among behavioral geneticists, the consensus is that most mental disorders "are not the result of a single gene with 'sledgehammer' effects on development. . . . Although evidence for genetic contribution to psychopathology continues to mount, current thinking is that heritable influences reflect the probabilistic impact of several or many genes rather than the control of single disease genes. . . . The genetic quest is not to find *the* gene for a psychiatric disorder or psychological trait, but to find the *many* genes that increase the likelihood of displaying the disorder or trait in a probabilistic rather than a predetermined manner" (Rende & Plomin, 1995, pp. 300, 307).

Within psychopathology, schizophrenia has long served as the prototypical scientific case. Researchers have searched for years for simple genes and simple neurochemical triggers that might produce onset of schizophrenia. What the evidence clearly shows, instead, is that although genetic vulnerability may predispose to schizophrenia, genetic factors by themselves cannot account for the disorder. This conclusion was already evident when Gottesman and Shields (1967) first applied the multifactorial polygenic model to schizophrenia. Their model assumed that a large number of genes contribute in an additive fashion to the liability for schizophrenia and that an episode of schizophrenia occurs when the liability exceeds a given threshold. Both familial and nonfamilial environmental influences were included in their seminal model and were assumed to combine additively with genetic influences.

Still today, in the case of schizophrenia researchers are unable to specify either a mode of inheritance, chromosomal locations for schizophrenia genes, or what function such genes might carry out. Even if the gene or genes for schizophrenia should be found, twin studies indicate that genetic vulnerability alone cannot account for all the variance; there is a clear opening for other (e.g., environmental) risk factors to operate. "Simplistic notions regarding gene expression in the activity of particular [brain] neurotransmitters have given way to a recognition of the many embryonic and developmental processes that must intervene between genetic change and a clinical phenotype" (Kety, 1996, p. 484). Boomsma, Anokhin, and de Geus summarize this research tradition as follows: "Large efforts have been made to map the genes responsible for major psychiatric diseases, and the first results were encouraging. However, after a series of failures to replicate initial findings, the excitement gave way to skepticism" (1997, p. 110).

Simple genetic and neurochemical answers remain elusive and highly unlikely in the domains of complex human behaviors. In modern Western society, serious diseases that result entirely from hereditary factors occur only rarely. A prominent behavior geneticist concludes, "There is as yet no firm evidence for a single-gene effect that accounts for a detectable amount of variation for any complex behavior . . . the widely publicized major gene effects for schizophrenia and manic–depressive psychosis may be limited to particular families" (Plomin, 1989, p. 110). In short, current genetic researchers are of a virtual consensus that, although single-gene effects can be devastating for affected individuals, no single gene has been shown to account for any of the multiple mental disorders classified in DSM-IV (American Psychiatric Association, 1994), including major mental disorders such as bipolar mood disorder and schizophrenia.

Modern genetic evidence demands changed viewpoints regarding physical disease as well. Findings even in regard to the biomedically prototypical *infectious diseases* cry out for more complex views of causality. For example, a suspension of cold virus sprayed directly into a person's nose and throat does not always result in a case of the common cold; some persons are more resistant than others. Also, tuberculosis, until very recently, had all but disappeared in the United States—though tubercular bacteria have not disappeared. Many persons today have small tubercular lesions in their lungs, yet never experience the disease. What medical researchers have discovered is that a set of factors associated with poverty—such as overcrowding, poor nutrition, poor sanitation, squalor, and stressful environments—need to be interactively present in order for the disease to be expressed. The upshot is that "doctors and scientists are rapidly abandoning the convenient but false and restrictive belief that most diseases are caused by simple factors. Now, they rarely claim that a particular illness is caused solely by one factor, like heredity, constitution, disordered chemistry or psychology, repressed emotions, or [infection]. The widest possible range of conditions are being implicated in the dynamic chain of cause and effect that eventually culminates in illness and death" (Foster, 1989).

In sum, a large number of physical diseases and virtually all prominent mental disorders are polygenic; they are influenced by many genes whose numbers, chromosomal locations, and degree of expression all are unknown. And, as is the case for all human polygenic traits or diseases, environmental factors are crucial for gene expression. Height can be codetermined by nutrition and diseases occurring during development. Intellectual expression can be influenced substantially by developmental factors such as sensory stimulation, nutrition, and human encouragement. In other words, genes contribute only partially to complex human behaviors, and the contribution is probabilistic rather than deterministic.

In almost all cases of psychopathology, the fact is that people do not inherit a mental disorder. Rather, people inherit a predisposition or tendency to develop a particular mental disorder. Individuals do not inherit schizophrenia; they inherit a predisposition to schizophrenia. A combination of environmental events over the course of the individual's development, together with his or her other genetic endowment, determine whether the tendency toward schizophrenia ever gets actualized. "Neither genes, viruses, nor drugs are sufficient to produce a schizophrenic episode; the symptoms must be acquired by social learning and human interaction" (Kringlen, 1996, p. 503). Similarly, individuals do not inherit chronic physical diseases such as diabetes or hypertension. A combination of environmental events, together with other genetic endowment, determines whether the vulnerabilities toward these physical diseases ever bear fruition. Specifically, a person with a genetic predisposition toward hypertension may increase his or her chances of getting the disease by eating too much salt or by smoking. Similarly, an individual with a tendency toward ("diathesis" for) schizophrenia may increase his or her vulnerability to onset of the disorder by being exposed during adolescence to a series of deaths, financial losses, or other stressors within the family. Environmental factors thus play a crucial role in the development and onset of both mental and physical disorders.

If we are ever to understand mental disorders, one inescapable conclusion from the science of behavior genetics needs to be engraved into our cognitive templates: In virtually all cases of mental disorder, genes and environment both make substantial contributions, on average contributing more or less equivalently, to the resulting human abnormal patterns. As we saw earlier, for the mental disorders studied to date, heritability estimates rarely exceed 50 percent, indicating that environments and genetic factors tend to be of similar magnitude. In some cases of major mental disorders (e.g., bipolar mood disorder), heredity may contribute relatively more variance (heritability indices are in the range of 60%, and perhaps more). Other major mental disorders such as schizophrenia reveal lower heritability indices in the range of 40 to 50 percent. In most instances of mental disorder, environmental influences seem to outweigh genetic contributions to various degrees.

An inescapable implication is that it is only with rare single-gene mental disorders that heredity causes or determines mental disorder. In all other instances (which are by far the huge majority), multiple genes (in the form of predispositions or diatheses) interact with multiple environmental events to shape resulting mental disorders. Accordingly, it makes much more sense to talk about "influences" on mental disorder, "contributory" causes, and, perhaps in a few instances, "necessary" causes. However, we need to retire permanently any use of "sufficient" causes or determinants, a term which implies a unilaterally overpowering determination of effect.

ENVIRONMENTAL INFLUENCES IN PERSONALITY AND PSYCHOPATHOLOGY

By the time they are adults, adoptive siblings who were reared in the same home will, on average, bear no resemblance to each other in personality. [Biological] siblings who were reared in the same home will be somewhat more alike, but still not very similar. Even identical twins reared in the same home will not be identical in personality. They will not be noticeably more alike than identical twins reared in separate homes.

—Harris, 1995, p. 458.

One of life's intriguing possibilities is that we all begin our journeys with the same clean cortical slate (a tabula rasa); how we turn out as adults exclusively results from the environment in which we are reared and the experiences it provides. From this perspective, any mentally disordered adult is the result of a series of unfortunate aversive environmental events, most typically beginning within the family context itself.

It may have been my bad luck that one or both of my parents ignored, abused, punished, or indulged me; were inconsistent and arbitrary in their discipline; or favored my older or younger siblings. In other unfortunate scenarios, my family may have been poor, discriminated against, or unhealthy; my family may have experienced severe losses, deaths, and other negative life events; or as a family we may gradually have lost all of our previous social support hookups in the community.

In the classic psychological analysis, family factors thought to be crucial to eventual adaptive or maladaptive outcomes affect everyone in the family equivalently. For example, it makes a huge difference to all family members whether parents apply democratic ideals in their discipline (versus authoritarian ones) or harsh and unyielding physical discipline (versus rational discussion accompanied by use of psychological rewards and punishments). Whether a particular family is well-to-do, highly educated, regulates itself by psychological discipline and rational discussion, has many books available in the home, engages in educational leisurely activities, and is easily accessible to top quality schools and teachers as well as to excellent health care has a primary and direct bearing on whether one of its members will become maladjusted or not.

The operative principle can be stated in various ways. Differences in parental behaviors result in differences in children's eventual personality traits. The environment shared by a family is critical in shaping children's eventual mental adjustment. Children growing up in the same family will have the same set of health-promoting or pathogenic experiences. Childhood experiences, especially those with the mothering individual, indelibly shape subsequent personality and mental adjustment. Peoples' destinies are controlled and shaped by the family environment they encountered while growing up.

Surprisingly, the findings of contemporary behavior genetics *negate* all these traditional notions. During the last two decades, multiple behavioral genetic studies of both personality and psychopathology have found little or no effect of the traditional familial environment. Findings indicate that the common or shared family environment is minimally related to and is mostly unimportant in determining family members' subsequent general maladjustment, specific mental disorder, or specific personality style. So far, the sole area in which common, shared environmental factors (e.g., socioeconomic status [SES], parental attitudes, and behavior) produce similar effects on children's behaviors is in the area of general intelligence—but only in the years before adolescence. From adolescence forward, even intellectual performance is affected relatively more by unique or unshared environmental experiences.

AT LEAST TWO FAMILY ENVIRONMENTS
MAKE UP OUR WORLDS

Although theorists in the behavioral sciences have long stressed the central role of the family in shaping emotional functioning and personality, empirical evidence from the growing science of human behavior genetics has found little support for this widely held view.
—Kendler, Walters, Neale, Kessler, Heath, & Eaves, 1995, p. 380.

What behavior genetic research has uncovered is the crucial distinction between common–shared versus unique–unshared environmental factors. The totally unanticipated finding is quite robust and trustworthy: The significant environment for development is found within experiences that are not shared by siblings within the same family (Dunn & Plomin, 1990; Hetherington, Reiss, & Plomin, 1994; Hoffman, 1991; Kendler, Walters, Neale, Kessler, Heath, & Eaves, 1995; Rowe & Plomin, 1981).

The *common–shared environment* encompasses the traditional notion of environment within the social sciences—namely, the common settings and experiences, advantages and disadvantages that we experience as the result of growing up as members of a particular family. Our family has a particular level of income and education that, together with a set of attitudes and values, constitute low, middle, or upper socioeconomic status. We grow up in a particular region of the country, in a particular town, in a particular neighborhood—all of which provide associated physical settings and social and interpersonal experiences to all family members. Our families are of varying sizes, led by parents with disciplinary approaches that range from lax democracy to harsh authoritarianism, with varying degrees of rational discussion, emotional expressivity, and physical punishment mixed in. Considerable psychological and sociological research has studied the relationship of many of these factors to general maladjustment and to specific mental disorder.

However, what is now clear is that common–shared environmental factors play a relatively small role in the genesis of mental disorders. One important reason for the modest effect has to do with the degree of both *vulnerability* or *resiliency* present for various individuals within a particular family who experience the same environmental stressors. We examine vulnerability and protective factors in detail in Chapter 7.

A landmark study (Loehlin & Nichols, 1976) involving nearly 800 pairs of adolescent twins concluded that virtually all of the environmental variance important in development of personality was of the nonshared variety. Plomin and Rende observed that "what runs in families is DNA, not experiences shared in the home" (1991, p. 180).

Other genetic evidence indicates that children growing up in the same family are not very similar. Actually, siblings show greater differences than similarities for three major psychological domains: heritabilities of about 40 percent for *cognitive abilities*, about 20 percent for *personality*, and less than 10 percent for *mental disorders*. The findings imply that "environmental influences important to behavioral development operate in such a way as to make children in the same family different from one another. That is, environmental influences do not operate on a family-by-family basis but rather on an individual-by-individual basis. They are specific to each child rather than general for an entire family" (Plomin, 1989, p. 109).

It has been robustly established, then, that the common–shared environment is virtually unimportant in regard to development of personality and mental disorder. Instead, it is the unique–unshared environment that is crucial for formative input into human development. Aspects of the environment that seem minimally influential are all those that are shared by children who grow up in the same home: their parents' personalities; the parents' philosophies of child rearing; the parents' physical presence or absence in the home; the number of books, TV sets, or personal computers the home contains; and whether the family attends church regularly.

Siblings in the same family are exposed to and/or experience considerably different environments in terms of factors such as parental treatment and their interaction with each other and with their peers. It is these unique–unshared environmental influences that are related substantially to the developmental outcomes of adult personality traits and patterns of adjustment or mental disorder. As Plomin concluded, "Behavioral genetic studies consistently point to nonshared environment as the most important source of environmental variance for personality and psychopathology and for IQ after childhood" (1990, p. 128).

What is this unique–unshared family environment? Quite simply, it consists of the often subtle differences in settings, social experiences, family circumstances, and parent–child and sibling–sibling interactions that are different from child to child in a given family. One prime contender lies in the fact that parents treat their children differently. Some of these differences may be unilaterally driven from the parent side; a parent might treat one child differently for personal reasons (e.g., the child was unplanned or bears a resemblance to a hated mother-in-law). Differences also can be driven mostly by the child's behavior; one child may be more attractive than his or her siblings, more difficult temperamentally, or continually racked with illness. Probably most differences in parental behaviors constitute transactional outcomes that involve reciprocal contributions from both parent and child; different treatment of one child may result from a troubling lack of fit or match (e.g., lack of interpersonal complementarity, Kiesler, 1983, 1996) between that child and a parent.

It is also likely that different children in the same family experience substantially different environmental conditions, including dissimilar neighborhoods, schools, friends, and financial advantages. Many of the traditional common environmental factors such as family income, neighborhood, and type and severity of parental discipline often change during the life of a family and over the developmental years of various children within the same family. Families with younger parents often experience lower levels of financial security and live in comparatively less than optimum neighborhoods; typically, they move to more affluent suburban settings and different schools as the family matures and later children arrive. Consider a case in which, during the elementary school years, an older son, in contrast to his much younger brother, had few if any close friends or was dismally unfortunate in teacher assignments. Add to this that his younger brother was lucky enough to have a sister close to his age with whom he became extremely close, did not physically resemble his father anywhere near the same degree, and was not held to the same achievement expectations as his older brother.

Even when these factors seem to change less dramatically during the life of a family, an overriding determinant of their effects is how these situational influences are perceived by a given child. It matters little if a group of observers agree that a given set of parents treat their children equivalently if the children themselves perceive dramatic (e.g., unfair, uneven, or inconsistent) patterns of difference. Indeed, from this perspective, it probably is impossible that parents' behaviors could ever achieve equivalent effects on their various children.

Other nonshared, unique environmental factors take the form of important differences among siblings themselves, such as gender, birth order, physical attractiveness, athleticism, and intelligence. These differences often are important in determining how parents respond to their children (e.g., the kind of discipline imposed, expectations carried, or degree of affection expressed) and how children respond to each other (e.g., as fierce competitors, with substantial positive support, as subservient admirers, or as malevolent dictators).

Finally, important stressful life events often occur randomly over the history of a particular family: deaths of grandparents, other relatives, and even immediate family members; debilitating physical illnesses or other accidental tragedies; financial reversals and job losses; or the significant absence of both parents.

Given the possible statistical permutations of these myriad environmental events and circumstances, it becomes easy to grasp that two children from the same family (supposedly an identical environment) may actually grow up in remarkably different environmental contexts, being exposed to surprisingly divergent life experiences. The luck of this environmental draw might gently nudge development of a younger brother in an entirely different direction from his older sibling. It also becomes much clearer why it is that common–shared environmental factors (such as SES at a given moment in time, or as an average family condition) are not likely to have identical or even similar effects on different children within the same family.

THE COMPLEX INTERACTION OF HEREDITY AND ENVIRONMENT

Nowhere do the conceptual boundaries between heredity and environment blur more than when investigators begin to study in detail the possibilities of interaction between hereditary predispositions within an individual and the environments in which those predispositions unfold.

During the last decade behavioral geneticists have drawn increasing attention to the various ways in which gene–environment reactions can arise (Kendler, 1995; Kendler & Eaves, 1986; Plomin & Bergeman, 1991; Rende & Plomin, 1992). Two leading alternatives are the *interaction* and *correlation–transaction* models. In the interaction model, the effects of environmental factors differ depending on genotype. For example, effects of few playmates in the neighborhood likely would be different for introverted than for extraverted children. Within a diathesis–stress framework, an environmental factor might serve as a stressor for one individual who carries a genetic propensity but would have little aversive affect on an individual in whom the diathesis is absent. For example, within the interaction model, schizophrenia can be interpreted as an outcome of combined biological vulnerabilities and environmental adversities (Rosenthal, 1970). A person born with the inherited diathesis will not become schizophrenic unless the environmental stress exceeds a certain level.

A much more dynamic interaction between genotype and environment is possible in the case of the correlation, transactional, or reciprocal gene–environment model, according to which the person and environment are interdependent. The key notion is that environments do not happen randomly, but are associated in consistent patterns with various genetic predispositions. Individuals shape and select their environments and genetic influences play a significant part in the process (Plomin, DeFries, & Loehlin, 1977; Plomin, Lichtenstein, Pedersen, & McClearn, 1990; Scarr, 1992; Scarr & McCartney, 1983; Rutter, 1997).

Individuals vary greatly in their exposure to risk factors in their environment (Rutter & Rutter, 1993). But considerable evidence can be found that people act in specific ways that influence the level of environmental risk that they experience. Studies show that controllable stressful life events involve substantial genetic influences (Plomin, Lichtenstein, Pedersen, & McClearn, 1990). Researchers need to understand better why some individuals suffer a host of environmental adversities, whereas others go through life with a string of mostly positive experiences. For now, what seems clear is that the creation of risk environments can be mediated in part by genetically influenced behaviors. Individuals also seem to create risk environments for psychopathology. Not all environmental risk factors happen by chance; rather, individuals play an active role in creating their own risky environments. For example, children with strong genetic predispositions toward schizophrenia may contribute to, or even evoke, dysfunctional reactions from their parents.

Monroe and Simons (1991) reviewed the literature indicating that certain kinds of stress may be influenced by specific individual predispositions or diatheses. For example, the Camberwell Collaborative Depression Study (McGuffin, Katz, & Bebbington, 1988) found that individuals who develop depressive disorders are also likely to engage in behaviors that help evoke negative life events that can precipitate an episode of depression. Hammen (1991) discovered that most of the severe life events found to precede depression (e.g., performing poorly at work or being hostile and withdrawn in interpersonal relationships) were not entirely independent of the depressed person's action or control. Hammen (1992) also reported that depressed mothers seemed to elicit more stress from the environment than did other mothers. In short, the mother contributed to her child's depression and the child's behavior reinforced the mother's depression.

In systematic empirical reviews, Bell (1968), Rheingold (1966), Sameroff (1993), and Sameroff and Chandler (1975) provided multiple examples of transactional processes between mother and child (each other's major social environments) during the process of development. Patterson (1986) and Olson (1992) each offered a transactional explanation of development and maintenance of antisocial behavior in childhood. Patterson described how a child's normal noncompliance behavior (e.g., whining, teasing, or yelling) elicits from inept parents negative coercive responses (e.g., harsh discipline, absence of positive reinforcement, and involvement with child); these negative parental responses then lead to further child noncompliance that escalates into aggressive behaviors, including sometimes physical attack. Olson described how an antisocial child in the classroom systematically converts his classmates from benign playmates into hostile combatants.

UNAVOIDABLE CONCLUSIONS FOR THE
TWENTY-FIRST CENTURY

Anyone wishing intelligently to discuss mental disorders and their origins needs at all times to keep "on the front burners" of his or her memory the following vital scientific learnings and conclusions.

First, *models of psychopathology that place total emphasis on genetic factors, such as the biomedical model, are invalid*, and "are going the way of models that focused exclusively on environmental factors" (Rende & Plomin, 1995, p. 291). Mental disorders, including major disorders such as schizophrenia, are best understood as "genetically *influenced* disorders rather than as genetically determined disorders" (Gottesman, 1991).

Second, in almost all cases of mental disorder *people do not inherit the disorder*; rather, when genetic factors are operative, *they inherit a predisposition or tendency* (*a diathesis*) to develop a particular mental disorder.

Third, *in virtually all cases of mental disorder, both genes and environment make substantial contributions*, on average contributing more or less equivalently to the resulting human abnormal patterns.

Fourth, for the huge majority of mental disorders, *multiple genes* (*in the form of predispositions or diatheses*) *interact with multiple environmental events* to shape particular mental disorders.

Fifth, *the common–shared family environment* is minimally associated with and *is mostly unimportant* in children's subsequent onset of a specific personality style or of a specific mental disorder.

Sixth, unique–unshared environmental influences are, however, associated substantially with the developmental outcomes of adult personality traits and patterns of adjustment or mental disorder. *The unique environments experienced by individuals within the same family encompass the significant causal influences for mental disorders.*

Overall we have to conclude that the major tenets of the biomedical model for mental disorders are contradicted by present-day scientific genetic evidence. Genetically determined biological brain abnormalities do not cause mental disorders.

At best, hereditarily transmitted biological abnormalities in the cortex and central nervous system are "necessary" causal factors for development of mental disorders. Most typically, genetically transmitted biological abnormalities are "contributory" causal factors or "influences" for mental disorders. In no case are genetically transmitted biological abnormalities "sufficient," much less "necessary and sufficient," causal factors for mental disorder.

All of us, scientists and members of the media, must take pains to communicate that mental disorders have multiple causes: biological, psychological, and psychosocial. The approach to study and treatment of mental disorders needs to be guided by the "doctrine of multiple causality" (Lipowski, 1975, 1980). In all cases of mental disorders, a configuration of interacting variables, including biological, psychosocial, and environmental factors, cumulatively exerts causal influences on the development, onset, course, and outcome of the particular psychopathology.

REFERENCES

American Psychiatric Association. (1994). *Diagnostic and statistical manual of mental disorders* (4th ed.). Washington, DC: Author.

Bell, R. Q. (1968). A reinterpretation of the direction of effects in studies of socialization. *Psychological Review, 75,* 81–95.

Boomsma, D., Anokhin, A., & de Geus, E. (1997). Genetics of electrophysiology: Linking genes, brain, and behavior. *Current Directions in Psychological Science, 6,* 106–110.

Bronfenbrenner, U., & Ceci, S. J. (1994). Nature–nurture reconceptualized in developmental perspective: A bioecological model. *Psychological Review, 101,* 568–586.

Carey, G., & DiLalla, D. L. (1994). Personality and psychopathology: Genetic perspectives. *Journal of Abnormal Psychology, 103,* 32–43.

Clarke, J. (1972). *The life and times of George III.* London: Weidenfeld & Nicolson.

Dunn, J., & Plomin, R. (1990). *Separate lives: Why siblings are so different.* New York: Basic Books.

Eisenberg, L. (1995). The social construction of the human brain. *American Journal of Psychiatry, 152,* 1563–1575.

Foster, H. D. (1989). Multiple sclerosis and schizophrenia: Some comments on similarities in their spatial distributions. *Journal of Orthomolecular Medicine, 4,* 11–13.

Gottesman, I. I. (1991). *Schizophrenia genesis: The origins of madness.* New York: Freeman.

Gottesman, I. I., & Shields, J. A. (1967). A polygenic theory of schizophrenia. *Proceedings of the National Academy of Science, 58,* 199–205.

Hammen, C. (1991). Generation of stress in the course of unipolar depression. *Journal of Abnormal Psychology, 100,* 555–561.

Hammen, C. (1992). The family–environmental context of depression: A perspective on children's risk. In D. Cicchetti & S. L. Toth (Eds.), *Developmental perspectives on depression: Rochester symposium on developmental psychopathology: Vol. 4* (pp. 252–281). Rochester, NY: University of Rochester Press.

Harris, J. R. (1995). Where is the child's environment? A group socialization theory of development. *Psychological Review, 102,* 458–489.

Hetherington, E. M., Reiss, D., & Plomin, R. (Eds.). (1994). *Separate social worlds of siblings: Impact of nonshared environment on development.* Hillsdale, NJ: Erlbaum.

Hoffman, L. (1991). The influence of family environment on personality. *Psychological Bulletin, 110,* 187–203.

Kendler, K. S. (1995). Genetic epidemiology in psychiatry: Taking both genes and environment seriously. *Archives of General Psychiatry, 52,* 895–899.

Kendler, K. S., & Eaves, L. J. (1986). Models for the joint effect of genotype and environment on liability to psychiatric illness. *American Journal of Psychiatry, 143,* 279–289.

Kendler, K. S., Walters, E. E., Neale, M. C., Kessler, R. C., Heath, A. C., & Eaves, L. J. (1995). The structure of the genetic and environmental risk factors for six major psychiatric disorders in women: Phobia, generalized anxiety disorder, panic disorder, bulimia, major depression, and alcoholism. *Archives of General Psychiatry, 52,* 374–383.

Kety, S. (1996). Genetic and environmental factors in the etiology of schizophrenia. In S. Matthysse, D. L. Levy, J. Kagan, & F. M. Benes (Eds.), *Psychopathology: The evolving science of mental disorders* (pp. 477–487). New York: Cambridge University Press.

Kiesler, D. J. (1983). The 1982 interpersonal circle: A taxonomy for complementarity in human transactions. *Psychological Review, 90,* 185–214.

Kiesler, D. J. (1996). *Contemporary interpersonal theory and research: Personality, psychopathology, and psychotherapy.* New York: Wiley.

Kringlen, E. (1996). Problems and paradoxes in research on the etiology of schizophrenia. In S. Matthysse, D. L. Levy, J. Kagan, & F. M. Benes (Eds.), *Psychopathology: The evolving science of mental disorders* (pp. 488–508). New York: Cambridge University Press.

Lander, E. S., & Schork, N. J. (1994). Genetic dissection of complex traits. *Science, 265,* 2037–2048.

Lipowski, Z. J. (1975). Psychiatry of somatic diseases: Epidemiology, pathogenesis, classification. *Comprehensive Psychiatry, 16,* 105–124.

Lipowski, Z. J. (1980). Organic mental disorders: Introduction and review of syndromes. In H. I. Kaplan, A. M. Freeman, & B. J. Saddock (Eds.), *Comprehensive textbook of psychiatry III* (Vol. 2). Baltimore: Williams & Wilkins.

Loehlin, J. C. (1992). *Genes and environment in personality development.* Newbury Park, CA: Sage.

Loehlin, J. C., & Nichols, R. C. (1976). *Heredity, environment, and personality.* Austin: University of Texas Press.

Mann, C. C. (1994). Behavioral genetics in transition. *Science, 264,* 1686–1689.

Mellon, C. D. (1997). *The genetic base of abnormal behavior.* Placitas, NM: Genetics Heritage Press.

McGuffin, P., Katz, R., & Bebbington, P. (1988). The Camberwell collaborative depression study III: Depression and adversity in the relatives of depressed probands. *British Journal of Psychiatry, 152,* 775–782.

McGuffin, P., Owen, M. J., O'Donovan, M. C., Thapar, A., & Gottesman, I. I. (1994). *Seminars in psychiatry genetics.* London: Gaskell.

McKusick, V. (1983). *Mendelian inheritance in man* (7th ed.). Baltimore: Johns Hopkins University Press.

Monroe, S. M., & Simons, A. D. (1991). Diathesis–stress theories in the context of life stress research: Implications for the depressive disorders. *Psychological Bulletin, 119,* 406–425.

Olson, S. (1992). Development of conduct problems and peer rejection in preschool children: A social systems analysis. *Journal of Abnormal Child Psychology, 20,* 327–350.

Pardes, H. J., Kaufman, C. A., Pincus, H. A., & West, A. (1989). Genetics and psychiatry: Past discoveries, current dilemmas, and future directions. *American Journal of Psychiatry, 146,* 435–443.

Patterson, G. R. (1986). Performance models for antisocial boys. *American Psychologist, 41,* 432–444.

Plomin, R. (1989). Environment and genes: Determinants of behavior. *American Psychologist, 44,* 105–111.

Plomin, R. (1990). *Nature and nurture: An introduction to human behavioral genetics.* Pacific Grove, CA: Brooks/Cole.

Plomin, R., & Bergeman, C. S. (1991). The nature of nurture: Genetic influences in "environment" measures. *Behavioral and Brain Sciences, 14,* 373–386.

Plomin, R., Chipuer, H. M., & Neiderhiser, J. M. (1994). Behavioral genetic evidence for the importance of nonshared environment. In E. M. Hetherington, D. Reiss, & R. Plomin (Eds.), *Separate social worlds of siblings: The impact of nonshared environment on development* (pp. 1–31). Hillsdale, NJ: Erlbaum.

Plomin, R., DeFries, J. C., & Loehlin, J. (1977). Genotype–environment interaction and correlation in the analysis of human development. *Psychological Bulletin, 84,* 309–322.

Plomin, R., DeFries, J. C., McClearn, G. E., & Rutter, M. (1997). *Behavioral genetics* (3d ed.). New York: Freeman.

Plomin, R., Lichtenstein, P., Pedersen, N. L., & McClearn, G. E. (1990). Genetic influence on life events. *Psychology and Aging, 5,* 23–30.

Plomin, R., & Rende, R. (1991). Human behavioral genetics. *Annual Review of Psychology, 42,* 161–190.

Reiss, D., Plomin, R., & Hetherington, M. (1991). Genetics and psychiatry: An unheralded window on the environment. *American Journal of Psychiatry, 148,* 283–291.

Rende, R., & Plomin, R. (1992). Diathesis–stress models of psychopathology: A quantitative genetic perspective. *Applied & Preventive Psychology, 1,* 177–182.

Rende, R., & Plomin, R. (1995). Nature, nurture, and the development of psychopathology. In D. Cicchetti & D. J. Cohen (Eds.), *Developmental psychopathology: Vol. 1, Theory and methods* (pp. 291–314). New York: Wiley.

Rheingold, H. L. (1966). The development of social behavior in the human infant. *Monographs of the Society for Research in Child Development, 31,* No. 1.

Rose, R. J. (1995). Genes and human behavior. *Annual Review of Psychology, 46,* 625–654.

Rosenthal, D. (1970). *Genetic theory and abnormal behavior.* New York: McGraw-Hill.

Rowe, G., & Plomin, R. (1981). The importance of nonshared environmental influences in behavior development. *Developmental Psychology, 17,* 517–531.

Rutter, M. L. (1997). Nature–nurture integration: The example of antisocial behavior. *American Psychologist, 52,* 390–398.

Rutter, M. L., Macdonald, H., LeCouteur, A., Harrington, R., Bolton, P., & Bailey, A. (1990). Genetic factors in child psychiatric disorders, II: Empirical findings. *Journal of Child Psychology and Psychiatry, 31,* 39–82.

Rutter, M. L., & Rutter, M. (1993). *Developing minds: Challenge and continuity across the life span*. New York: Basic Books.

Sameroff, A. J. (1993). Models of development and developmental risk. In C. Zeanah (Ed.), *Handbook of infant mental health* (pp. 3–13). New York: Guilford.

Sameroff, A. J., & Chandler, M. J. (1975). Reproductive risk and the continuum of caretaking causality. In F. D. Horowitz, M. Hetherington, S. Scarr-Salapatek, & G. Siegel (Eds.), *Review of child development research* (Vol. 4, pp. 187–244). Chicago: University of Chicago Press.

Scarr, S. (1992). Developmental theories for the 1990s: Development and individual differences. *Child Development, 63,* 1–19.

Scarr, S., & McCartney, K. (1983). How people make their own environments: A theory of genotype–environment effects. *Child Development, 54,* 424–435.

Susser, M. (1973). *Causal thinking in the health sciences*. New York: Oxford University Press.

Vandenberg, S. G., Singer, S. M., & Pauls, D. L. (1986). *The heredity of behavior disorders in adults and children*. New York: Plenum.

Weatherall, D. (1992). *The Harveian oration: The role of nature and nurture in common diseases—Garrod's legacy*. London: The Royal College of Physicians.

Chapter 5

Scientific Evidence Invalidates the Environmental Model: Findings from Psychological Research

> Every parent of one child is an environmentalist, and every parent of more than one becomes a geneticist.
>
> —Rowe, 1987.

We have just learned that the biomedical model for mental disorders is contradicted by present-day scientific evidence from behavioral genetics. We will now examine the polar-opposite, competing stance, which is referred to as environmentalism or situationism.

Environmentalism asserts that the primary determinants of mental disorder are external situational events found within the family, neighborhood, and culture. Beginning at birth and continuing throughout life, these environmental events produce formative effects on personality and mental health. Mental disorder results from factors such as early child abuse, marital discord, family disruption, neighborhood deterioration, and "sick" societal values and institutions—all of which form the context for faulty or undesirable learning experiences.

The social sciences (sociology, anthropology, and psychology) have been the major disciplines advocating this perspective for mental disorders. Behavioristic psychology, especially the radical behaviorism of B. F. Skinner, has been prominent in insisting upon the sole primacy of the environment in the determination of human and animal behavior.

We need to ask the same vital question of the environmental model that we just addressed to the disease model: What does the scientific evidence indicate? Is this exclusive environmental emphasis justified and warranted in light of the empirical research?

We must first acknowledge that the behavioral genetic evidence reviewed in Chapter 4 invalidates any monocausal model of human behavior. Accordingly, behavioral genetic evidence in an of itself invalidates any environmental theory, including behavioristic psychology, that advocates sole situational determination of human behavior and its abnormal manifestations.

This chapter will expand our perspective further by reviewing scientific evidence relevant to behavioristic psychology other than genetic research—empirical findings from within psychology itself. These findings necessitate the same conclusion: any environmental theory of human behavior—any solely behavioral explanation of mental disorders—by itself is no longer adequate. To provide valid explanations of mental disorders, theories that incorporate only environmental or psychological causal factors must be expanded to include important biological (and sociocultural) causal influences.

SCIENTIFIC PSYCHOLOGY AND BEHAVIORISM

John Watson (1913, 1925), the founder of behavioristic psychology, considered hereditary influence crucial only for physical traits—not for behavioral traits (those patterns operative, for example, in personality and maladjustment). Watsonian behaviorism advocated the centrality for human behavior of environmental events (external to the individual) that could be objectively observed and measured. Valid explanations of human behavior could be found in these external situations or settings in which individuals' developmental histories and current activities are imbedded.

Subsequent to Watson's introduction of behaviorism, the most extreme psychological theory extolling the centrality of environmental events for understanding human behavior was the "radical behaviorism" of B. F. Skinner (1938, 1953, 1957, 1974, 1989; Delprato & Midgley, 1992). One of the most famous of American psychologists, Skinner almost singlehandedly made "reinforcement" (a property of the external environment) a household word. Under his influence, human maladjustments (under the biomedical model they are regarded as mental illnesses) became transformed into "behavior disorders." Today, the term "behavior therapy" describes a vast armamentarium of interventions and techniques applied by behavioral and other therapists to individuals presenting with DSM mental disorders.

Skinner's basic stance was that the important factors controlling (influencing or determining) human behavior are found exclusively outside the person (or organism)—they reside in the external situation or environment. He objected strongly to claims that private events can explain overt behavior. Rather, he considered anything occurring inside the person–organism irrelevant to what that person eventually does: "We can predict and control behavior without knowing anything about what is happening inside" (Skinner, 1989, p. 130). The organism is irrelevant either as a site of physiological processes or as the locus of mental activities.

In Skinner's theory, all behavior is determined by "contingencies of reinforcement" that can be identified in the environmental context. In any situation our behavior depends on and is determined by the kind or frequency of positive and negative reinforcements we have received in similar situations in our past. We are apt to repeat behaviors that have been reinforced, less apt to repeat those that have not been reinforced or that have been punished. All the information one needs to predict behavior can be found among factors within the environmental context; no relevant information is needed from inside the person's skin, from within his or her brain. Skinner did not deny the existence of brain events (internal events such as conscious feelings, intentions, thoughts, or fantasies); he simply dismissed them as irrelevant and unimportant for predicting what humans (or other organisms) may do. In short, human behavior is conditioned.

Maladaptive behavior is simply the product of inadequate or unsuccessful conditioning. Our different conditioning histories mold our responses into different forms. None of these responses, by itself, can be called either sick or healthy. Some responses simply work better than others within the context of a particular setting or society. Those that initially don't work can be remolded, using reconditioning procedures, so that they work more adaptively.

From Skinner's perspective, personality also is a somewhat useless term. Personality simply is the totality of one's behavior. When we are not performing some act, our personalities do not exist—except as learned residues from our past histories. My personality, accordingly, is my life history of reinforcements that occurred in the situations of my life. Personality simply is an individual's repertoire of behavior which, in turn, is exclusively the historical product of environmental contingencies of reinforcement. Similarly, a person's abnormal, maladjusted behaviors are similarly the product of environmental contingencies of reinforcement. His or her maladjusted behaviors can be changed simply by altering the operative environmental contingencies of reinforcement.

One would be hard pressed to find a theoretical position that represents a more contrasting conceptual position to the biomedical model reviewed in Chapter 2. Above all else, Skinner's theory is an example of extreme environmental determinism or causality. His radical situation or environment position can be summarized with the following three themes. (1) Causal (controlling) factors are external to the behaving human; situational factors are the main determinants or causes of human behavior. (2) A person consists of a large number of response patterns attached to particular situations; except to summarize a person's repertoire of behaviors, the term "personality" is of little use. (3) A person's behavior changes from one situation to the next, depending on the contingencies present; there should be little consistency in a person's behavior over time and across various situations. Since a person's behavior develops through the contingencies of reinforcement experienced as he or she grows up (summarized in a reinforcement history), the only biological structures and events that are important are those that reflect and store this learned environmental experience.

The remainder of this chapter will review the evidence for each of these three radical behavioral assumptions. Since the second and third assumptions are closely interlaced, they will be discussed together.

SITUATIONAL–ENVIRONMENTAL FACTORS
ARE THE MAJOR CAUSES OF HUMAN BEHAVIOR:
THE EVIDENCE

Behavioral Genetics

Chapter 4 reviewed the conclusions from contemporary behavioral genetic research that disprove the exclusively biological position of the biomedical model. These conclusions equally invalidate the environmental position of radical behaviorism.

A major behavioral genetic conclusion was that, in adult personality and in virtually all cases of mental disorder, both genes (nature) and environment (nurture) make substantial contributions, on average contributing more or less equivalently to the resulting human behavior patterns. The evidence is overwhelming, then, that hereditarily transmitted mental mechanisms develop and function continuously from life in the womb onward. Robert Plomin (1989), one of the major behavioral genetics authorities, admonished us—whether we are concerned about intelligence, personality, or mental disorder—to ask not what is heritable, but rather to ask what is not.

If genetic contribution is the order of the day for these behavioral domains, then some stable biological substrate is continuously present and functioning within us as we mature and develop throughout life. A major feature of this substrate is that it shows stability over time, while still permitting change and development as we interact with environmental factors. This substrate involves cognitive, emotional, and other functioning occurring via the human cortex and central nervous system. At the human adult level this biological substrate is manifested importantly as human intellectual and personality "traits"—enduring human characteristics that are expressed in a relatively wide range of contexts and environments.

Another behavioral genetic conclusion from Chapter 4 is equally devastating to a radical behavioristic position: Unique—unshared family environmental influences are related substantially to the developmental outcomes of adult personality traits and patterns of adjustment or mental disorder—common–shared family environmental factors are not. In the present context, common environmental factors are equivalent to the external situation or external environment. The behavioral genetic evidence is abundant that the common family environment—for example, the external situation as rated by a group of observers—is unrelated to development of personality or maladjustment. Instead, the literature suggests that it is the unshared "internal" environment—the family environment as uniquely perceived and interpreted by the individual—the environment that the individual uniquely changes or shapes—that is crucial.

In short, the scientific behavioral genetic evidence summarized in the previous chapter pulls the rug from beneath any continued advocacy by behavioristic psychology for causal exclusivity of the external environment. If, in the case of personality and mental disorder, heredity is half the story, then environment cannot be the full story. Not only is environment just half the story, most of its influence seems to occur from inside the person (inside the "black box") as a unique, unshared, perceived environment.

Social Learning Theory

Some relatively recent developments within behavioristic psychology itself challenge radical behavior's exclusive emphasis on the external environment. These include emergence of social learning theory and the cognitive revolution within experimental and clinical psychology.

The original framework of social learning theory was offered by Julian Rotter (1954; Rotter, Chance, & Phares, 1972), but gained significant momentum with the research and writings of Albert Bandura (1969, 1977). In applied clinical settings, it expanded earlier Skinnerian "behavior therapy" (Ullmann & Krasner, 1969) into what is known popularly today as "cognitive–behavioral therapy" (Mahoney, 1974; Meichenbaum, 1977).

The major premise of social learning theory is that an individual's perception of external stimulus events (what Rotter called the "psychological situation") supersedes external events themselves in determining or causing human behavior. As advocated also by phenomenological psychology (Spinelli, 1989; Thines, 1977; Wann, 1964) and by the personologist Murray (1938), social learning theory located primary causation of human behavior in the "subjective" environment—in the environment as perceived by the individual. In contrast, the "objective" environment—the "real" aspects of the external environment that a group of observers might agree are present and relevant in a particular instance—was considered to have considerably less importance in determining what an individual may or may not do.

What distinguished Rotter's theory was his heavily cognitive formulation that a person's behavior is determined by the person's expectancy of the value and probability of occurrence of a reinforcement. The central ingredient, then, was not the external reinforcement per se, but rather the meaning the reinforcement represented to the individual in question.

Empirical studies of human learning were simultaneously uncovering serious problems with the behavioristic notion of external reinforcement. Studies of "verbal reinforcement" (in which smiling or saying "good" are used as positive reinforcers to increase a person's use of certain targeted words) demonstrated convincingly that these reinforcements were unsuccessful unless the person being conditioned became aware of the connection. Other studies of Pavlovian or classical conditioning with humans similarly demonstrated that only those subjects who become aware of the regular relationship between conditioned and unconditioned stimuli (e.g., every time a light flashes, I get shocked) actually condition their skin resistance or other physiological reactions in the form of anticipatory anxiety responses. In short, human research in both operant and classical conditioning was also demonstrating that some cognitive representation of stimulus–response connections had to occur internally (within an individual's subjective environment) before the reinforcing event could determine the result.

Another series of studies compared the effectiveness of "actual" schedules of reinforcement (e.g., reinforcements occurring randomly) to "expected" schedules of reinforcement (e.g., being told that reinforcement would occur once every fourth behavioral occurrence). Subjects' responses were found to be controlled, not by the actual external state of affairs (e.g., randomness), but by their expectations based on incorrect information provided to them. Once again, the key determining factor was the subjective environment, in this case in the form of a cognitive expectation planted by the experimenter.

Bandura (1969, 1977) was instrumental in establishing the social learning perspective with his innovative and creative studies of human "modeling" (observational or imitation learning). What he and his colleagues demonstrated was that it is vital to distinguish between learning and performance. *Performance* defines the overt event, a person's actions, which are controlled by reinforcing outcomes. In contrast, *learning* refers to the covert, internal event—a person's cognitive images, expectations, and interpretations. What Bandura demonstrated unequivocally in his experiments on human modeling was that learning could take place without the learner having to perform any action. A child, for example, learns many things by simply watching, observing others' actions and the outcomes that follow. Cognitive representations (images, expectations) of associated situations and consequences, then, are essential to the learning process; actual performance is not. In the case of modeling, further, actual external reinforcement is necessary only to elicit performance of previously cognitively learned behavior.

The upshot of all these developments was an unavoidable conclusion: external events and outcomes are not the crucial causal factors in human conditioning and learning. Instead, prepotent determinants are individually perceived events and anticipated outcomes. The determinants of a person's behavior are his or her perceptions, expectations, and interpretations of events and outcomes—not the objective, external facts.

The Cognitive Revolution

Since the 1970s, a strong shift away from behaviorism also occurred within basic experimental psychology—a shift that came to be referred to as the "cognitive revolution in psychology" (Baars, 1986; Dember, 1974; Gardner, 1985; Joynson, 1970; Palermo, 1971). The field rather quickly shifted from behavioristic experimental psychology toward a new point of view called "cognitive" or "information-processing" psychology.

Behaviorism, especially Skinner's radical version, insisted on the centrality of observable external behaviors and situations and denied the importance of (inner) conscious experience. In contrast, theorists central to the cognitive revolution (Miller, Galanter, & Pribram, 1960; Neisser, 1967; Newell & Simon, 1972; Norman, 1967) insisted that people primarily make inferences about cognitive factors (e.g., memories, meanings, ideas, and plans) that underlie and explain overt patterns of human activity. As Baars observed, cognitive psychologists distinctively emphasized "the *representations* that organisms can have of themselves and of their world, and about the transformations that these representations undergo" (1986, p. 7). Information processing (transformations of representations), moreover, can occur at both conscious and unconscious levels.

These cognitive themes are well established within present-day experimental psychology. Not surprising, they have also become established in behavior therapy within clinical psychology. Originally tied closely to radical behaviorism, the behavior therapy movement insisted adamantly on avoiding any concepts that targeted inner (covert) human events or experiences (Ullmann & Krasner, 1969). Clinical behaviorists indeed were determined to eliminate any unobservable (e.g., conscious experience, and certainly unconscious activity) or "psychodynamic" constructs.

It was perhaps inevitable that behavior therapy, grounded as it had been in the behavioral learning tradition of experimental psychology, would eventually incorporate the theoretical shifts necessitated by the cognitive revolution occurring within that same experimental psychology. The fact is that much of contemporary behavior therapy has arrived at a conglomerate cognitive–behavior therapy (Mahoney, 1974; Meichenbaum, 1977), without explicitly recognizing that, historically, "cognitive behavioral" is a true oxymoron.

The evidence from behavioral genetics, together with recent theory and research within social learning and cognitive psychology, consistently underscores the validity and prepotency of the subjective environment (stable cognitive factors or activities residing within the individual) as causal factors for human behavior. In comparison, the external environment per se makes relatively impotent causal contributions.

PERSONALITY EXISTS AND IS STABLE ACROSS TIME AND SITUATIONS

Personality Exists

We can now examine the second and third central tenets of environmentalism or "situationism" in psychology. The second tenet was that little need or use exists for the notion of personality (enduring human characteristics that are expressed in a relatively wide range of contexts and environments); rather, as a result of idiosyncratic learning histories, each person consists of a large number of response patterns attached to, and elicited in, particular situations. The third tenet was that a person's behavior should change when a different situation is encountered; no stabilities in human behavior are expected.

The first source of rebuttal of these tenets is the evidence from behavior genetics that robustly supports the genetic transmission of personality traits. Broad personality traits (e.g., neuroticism, extraversion), specific behaviors such as smoking cigarettes, and even subjective states such as happiness all show substantial heritability in the 40 to 60 percent range (Bouchard, 1994; Brody, 1988, 1994; Carey & DiLalla, 1994; Cloninger, Adolfsson, & Svrakic, 1996; Eysenck, 1990; Loehlin, 1992; Loehlin, Willerman, & Horn, 1988; Mann, 1994; Plomin, DeFries,

McClearn, & Rutter, 1997; Rose, 1995; Rowe, 1989, 1997). Kety had earlier observed, "If schizophrenia is a myth, it is a myth with a strong genetic component" (1974, p. 961). If personality is a myth, as behaviorism often has advocated, we now know that it is a myth with a strong genetic component. That which is genetically transmitted has to be in the form of dispositions or "traits" or some similar stable person variables—stable cortical mechanisms and/or psychological processes that continue to guide our actions in characteristic directions.

Within the last decade or so, scientific findings from personality researchers have resulted in a growing consensus that five major personality dispositions or traits can be reliably identified for human subjects; apparently universal, they are found also in most countries throughout the world (Costa & McCrae, 1985; Deary, 1996; Digman, 1990; Goldberg, 1990; John, 1990; Krug & Johns, 1986; McCrae & Costa, 1987; Norman, 1963; Tupes & Christal, 1961/1992; Wiggins & Pincus, 1992). These five personality traits include the degree to which a person is surgent (assertive, leader-like, sociable, and gregarious), agreeable (cooperative, good-natured, and sympathetic), emotionally stable (calm, steady, self-confident, and cool), conscientious (hard-working, persevering, organized, and responsible), and intellectually creative and open (curious, imaginative, cultured, and broad-minded). Humans can be described and differentiated in terms of their rankings on these broad five dimensions, as well as on the set of more specific dimensions ("facets") that are subsumed under each of the five. Within psychology these basic dimensions of personality have come to be referred to as the "Big Five Factors."

Considerable evidence supports the following conclusions. (1) The Big Five dimensions of personality underlie the multiple personality tests and instruments that have been developed and used within psychology; hence the Big Five Factors provide a powerful model for understanding and integrating the findings of personality research. (2) The five personality dimensions are independent of (uncorrelated with) each other so that a person who is strong (or weak) on one factor can also be either strong, moderate, or weak on another. (3) A person's positions on the Big Five dimensions are genetically determined. (4) At least some of the Big Five trait dimensions are associated with differences in biological brain structure and/or functioning.

In sum, the bulk of scientific evidence suggests that personality indeed exists in the form of the Big Five personality traits. These five broad human dimensions that affect our basic social and interpersonal functioning can be found in humans throughout the world. The Big Five dimensions have a clear genetic basis and may be anchored in biological brain mechanisms.

Personality Is Stable across Time and across Situations

Though personality traits have only recently been found to organize themselves around the Big Five factors, for years psychological understanding of human personality and maladjustment was based heavily in personality trait theory. Basic tenets of the classic trait ("person") model are as follows. (1) Traits are internal dispositions that are relatively stable over time and across situations. (2) Human traits are continuous dimensions of behavior on which people can be reliably scored and differentiated. (3) These inherent dispositions found in the person (these traits) are primary determinants of behavior; responses in different situations reflect these latent disposition of the individual and are affected little by environmental factors. (4) A person's behavior tends to be relatively stable across chunks of time (transtemporal stability) and across a range of situations (transsituational stability).

One of the early social learning theorists, Mischel (1968), rejected these tenets of trait theory and thereby set a challenge to the fields of both clinical and personality psychology. His 1968 book examined the existing research literature and concluded that little evidence existed for the claims of personality trait theory. He documented that traits are not substantial attributes of persons that are central to understanding human behavior; rather they can be more usefully considered as products of an observing person's (interactant or scientist) categorizing behavior. He concluded that personality traits are no more than convenient but misleading labels about other people that exist only in the mind of the observer.

Mischel decreed that psychology needed to abandon the relatively useless notion of traits and adopt instead the perspective of social learning theory. His basic reason for the uselessness of personality traits was his documentation that human behavior is not very consistent from one situation (environmental context) to another. Rather, as social learning theory indicates, human behavior is much more situationally specific—shaped largely by the conditions and outcomes that occur in given environmental contexts. What really determines a person's reactions in these different situations is not some nonexistent enduring trait organization within the person—rather the sole determinant is the residue of a person's history of reinforcements in past similar situations. Mischel concluded, "With the possible exception of intelligence, highly generalized behavioral consistencies have not been demonstrated, and the concept of personality traits as broad dispositions is thus untenable" (1968, p. 146).

As is common within psychology, a series of replies and counter-replies appeared (for an earlier summary of the dialogue see Endler &

Magnusson, 1976; Magnusson & Endler, 1977) in what came to be known as the "person–situation" debate. One indisputable effect of Mischel's arguments was that personality theory and research stayed on the defensive for the next several decades.

Summaries of the person–situation controversy (Endler & Magnusson, 1976; Kenrick & Funder, 1988, 1991; Magnusson & Endler, 1977; Pervin, 1985; Ross & Nisbett, 1991) now make it clear that the issue was a pseudoissue, and that interactionism is a more valid model. Mischel (1973) admitted the same point five years after appearance of his book, and basically recanted and reshaped his earlier polemic themes. What also emerged from the controversy was a series of clearer understandings and insights regarding the issue and, more important, a set of learnings as to how personality scientists could better conduct future theory and research (Kenrick & Funder, 1988).

A major result of the controversy was that the fields of personality and clinical psychology moved toward an "interactionist" position (Endler & Magnusson, 1976; Magnusson, 1990) that combines the strengths of the situation (social learning) and person (trait) traditions. The central interactionist tenet is that human behavior is jointly determined by both genetically shaped person and environmentally presented situation factors; by itself, neither person nor situation variables can provide a sufficient explanation. Second, persons and situations interact continuously in a dynamic manner in which each affects and alters the other. Third, persons are intentional, proactive agents in this interaction process, not mere reactants; humans actively interpret situations they encounter, choose to be situations that represent distinctive matches to their characteristics, and through interaction, alter and change the situations. Finally, the psychological meaning of a situation to the individual, the subjective environment, is the essential determinant of that person's behavior. The bottom line is that neither the setting alone nor the person alone provides an adequate account of human behavior; personality traits and situations interact with each other to influence what we humans do.

From longitudinal studies of personality across the adult years, it has now also become clear that personality traits demonstrate substantial stability over time (Brody, 1988; Carver & Scheier, 1992; Costa & McCrae, 1997; McCrae & Costa, 1990). Costa and McCrae summarized the evidence as follows: "In the course of adult life individuals . . . age biologically and face acute and chronic disease. They pass through a variety of social roles, from novice parents and workers to grandparents, widows, and retirees. They share with others the impact of great social and cultural changes, and face their own personal history of triumphs and tragedies. Yet all these events have little or no impact on basic personality traits. . . . Personality is not a product of the life course . . . but a robust and resilient set of dispositions within the individual that themselves help shape the life course" (1997, p. 283).

The upshot, then, is the same conclusion we keep returning to. External situational–environmental factors are not the primary determinants or causes of human behavior. Genetically transmitted person factors (in the form of personality traits and/or other enduring cognitive processes) are at least equally determining, while the dynamic interaction of the person and environmental factors is the most important factor of all.

DYNAMIC INTERACTION OF
PERSONALITY AND SITUATION

Persons interact dynamically with the social and other environments in which they conduct their lives. Interactionism and interpersonal transactional perspectives (Kiesler, 1996) are strongly established in much of scientific psychology. The basic thrust of these developments is to render historically naive and remote the notion that humans are relatively passive agents whose behaviors are governed predominantly by environmental circumstances and contingencies.

An individual's behavior instead is influenced by significant perceived features of situations. The individual chooses the situations in which he or she performs, attends to and interprets significant aspects that serve as cues for his or her activities in the situations, and subsequently actually affects the character of these situations. The bottom-line notion of "dynamic" interactions between person and environment is that humans, far from being passive reactants, constantly act on their environmental settings. Several essential components of this activity have been delineated.

First, humans constantly attend to and perceive certain (probably distinctive) aspects of their external environments and constantly construe and interpret the meanings that are most relevant to them. Hence, dynamic interaction implies the priority of the subjective (versus objective) external environment. The environment that most determines our actions and reactions is that particular environment that we perceive (regardless of what anyone else in the same external environment might perceive). The validity of this notion has been confirmed robustly by the recent findings of behavioral genetics that it is the unique, unshared family environment that is central for development of personality and mental disorder.

Second, humans act on their environments by, whenever at all possible, choosing (selecting) the situations and settings into which they will enter. The choices that people make depend in part on personality characteristics (Brandstatter, 1983; Buss, 1984, 1987; Cantor, 1990;

Emmons & Diener, 1986; Emmons, Diener, & Larsen, 1986; Ickes, Snyder, & Garcia, 1997; Scarr & McCartney, 1983; Snyder & Gangestad, 1982). We all tend to avoid certain situations: some of us, for example, can only be "dragged screaming" into large group or party situations; others literally suffocate if isolated even momentarily somewhere on a mountain trail. We each have characteristic "comfortable" and "uncomfortable" settings, the former probably being those situations that we found in the past to permit easy and safe expression of our basic personalities (selves). Our personalities are reflected directly and prominently in the pattern of situations we recurrently enter or avoid while living our lives.

Third, interpersonal theory insists that the most important situations we respond to in life are the people with whom we interact within the environmental settings of our life: within our homes, our jobs, our neighborhoods, our churches, and our recreational activities (Kiesler, 1996). An additional aspect of selection of environments is our preference for and fit with the people most commonly found in those environments. We attend to and choose to interact with only certain people within a particular setting; and among the people with whom we choose to interact we likely attend to and interpret only selective aspects of their behaviors and personalities. Regardless, as humans we interact primarily with other persons present in situations, and carry on internal dialogues even with fantasized persons who may not be actually present within the setting.

Fourth, to substantial degrees people make or create their own environments (Buss, 1984, 1987; Buss, Gomes, Higgins, & Lauterbach, 1987; Cantor, 1990; Kiesler, 1983, 1996; Scarr & McCartney, 1983; Thorne, 1987). Recent evidence supports that genetically determined personality traits can increase the probability that individuals will experience stressful life events (McGue & Lykken, 1992; Saudino, Pedersen, Lichenstein, McClearn, & Plomin, 1997). We act on environments by transacting with them. People differ in the kind of responses they evoke from others. Our characteristic behaviors within settings can change those settings and, crucially from an interpersonal viewpoint (Kiesler, 1996), can shape and alter the behavior of other persons within that environment. Negotiations or transactions continuously occur so that Person A can evoke reactions in Person B, which in turn evoke altered behaviors in Person A. All these effects on other persons serve to change the situation, so that the "same" environment may be different from one person to another.

Fifth, the match or fit of an individual with congruent environments appears crucial for optimal performance, minimal stress, and general adjustment. Person–environment congruence tends to be associated with satisfaction, productivity, creativity, personal stability, and vocational stability and satisfaction. Complementary person–environment links are considered to be reinforcing and satisfying; noncomplementary life events are considered to be punishing and contributing to change (Holland, 1985; Jahoda, 1961; Kiesler, 1983; Pervin, 1968).

In sum, recent psychological research has arrived at a dramatically different notion of the relative importance of person (nature) versus environmental (nurture) factors for human behavior, personality, and mental disorders. Persons constantly are in dynamic interaction with environments: whenever possible, they select their environments; while in environments, they react to the meanings of environmental events as individually perceived and interpreted by them; while in environments, the events that are most attended to and salient are the interpersonal ones (actions of other people); and while in environments, they constantly transact with, evoke from, and have effects on the persons and environment, leading to ongoing reciprocal cycles of action and reaction.

Within this new psychological perspective, persons with mental disorders are those who develop deficiencies in their dynamic interactions with the environment (Kiesler, 1996). Their "dynamic" patterns increasingly become rigid and extreme, unreactive to the characteristics of the various situations in which they live their lives. They dramatically narrow their selection of life situations so that their settings become rigidly predictable. They develop rigid and invalid cognitive templates that result in invalid and distorted perceptions and interpretations of external events (and act from distorted, invalid, nonrepresentative subjective environments). They rigidly choose to interact on some continuing basis with only a restricted sample of people—interactants from whom their rigid and extreme interpersonal behaviors seek to evoke self-confirming reactions. But to accomplish this, they must continually overpower even these persons with their extreme and rigid presentations that inevitably evoke both compliance and resentment from these very interactants.

The thesis of this chapter is that the multiple facets of this dynamic interaction between person and situation are rooted in the genetic and biological underpinnings of the person. From birth onward, these personality characteristics dynamically interact with the interpersonal, family, social, and cultural factors that operate within the environmental settings of human living. A valid explanation of human living, then, always needs to consider multicausal factors: biological, psychological, and sociocultural.

CONCLUSION

Until recently, situational or environmental causation of human behavior has been the hallmark of scientific psychology, especially the erstwhile predominant camps of behaviorism and radical behaviorism. What this chapter demonstrates is that environmentalism per se no longer washes. Psychology can no longer validly maintain a perspective about human behavior that is contradicted so convincingly by developments within contemporary cognitive experimental psychology itself, by social learning theory and research, by personality theory and research, and by evidence from contemporary behavioral genetics.

Certainly interpersonal, family, group, and societal environments (situations and settings) are important, especially as they dynamically interact with the person. But neither psychological nor sociological theory can any longer omit theoretical formulations that target important genetically transmitted, enduring human characteristics and processes that determine a person's perception, selection, and alteration of that environment. These enduring processes, in turn, have to be anchored within some enduring biological substrate found somewhere in the brain and central nervous system.

In the case of mental disorders, similarly, environmental factors alone no longer can suffice as respectable explanations of the various abnormal conditions. Starting at birth with the presence of genetically determined temperamental differences, humans constantly mature and develop through interactions with important social environmental factors—through transactions with important persons in their lives. These social and cultural environmental factors include major and minor environmental "stressors" that can interact with personality factors to precipitate episodes of mental disturbance. The "social" (sociocultural) part of the biopsychosocial perspective consists of primarily social environmental events that occur within a hierarchy of systems ranging from individuals, dyads, and families all the way to larger groups, subcultures, and cultures.

We must conclude that the external environment cannot be the whole story of human behavior and maladjustment. The human organism, far from being empty, is a hotbed of important activity. This activity, at least in the form of personality traits, is hereditarily transmitted, with heritability coefficients being in the same range (about 50%) that we found on average for mental disorders. We have learned that the way the external environment continues to be important in mental health and disorder is (a) as being primarily social and interpersonal; (b) as perceived uniquely by each person; (c) as transacted with, shaped, and changed by the person; and (d) within the family context at least, as unique and unshared with siblings.

Once more we are forced to conclude that both nature and nurture, in this case both person and situation, are required for an adequate understanding and explanation of human behavior, personality, and mental disorder.

REFERENCES

Baars, B. J. (1986). *The cognitive revolution in psychology.* New York: Guilford.

Bandura, A. (1969). *Principles of behavior modification.* New York: Holt, Rinehart & Winston.

Bandura, A. (1977). *Social learning theory.* Morristown, NJ: General Learning Press.

Bouchard, T. J. (1994). Genes, environment and personality. *Science, 264,* 1700–1701.

Brandstatter, H. (1983). Emotional responses to other persons in everyday life situations. *Journal of Personality and Social Psychology, 45,* 871–883.

Brody, N. (1988). *Personality: In search of individuality.* San Diego, CA: Academic Press.

Brody, N. (1994). Heritability of traits. *Psychological Inquiry, 5,* 117–119.

Buss, D. M. (1984). Toward a psychology of person–environment correlation: The role of spouse selection. *Journal of Personality and Social Psychology, 47,* 361–377.

Buss, D. M. (1987). Selection, evocation, and manipulation. *Journal of Personality and Social Psychology, 53,* 1214–1221.

Buss, D. M., Gomes, M., Higgins, D. S., & Lauterbach, K. (1987). Tactics of manipulation. *Journal of Personality and Social Psychology, 52,* 1219–1229.

Cantor, N. (1990). From thought to behavior: "Having" and "doing" in the study of personality and cognition. *American Psychologist, 45,* 735–750.

Carey, G., & DiLalla, D. L. (1994). Personality and psychopathology: Genetic perspectives. *Journal of Abnormal Psychology, 103,* 32–43.

Carver, C. S., & Scheier, M. F. (1992). *Perspectives on personality* (2d ed.). Needham Heights, MA: Allyn & Bacon.

Cloninger, C. R., Adolfsson, R., & Svrakic, N. M. (1996). Mapping genes for human personality. *Nature Genetics, 12,* 3–4.

Costa, P. T., Jr., & McCrae, R. R. (1985). *The NEO Personality Inventory manual.* Odessa, FL: Psychological Assessment Resources.

Costa, P. T., Jr., & McCrae, R. R. (1997). Longitudinal stability of adult personality. In R. Hogan, J. Johnson, & S. Briggs (Eds.), *Handbook of personality psychology* (pp. 269–290). San Diego, CA: Academic Press.

Deary, I. J. (1996). A (latent) big five personality model in 1915? A reanalysis of Webb's data. *Journal of Personality and Social Psychology, 71,* 992–995.

Delprato, D. J., & Midgley, B. D. (1992). Some fundamentals of B. F. Skinner's behaviorism. *American Psychologist, 47,* 1507–1520.

Dember, W. (1974). Motivation and the cognitive revolution. *American Psychologist, 29,* 161–168.

Digman, J. M. (1990). Personality structure: Emergence of the five-factor model. *Annual Review of Psychology, 41,* 417–440.

Emmons, R. A., & Diener, E. (1986). Situation selection as a moderator of response consistency and stability. *Journal of Personality and Social Psychology, 51,* 1013–1019.

Emmons, R. A., Diener, E., & Larsen, R. J. (1986). Choice and avoidance of everyday situations and affect congruence: Two models of reciprocal interactionism. *Journal of Personality and Social Psychology, 51,* 815–826.

Endler, N. S., & Magnusson, D. (Eds.). (1976). *Interactional psychology and personality.* New York: Wiley.

Eysenck, H. J. (1990). Genetic and environmental contributions to individual differences: The three major dimensions of personality. *Journal of Personality, 58,* 245–261.

Gardner, H. (1985). *The mind's new science: A history of the cognitive revolution.* New York: Basic Books.

Goldberg, L. R. (1990). An alternative "description of personality": The Big Five factor structure. *Journal of Personality and Social Psychology, 59,* 1216–1229.

Holland, J. L. (1985). *Making vocational choices: A theory of vocational personalities and work environments* (2d ed.). Englewood Cliffs, NJ: Prentice Hall.

Ickes, W., Snyder, M., & Garcia, S. (1997). Personality influences on the choice of situations. In R. Hogan, J. Johnson, & S. Briggs (Eds.), *Handbook of personality psychology* (pp. 165–195). San Diego, CA: Academic Press.

Jahoda, M. (1961). A social–psychological approach to the study of culture. *Human Relations, 14,* 23–30.

John, O. P. (1990). Searching for the basic dimensions of personality: Review and critique. In P. McReynolds, J. C. Rosen, & G. J. Chelune (Eds.), *Advances in psychological assessment* (Vol. 7). New York: Plenum.

Joynson, R. B. (1970). The breakdown of modern psychology. *Bulletin of the British Psychological Society, 23,* 261–269.

Kenrick, D. T., & Funder, D. C. (1988). Profiting from controversy: Lessons from the person–situation debate. *American Psychologist, 43,* 23–34.

Kenrick, D. T., & Funder, D. C. (1991). The person–situation debate: Do personality traits really exist? In V. J. Derlega, B. A. Winstead, & W. H. Jones (Eds.), *Personality: Contemporary theory and research* (pp. 149–174). Chicago: Nelson-Hall.

Kety, S. (1974). From rationalization to reason. *American Journal of Psychiatry, 131,* 957–963.

Kiesler, D. J. (1983). The 1982 Interpersonal Circle: A taxonomy for complementarity in human transactions. *Psychological Review, 90,* 185–214.

Kiesler, D. J. (1996). *Contemporary interpersonal theory and research: Personality, psychopathology, and psychotherapy.* New York: Wiley.

Krug, S. E., & Johns, E. F. (1986). A large scale cross-validation of second-order personality structure defined by the 16PF. *Psychological Reports, 59,* 683–693.

Loehlin, J. C. (1992). *Genes and environment in personality development.* Newbury Park, CA: Sage.

Loehlin, J. C., Willerman, L., & Horn, J. M. (1988). Human behavior genetics. *Annual Review of Psychology, 39,* 101–133.

Mahoney, M. J. (1974). *Cognition and behavior modification.* Cambridge, MA: Ballinger.

Magnusson, D. (1990). Personality development from an interactional perspective. In L. A. Pervin (Ed.), *Handbook of personality: Theory and research* (pp. 193–222). New York: Guilford.

Magnusson, D., & Endler, N. S. (Eds.). (1977). *Personality at the crossroads.* Hillsdale, NJ: Erlbaum.

Mann, C. C. (1994). Behavioral genetics in transition. *Science, 264,* 1686–1689.

McCrae, R. R., & Costa, P. T., Jr. (1987). Validation of the five-factor model of personality across instruments and observers. *Journal of Personality and Social Psychology, 52,* 81–90.

McCrae, R. R., & Costa, P. T., Jr. (1990). *Personality in adulthood.* New York: Guilford.

McGue, M., & Lykken, D. T. (1992). Genetic influence on risk of divorce. *Psychological Science, 3,* 368–373.

Meichenbaum, D. H. (1977). *Cognitive–behavior modification.* New York: Plenum.

Miller, G. A., Galanter, E., & Pribram, K. H. (1960). *Plans and the structure of behavior.* New York: Holt, Rinehart & Winston.

Mischel, W. (1968). *Personality and assessment.* New York: Wiley.

Mischel, W. (1973). Toward a cognitive social learning reconceptualization of personality. *Psychological Review, 80,* 252–283.

Murray, H. A. (1938). *Explorations in personality: A clinical and experimental study of fifty men of college age.* New York: Oxford University Press.

Neisser, U. (1967). *Cognitive psychology.* New York: Appleton-Century-Crofts.

Newell, A., & Simon, H. A. (1972). *Human problem-solving.* Englewood Cliffs, NJ: Prentice Hall.

Norman, D. A. (1967). *Memory and attention: An introduction to human information processing.* New York: Wiley.

Norman, W. T. (1963). Toward an adequate taxonomy of personality attributes: Replicated factor structure in peer nomination personality ratings. *Journal of Abnormal and Social Psychology, 66,* 574–588.

Palermo, D. (1971). Is a scientific revolution taking place in psychology? *Scientific Studies, 1,* 135–155.

Pervin, L. A. (1968). Performance and satisfaction as a function of individual–environment fit. *Psychological Bulletin, 69,* 56–58.

Pervin, L. A. (1985). Personality: Current controversies, issues, and directions. *Annual Review of Psychology, 36,* 83–114.

Plomin, R. (1989). Environment and genes: Determinants of behavior. *American Psychologist, 44,* 105–111.

Plomin, R., DeFries, J. C., McClearn, G. E., & Rutter, M. (1997). *Behavioral genetics* (3d ed.). New York: Freeman.

Rose, R. J. (1995). Genetics and human behavior. *Annual Review of Psychology, 46,* 625–654.

Ross, L., & Nisbett, R. E. (1991). *The person and the situation: Perspectives of social psychology.* New York: McGraw-Hill.

Rotter, J. B. (1954). *Social learning and clinical psychology.* New York: Prentice Hall.

Rotter, J. B., Chance, J. E., & Phares, E. J. (Eds.). (1972). *Applications of a social learning theory of personality.* New York: Holt, Rinehart & Winston.

Rowe, D. C. (1987). Resolving the person–situation debate: Invitation to an interdisciplinary dialogue. *American Psychologist, 42,* 218–227.

Rowe, D. C. (1989). Personality theory and behavioral genetics: Contributions and issues. In D. M. Buss & N. Cantor (Eds.), *Personality psychology: Recent trends and emerging directions* (pp. 294–307). New York: Springer-Verlag.

Rowe, D. C. (1997). Genetics, temperament, and personality. In R. Hogan, J. Johnson, & S. Briggs (Eds.), *Handbook of personality psychology* (pp. 367–386). San Diego, CA: Academic Press.

Saudino, J. J., Pedersen, N. L., Lichenstein, P., McClearn, G. E., & Plomin, R. (1997). Can personality explain genetic influence on life events? *Journal of Personality and Social Psychology, 72,* 196–206.

Scarr, S., & McCartney, K. (1983). How people make their own environments: A theory of genotype–environment effects. *Child Development, 54,* 424–435.

Skinner, B. F. (1938). *The behavior of organisms.* New York: Appleton-Century-Crofts.

Skinner, B. F. (1953). *Science and human behavior.* New York: Macmillan.

Skinner, B. F. (1957). *Verbal behavior.* Englewood Cliffs, NJ: Prentice Hall.

Skinner, B. F. (1974). *About behaviorism.* New York: Knopf.

Skinner, B. F. (1989). *Recent issues in the analysis of behavior.* Columbus, OH: Merrill.

Snyder, M., & Gangestad, S. (1982). Choosing social situations: Two investigations of the self-monitoring process. *Journal of Personality and Social Psychology, 43,* 123–135.

Spinelli, E. (1989). *The interpreted world: An introduction to phenomenological psychology.* Newbury Park, CA: Sage.

Thines, G. (1977). *Phenomenology and the science of behavior.* Winchester, MA: Allen & Unwer.

Thorne, A. (1987). The press of personality: A study of conversations between introverts and extraverts. *Journal of Personality and Social Psychology, 53,* 718–726.

Tupes, E. C., & Christal, R. E. (1961/1992). Recurrent personality factors based on trait ratings. Technical Report No. ASD-TR-61-97, US Air Force, Lackland US Air Force Base, TX. *Journal of Personality, 60,* 225–251.

Ullmann, L. P., & Krasner, L. (1969). *A psychological approach to abnormal behavior.* Englewood Cliffs, NJ: Prentice Hall.

Wann, T. W. (Ed.). (1964). *Behaviorism and phenomenology.* Chicago: University of Chicago Press.

Watson, J. B. (1913). Psychology as the behaviorist sees it. *Psychological Review, 20,* 158–177.

Watson, J. B. (1925). *Behaviorism.* New York: Norton.

Wiggins, J. S., & Pincus, A. L. (1992). Personality: Structure and assessment. *Annual Review of Psychology, 43,* 473–504.

Chapter 6

Scientific Evidence:
Stressful Environmental Events
Affect the Development and Onset
of Mental Disorders

Chapters 4 and 5 reviewed the behavioral genetic and other scientific evidence that invalidates the viewpoint that the environment is the major and primary determinant of human behavior. They concluded confidently that the notion of environmentalism as the sole or primary determinant of our daily actions is an untenable position. In the specific case of mental disturbance, we know that environmental factors are not "sufficient" in themselves to produce mental disorder, although they certainly can provide "contributory" and even "necessary" influences.

Other recent evidence indicates that a central way in which the environment *is* crucial to adjustment and maladjustment is in the form of stressful events that occur throughout an individual's entire life span. Stress originates within the external environment in the form of negative life events. These stressful life events, in turn, can have substantial effects (both formative and precipitative) on development of mental disorders. We encountered these notions in Chapter 3, which introduced early diathesis–stress and vulnerability–stress models of mental disorder.

This chapter's review of stressful life events confirms many of the same principles uncovered in the previous chapter. First, the effects of negative life events depend very much on characteristics of the individual person. The person dynamically mediates both occurrences and effects of stressful external environments. Second, the important components of external events are the ones subjectively perceived and appraised by the individual. Third, the most salient stressful external events are those that involve other persons (the social and interpersonal environment). Fourth, the individual *transacts* with stressors, not only by shaping and changing them, but also by actually participating in their evocation. Sixth, those aspects of the nuclear family environment that constitute stressful events (influencing, in turn, development of personality and psychopathology) are family experiences that are unique to an individual child and unshared with his or her siblings.

This chapter examines the research evidence for the importance of environmental stressors in the development and precipitation of mental disorders. I will conclude that any adequate theory of mental disorder must include stressful environmental events as central formative and precipitating influences in the development and onset of mental disorders.

IMPORTANT CONCEPTIONS OF THE ENVIRONMENT

Before addressing the nature of stressful environmental events, we need to keep in mind several important distinctions of the term *environment*.

Subjective versus Objective Environments

We saw earlier that the *objective environment* denotes "objective reality," aspects of the external environment that are "really out there"—aspects that any group of people would perceive as most relevant in a particular setting. If a researcher wants to know what important situational factors are prompting an individual's actions, the researcher might ask a group of individuals to report the important aspects of a particular setting and then calculate their major points of agreement. The *subjective environment*, in contrast, is the environment as perceived by a particular individual. In this instance, a researcher can identify the important situational factors that are prompting an individual's actions only by asking the individual himself or herself (self-report).

We saw in Chapter 5 that one of the major contributions of contemporary social learning theory was to shift the locus of primary causation of human behavior to the subjective environment. Though the objective environment may make contributions, the prepotent influence regarding what a person does is a person's perception and interpretation of the salient aspects of a particular setting. Actually, as Henry Murray (1938) suggested earlier, it likely is most profitable to study the environment by measuring both perspectives (what he called *alpha press* versus *beta press*).

Stress researchers have been plagued by the same issue and emphasize the same distinction. Like the rest of psychological science, stress researchers struggle to find optimal ways to blend the subjective and objective perspectives in their assessment of stressful events. The stress literature is unanimous also that external events cannot be considered stressful until they are appraised as such by the particular individual involved.

Common–Shared versus Unique–Unshared Family Environments

Chapter 4 reported that one of the major findings of modern behavioral genetic research involves the necessity of distinguishing between common and unique family environments. The *common–shared* family environment denotes the common settings and experiences, the shared advantages and disadvantages, that siblings experience growing up as members of the same family. A particular family has a given level of income and education; resides in a particular neighborhood, in a particular town, in a particular region of the country, within the United States; is run by parents with specific disciplinary approaches.

In contrast, the *unique–unshared* family environment denotes the environmental experiences (both subjective and objective) that are different from child to child in a given family. These consist of often subtle differences or changes in settings, social experiences, family circumstances, and parent–child and sibling–sibling interactions. The notion of unique family environment recognizes the fact that different children in the same family often experience substantially different environmental events. What Chapter 5 reveals is that unique environmental experiences are related substantially to development of personality and mental disorder; the common environment is virtually irrelevant to these developmental outcomes.

Stress researchers have only begun to include this important distinction regarding family stressors in their research designs and methods. Any seminal attempt to include this distinction in empirical studies can only lead to much more sophisticated questions and answers. The crucial point is that the *family environmental stressors that likely are crucial for development of personality and mental disorder are those that are unique to particular siblings within the same family*. Accordingly, stress research will not likely uncover important formative and precipitating stressful events that are common to, or shared by, all the siblings within a given family.

Stressful versus Nonstressful Environments

Throughout our lives, the settings in which we find ourselves make greater or less demands on us for survival, either physical or psychological (e.g., demands for mistake-free performance, for proving our worth, or for safe-guarding our identities). From birth to death our momentary real life environments are, to the extent that they make demands on our personal resources, more or less "stressful" to our psychological and physical existence. Our childhoods constitute the developmental period that probably is most saturated with stress, with new demands for performance and growth presenting themselves almost daily.

Stress refers to the situation in which the environment places demands, pressures, or forces on a person that threaten the person's well-being. According to a widely accepted definition, *stress* refers to "a particular relationship between the person and the environment that is appraised by the person as taxing or exceeding his or her resources and endangering his or her well-being" (Lazarus & Folkman, 1984, p. 19).

Obviously, the stressfulness of a particular situation is not an either–or characteristic; rather, the degree of stress present varies from nonexistent, through minimal and moderate, to severe and extreme. Some environments clearly facilitate healthy development and adjustive living. For example, we tend to seek out environments that feel comfortable and provide good matches to our personalities and strivings. In initially poor-fit settings, also, we tend to act in ways designed to shape or modify the environment in directions that would make it a better match.

The "individual–environmental fit" hypothesis (Jahoda, 1961; Pervin, 1968) stipulates that when we are in our best-fit environments, we perform most easily and effectively, are satisfied, and feel congruent and authentic—generally, we experience minimum personal stress. In contrast, while in our worst-fit or poor-fit environments, we perform poorly and with difficulty, are dissatisfied, and feel ungenuine and unauthentic—generally experience high personal stress.

Contemporary interpersonal theory (Kiesler, 1996; Sullivan, 1953) distinguishes between *conjunctive* and *disjunctive* human relationships. When we are with persons who endorse our self-definitions wihout qualification and complement our interpersonal behaviors (conjunctive situations), we feel minimal stress. We feel maximal stress when interacting with persons who negate our self-definitions and abrasively challenge our interpersonal behaviors.

In sum, situations vary in degree of stress, likely depending on the degree to which they are conjunctive or best-fit for a particular individual (to the extent that they facilitate optimal performance, elicit creative integrations of resources, and maximize well-being). Hence, although stress researchers seldom make the point, it is likely that one major aspect of environments that is highly relevant for development and adjustment is found on a continuum ranging from "extreme stress" at one pole to "extreme best-fit" at the other, with a "neutral" point that represents an absence of both stress and best-fit.

Formative versus Precipitative Environmental Stressors

The distinction between formative and precipitative stressors is crucial for a comprehensive theory of mental disorder. *Formative* environmental factors (including stressful events) refer to those environmental experiences that contribute to the predisposition of an individual to incur a particular disease or disorder. That is, formative factors increase *or* decrease an individual's vulnerability to subsequent disease or disorder. Formative factors are "remote" environmental events that occur during an individual's childhood and adolescence and that constitute either risk or protective factors for that individual in regard to occurrence (or nonoccurrence) of disease or disorder. In short, important environmental events occur during our growing years that have a formative affect on our predisposition to subsequent illness or disorder.

At the other end of the time spectrum are environmental events, occurring most typically during late adolescence and adulthood, that contribute directly to the onset of an episode of a particular illness or disorder. These precipitating (or triggering) environmental events are "recent" stressful events that tax a person's capacity for survival or adaptation. Triggering events may elicit an episode of disorder, and may or may not significantly influence the probability of further future episodes. In short, when precipitating stressors exceed some threshold level, the individual's adaptation breaks down and an episode of disease or disorder ensues.

Formative environmental events contribute to a person's diathesis or predisposition toward a particular disorder. Precipitating stressful environmental events represent the contemporary causal input for onset of disorder. It is important to note, then, that stressful environments can have "contributory" or "necessary" causal effects both during the development of personality in childhood and adolescence (formative events) and during adulthood prior to an episode of disorder (precipitative or triggering events). Environmental events shape both diathesis and stress in diathesis–stress models of mental disorder.

TWO MAJOR COMPONENTS OF STRESS

Any stressful event consists of two essential processes: one environmental (external), and the other occurring within the person. Various terms have been used in the stress literature to make this universally found differentiation.

I will use the term *stressful events* to refer to the external demands, pressures, or forces existing in the environment that threaten the person's well-being. I will use the term *strain process* to denote the internal physiological and psychological reactions of a person that are triggered in response to the external demands or threats. The term *stress* will refer to the overall process, involving occurrence of both stressful events and the strain process. As Bloom observed, "Stress cannot be measured without measuring strain. Since stress, by definition, produces strain, its study is interactional—the study of the individual in the environment" (1988, p. 75).

Stressful Events

"Life Events" research began when Holmes and Rahe (1967) published the first inventory of stressful life events, the Social Readjustment Rating Scale (SRRS). The SRRS asks a subject to indicate, among a list of stressful life events, those they have encountered during the preceding six months or one year. Items range from events that are quite stressful (e.g., death of a spouse, divorce, or loss of job) to those least stressful (e.g., vacation or minor violations of the law).

Together with other early workers in the area, Holmes and Rahe (1967) believed that onset of illness or disorder was influenced by the extent to which life event occurrences disrupted a person's routine, thereby demanding some degree of readjustment. The more change an individual experienced, regardless of its apparent positive or negative quality, the more likely body resistance (one aspect of the strain process) would be overtaxed, and illness would result. In line with this notion, either a job promotion or a divorce can induce considerable strain within a person.

Subsequent research has refuted this early view. Study after study found that it was *undesirable* events (e.g., death of a child)—not desirable ones (e.g., birth of a child), or change per se (e.g., moving into a new home)—that cause distress and illness. Only negative life events have been empirically associated with stress (Blaney, 1985). As opposed to Holmes and Rahe's (1967) SRRS, Sarason, Johnson, and Siegel (1978) introduced the Life Experiences Survey to assess only negative life events.

Hence, it is not simply the degree of disruption of routine induced by a life event that is etiologically influential for development of subsequent illness and disorder. Rather, the key etiological factors are (a) the unpleasant (negative) quality of the external stressful event and (b) the unpleasant (negative) emotional arousal induced within the individual (part of the strain process). A first aspect of stressful events that seems to be key in subsequent induction of illness and disorder is the undesirability or unpleasantness of the change occurring in one's life, not simply the degree of change involved.

A second conclusion from stress research, at first glance, appears counter-intuitive. Negative events over which a person has no control (e.g., disability following a randomly occurring accident or destruction of one's home by a tornado) are more stressful and relevant to subsequent illness or disorder than ones in which the person has played a part or had some choice (e.g., leaving an unsatisfying job or initiating a divorce). This finding has been demonstrated "hundreds of times, with many different species, with similar results. In general, the less control that the organism has over a stressor, the more severe the health outcomes; and, conversely, the more control an organism has over a stressor, the better the health outcomes" (Auerbach & Gramling, 1998, p. 97).

One might expect the reverse to be the case, "because fate, rather than oneself, can easily be blamed. Events outside a person's control suggest less personal inadequacy and thus minimally threaten self-esteem. . . . [The actual case, however, is that negative events seem to] leave people with the demoralizing sense that they are at the mercy of the environment; that no action will be effective in preventing bad things from happening in the future" (Mirowsky & Ross, 1989, p. 93).

Negative events also can take the form of either acute or chronic stressors. *Acute* negative life events (e.g., sudden death of a loved one) tend to be major ones; they involve a relatively brief, intense temporal exposure to a life event that has a clear starting (onset) and stopping (offset) point. Acute stress often represents a crisis, in that the stressful situation tends to approach or exceed the adaptive capacities of the person. *Chronic* negative stressors can also be major (e.g., long-standing marital conflict), but most distinctively involve an accumulation of minor life events—of "daily hassles" (e.g., daily traffic, neighborhood vandalism and theft, routine required shopping, or noise pollution). Exact onset and offset times for chronic stressors often cannot be clearly demarcated, and a person's exposure to the stressor(s) can persist for extended periods of time. Accumulation of relatively ordinary and frequent stressful incidents in one's life can be more pathological than exposure to an extreme but short-lived event, such as a natural disaster. Hence, *life events associated with subsequent illness and disorder can take the form of acute and/or chronic and major and/or minor negative stressors.*

Finally, the field has reached considerable consensus that it is not the mere occurrence of a negative event that initiates the strain response. The crucial factor is the person's interpretation or appraisal of the meaning of the event within the particular context of its occurrence. An individual's unique perception (the subjective environment) is crucial, independently of whether others might agree (the objective environment). As Lazarus and Folkman (1984) noted, the negative environmental event "is appraised by the person as taxing or exceeding his or her resources and endangering his or her well-being" (p. 19). In short, the overall human stress process includes both person and environmental components.

Strain: The Inner Response to Stressful Events

That a person appraises a life event as a threat or danger to his or her well-being is the first major component of stress and a necessary condition for triggering the person's internal strain response (the second major component).

The same stressful event may evoke a strain response in one individual but not in another. The same stressful event may elicit a stress response in the same individual at one time, but not at another. The same or equivalent stressful event may place one person, but not another, at risk for a particular disease or disorder. The same stressful event can place the same person, or a group of persons, at risk for a variety of different diseases and disorders. The general rule is that stressful events by themselves do not linearly determine organismic effects experienced by humans.

Three body systems seem to be centrally involved in the strain process—in the internal stress response (Auerbach & Gramling, 1998; Kaplan, Sallis, & Patterson, 1993). In response to stressors, all three systems interact in concert. The central notion is that intense and/or chronic stress can directly produce or exacerbate dysfunction in some organs or can produce a suppressive effect on immune functioning—either of which over time can increase vulnerability to illness and disorder.

(1) Appraisal of stressful events activates the *nervous system*, especially the sympathetic and parasympathetic branches of the autonomic nervous system (ANS). Quickly triggered are "fight or flight" physiological arousal responses (e.g., increased heart rate, palmar sweating, and irregular breathing). Under chronic stress, these ANS reactions can directly affect organ functioning and produce susceptibility to dysfunction (e.g., cardiopulmonary disorders).

(2) ANS reactions also may induce susceptibility to other diseases (e.g., viruses or tumors) by affecting the immune response (through activation of the *endocrine and catecholamine systems*). The endocrine system consists of interacting glands located primarily in the peripheral nervous system, which influence other body systems by releasing hormones into the bloodstream. During stress the hypothalamus secretes stress hormones that activate additional secretions from the pituitary and adrenal glands (the HPA: hypothalamus–pituitary–adrenal pathway) that have widespread fueling or energizing effects.

Under stress, individuals release more of these stress hormones (e.g., cortisol, ACTH, and beta endorphin) resulting in decreased immune activity. One early hypothesis was that excessive activation of the HPA pathway leads to adverse health outcomes. Stress also activates the catecholamine system to releases two hormones, adrenaline and nora-drenaline, which have major action on the cardiovascular system. Under stress, release of these two hormones accelerates blood pressure and heart rate, in turn reducing immune responsiveness.

(3) The third component of the strain response triggered by stressful events is the *immune system* which, as we just saw, is activated by the endocrine and catecholamine systems. Daily we are exposed to infectious and toxic agents (antigens) such as bacteria, viruses, fungi, and parasites. Unchecked, these agents can result in a wide variety of diseases ranging from colds to cancer. Fortunately, the body has an immune system that fights and destroys these omnipresent disease-causing agents.

Our white blood cells (leukocytes) are the major combatants in the war against destructive antigens. Leukocytes are produced in the lymph nodes, bone marrow, spleen, and parts of the gastrointestinal tract. Two lymphoid organs produce Thymus (T) lymphocytes (including helper cells that tell the system to turn on in the face of a virus and suppressor cells that tell the system to slow down) and Bursa (B) lymphocytes; both T and B lymphocytes can mount an attack on harmful substances produced within the body. A third, Natural Killer (NK), leukocyte destroys cells that have been invaded by foreign substances (e.g., viruses, bacteria).

Essentially, the immune system protects the body from harmful substances that either invade it from outside or that are created internally (e.g., mutant cells). The degree to which the immune system is active and effective is referred to as the individual's level of *immunocompetence*. Prolonged and/or intense stress reduces immunocompetence, producing a suppressive effect on immune functioning which over time can affect health status and increase vulnerability to illness and disorder.

A new discipline, psychoneuroimmunology, studies the impact of stress and other psychological process on the immune system. It has provided some early and promising findings. First, recent evidence from a wide variety of sources strongly suggests that both psychological and physiological factors can have important effects on a person's level of immunocompetence (Cohen & Herbert, 1996; Maier, Watkins, & Fleshner, 1994). Second, studies show that a variety of stressors impair the immune response in animals as well as in humans (Borysenko & Borysenko, 1982; Palmblad, 1981). Studies with animals permit examination of the effects of more intense stressors (e.g., overcrowding of mice, long periods of intermittent foot-shock) than those that can be used with humans. "Animal studies . . . provide some of our best support for the link between stress, . . . disturbed immune function and, in the long term, a higher incidence of disease (e.g., tumor growth)" (Auerbach & Gramling, 1998, p. 84).

Third, psychological stress causes a decrease in the functioning of the immune system, probably through some type of brain mediation (Andersen, Kiecolt-Glaser, & Glaser, 1994; Antonini, Schneiderman, Fletcher, & Goldstein, 1990; Cohen, Delahanty, Schmitz, Jenkins, & Baum, 1993; Geiser, 1989; Glaser & Kielcolt-Glaser, 1994; Herbert & Cohen, 1993a, 1993b; Jemmott & Locke, 1984; Kiecolt-Glaser & Glaser, 1992; O'Leary, 1990; Weisse, 1992). For example (cf. Cohen, 1996), immunosuppression has been found among persons who are clinically depressed; taking important exams; caring for relatives with chronic diseases; living near the site of a serious nuclear power plant accident; suffering marital conflict; reporting relatively high levels of unpleasant daily events, negative moods, or perceived stress; and responding to acute laboratory stressors or delivering public speeches. However, other evidence indicates that the immune responses of stressed persons actually may fall within normal ranges (Rabin, Cohen, Ganguli, Lysle, & Cunnick, 1989).

Fourth, a growing body of research suggests that stress can increase the body's susceptibility to diseases that are under the control of the immune system (Kiecolt-Glaser, Fisher, Ogrocki, Stout, Speicher, & Glaser, 1987; Riley, 1981). Specifically, stress has been demonstrated to reduce the body's resistance to acute respiratory infections such as the common cold and influenza (Cohen, 1996) and tumors (Adler, 1981).

In sum, routine commonplace stressors (e.g., final exams in medical school) are associated with transient impairments in immune functioning. Whether, or the extent to which, transient changes in immune functioning are related to health outcomes remains unclear. Exposure to either acute or chronic stressors can suppress a person's immune system (disrupt its equilibrium, making it overactive or underactive) and ultimately can make the person more vulnerable to disease and disorder.

Herbert and Cohen used meta-analysis to review the association between stressors and changes in human immunity. They concluded that "relatively strong and consistent associations" exist between stress and the human immune reaction. They add that "objective stressful events are related to larger immune changes than subjective self-reports of stress" and "interpersonal events [stressors] are related to alterations in different immune outcomes than nonsocial events" (Herbert & Cohen, 1993b, pp. 374, 375).

In general, the literature indicates that a stressful event can generate a severe and/or chronic strain process that includes chronic activation of the central and autonomic nervous systems and of the endocrine and catecholamine systems leading to chronic suppression of the immune response. However, not all studies have reported consistent findings. Whether immunosuppression occurs—whether a stressful event contributes to disease or disorder—depends on the meaning the event has for the stressed person, his or her manner of coping with it, his or her adaptive capacities, and his or her available social support network.

EFFECTS OF STRESS ON PHYSICAL DISEASE AND MENTAL DISORDER

Recent explosion of scientific knowledge and theory in medicine and psychopathology has resulted in a wide acceptance of the notion that stressors are significantly associated with both physical disease and mental disorder. Stressful events such as job loss, bereavement, and marital disruption can increase the risk not only of mental disorders such as unipolar depression, but also of minor infections and many other more serious physical illnesses.

Findings from several hundred studies support the hypothesis that life stressors of all types place individuals at greater risk for a variety of physical and mental disorders (Aneshensel, 1992; Brown & Harris, 1989; Dohrenwend & Dohrenwend, 1981; Elliott and Eisdorfer, 1982; Harris, 1989; Jenkins, 1978; McQueen & Siegrist, 1982; Miller, 1989; Monroe, 1992; Paykel, 1978; Sklar & Anisman, 1981). Among physical diseases, the evidence is strongest for cardiovascular disease, infectious disease, and pregnancy complications. Evidence for the role of stress in the etiology of cancer and endocrine diseases (such as diabetes, thyroid disorder, and Cushing's disease) is not as substantial (Adler & Matthews, 1994).

An important conclusion seems to be supported empirically. *Development or precipitation of physical disease or mental disorder can occur as the result of severe and chronic strain states that are induced by stressful events.* The period of childhood is a high-risk stage during which stressful events (and the consequent strain process) are likely to have formative influences on subsequent development of disease or disorder. Throughout life severe and/or chronic strain states (elicited by stressful events) also can precipitate or trigger an episode of illness or disorder.

Stress and Physical Disease

The stress literature provides ample examples of health outcomes and physical diseases that seem to be affected dramatically by stressful events. For example, Rozanski et al. (1988) demonstrated that mental stress produced serious abnormalities of heart function in patients with known heart disease. These abnormalities, moreover, were comparable in magnitude and clinical significance to those produced by demanding physical exercise.

Another study followed up a sample of over 1,500 bright California children and examined death certificates for the half of the sample who had died. Several psychosocial factors emerged as leading risks for premature mortality (occurring from all causes). Children of divorced parents faced a one-third greater risk of death than people whose parents remained married, at least until they reached age twenty-one. People who remained married to the same partner were at a lower risk for premature death than were those who had separated or divorced. Children who had been rated by their parents and teachers as socially dependable and conscientious lived significantly longer. In light of these and other detailed findings, the authors concluded that problems in psychosocial adjustment "are a key general risk factor for all cause mortality" (Friedman et al., 1995, p. 76).

Extensive research on cardiovascular disease, one of the leading causes of disability and death in the United States, links the disease to a variety of lifestyle components peculiar to the industrialized twentieth century. Findings suggest that a set of illness behaviors (smoking, little or no exercise, diets high in saturated fat and cholesterol, and chronic stress) represent significant risk factors for high blood pressure, high blood cholesterol, and obesity. These latter conditions, in turn, are all associated with increased risk of cardiovascular disease.

Petersen (1984) summarized the effects of acute and chronic stress on work-related accidents and concluded that high stress levels are indeed an important risk factor. Sklar & Anisman's (1981) concluded that findings they reviewed support the notion that cancer growth is significantly augmented by stress and a sense of helplessness (perhaps via stress-related changes in the immune system). Cohen and Williamson's (1991) review concluded that stress (a) is associated with an increase in illness behaviors (such as smoking, drinking, and/or sedentary activity) and (b) may be associated with onset and reactivation of infectious diseases (such as upper respiratory, herpes virus, and bacterial infections). Studies have demonstrated that stress also reduces the body's resistance to acute respiratory infections (McClelland, Alexander, & Marks, 1982) and tumors (Adler, 1981). Other researchers (Rabkin & Struening, 1976) concluded that the association between stress and illness is more typically weak. Such weak links have been interpreted as reflecting individual differences in susceptibility to stress; dispositional factors make a person more or less susceptible to the pathogenic effects of stressors.

Zegans (1982) conceptualized the link between stress and physical illness as consisting of the following sequential elements. First, stress induces an alteration in physiological functioning (e.g., changes in the autonomic nervous system, the neuromuscular system, endocrine function, or neurotransmitter integrity). Second, these enduring physiological changes lead to a generalized increase in vulnerability to illness (e.g., reduction of the organism's resistance to disease, compromising the integrity of the immune system). Third, reduced immunocompetence leads to a neurological hypersensitivity or excitation (perhaps in the brain limbic system) in predisposed individuals. Fourth, the neurological changes occur only when the individual's ability to cope effectively with the stressor is exceeded.

Auerbach and Gramling conclude that human and animal studies "converge to present a convincing picture that stress plays an important role in the development and exacerbation of illness in humans . . . most researchers agree that stress is an influential variable in the development and maintenance of many physical problems" (1998, pp. 87, 95).

In general, evidence indicates that stressful life events and resulting strain can have deleterious effects on physical health (Kaprio, Koskenvuo, & Rita, 1987; Miller, 1983). Miller included in his list of verified affected conditions gastrointestinal disorders, sudden cardiac death, myocardial infarction, hypertension, stroke, diabetes, cancer, multiple sclerosis, tuberculosis, influenza, pneumonia, headaches, and insomnia. So far, the effects seem to be nonspecific; that is, stress constitutes an increased risk for a wide variety of medical conditions or diseases. Also, studies differ regarding the degree to which stress influences the development of medical problems.

Stress and Mental Disorder

The strongest evidence that environmentally induced stress can produce adverse changes in health, including mental health, comes from studies of extreme situations and stressors such as laboratory administered electric shocks and wartime combat (for a review of the combat evidence, see Dohrenwend & Egri, 1981). These more extreme stressful events occur relatively rarely, in contrast to more common and moderate stressors such as separation and divorce, loss of job, or death of loved ones.

Since 1980 (American Psychiatric Association, 1980), the DSM allows, in addition to a diagnosis of a specific mental disorder, a rating (on what is called Axis IV) of the type and/or severity of psychosocial stressors that may be contributory to an individual's present episode. Axis IV was added to encourage all future diagnoses of mental disorder to consider carefully the contribution of stressful life events to the person's current episode.

The latest version of the diagnostic manual, DSM-IV (American Psychiatric Association, 1994) contains a number of diagnostic groups that have as a defining criterion the reaction of an individual to stressful life events. The first group includes the classic stress reaction diagnoses of Post Traumatic Stress Disorder (PTSD) and Acute Stress Disorder. For both disorders the key diagnostic feature is development of distinctive symptoms following exposure to an universally extreme traumatic stressor.

A second group of stress-reaction disorders are the Adjustment Disorders, which are characterized by a variety of symptoms including anxiety, depression, and impulsive and aggressive behavior. A key diagnostic feature of Adjustment Disorders is that the respective symptoms develop in response to a clearly identifiable psychosocial stressor(s)—a stressor that is typically more moderate and less extreme than for PTSD and Acute Stress Disorder.

A third DSM-IV group of stress-reaction disorders is found under the major diagnostic group of schizophrenia and other psychotic disorders. Brief Psychotic Disorder denotes an episode of schizophrenia that lasts less than one month, at the end of which time the individual gradually returns to his or her premorbid level of functioning. A key diagnostic requirement for Brief Psychotic Disorder is that the episode be preceded by clearly identifiable negative life events.

In sum, DSM-IV (American Psychiatric Association, 1994) recognizes three distinct mental disorders that take the form of stress-reaction disorders. Their defining features are that the particular mental disturbance has a relatively sudden onset, after occurrence of identifiable stressful life events, in individuals who show relatively normal adjustment before, and often after remission of the episode. Also, by including Axis IV (the rating of precipitating stressor) as a routine part of diagnosis, DSM-IV explicitly emphasizes that stressful life events often play an important role, predominantly precipitative, in the onset of many mental disorders. These DSM additions are consistent with the expanding and convincing empirical evidence that stressful life events have both formative and precipitative influences on the occurrence of mental disorder (Avison & Turner, 1988; Barrett, 1979; Eckenrode, 1984; Link, Dohrenwend, & Skodel, 1986).

Studies during the 1960s and 1970s demonstrated a strong association between life events and incidence of mental disorders. By far the majority of the studies focused on the major diagnostic groups of mood disorders and schizophrenia. One of the earlier reviews of *schizophrenia* (Rabkin, 1980) suggested that the most probable role of life events in schizophrenia was that of triggering schizophrenic episodes or relapse. Subsequent reviews of the literature on life events and schizophrenia (Brown & Birley, 1968; Day, 1981; Day, Zubin, & Steinhauer, 1987; Dohrenwend & Egri, 1981; Jacobs, Prusoff, & Paykel, 1974) echoed the same theme, revealing a significant increase in patients' report of life events during the two to three-week period preceding the appearance of acute episodes of schizophrenia. In the definitive review to date of psychosocial environmental conditions, Lukoff, Snyder, Ventura, and Nuechterlein (1984) concluded that a variety of stressors contribute to the onset, exacerbation and/or relapse of schizophrenia. Stressors they identified were life-change events, aversive family interactions, impoverished or aversive hospital environments, the social stigma associated with patienthood, and occupational and educational disadvantages. The authors also concluded that so far no evidence could be found that these influences were specifically tied to schizophrenia. Hence, studies of schizophrenia offered no support for the "specificity hypothesis," namely, that specific types of psychosocial stressors are distinctively associated with specific mental disorders.

In the case of the mood disorders, the evidence suggests that life events have both formative and precipitating influence on both bipolar and unipolar episodes of mood disorder (Ellicott, Hammen, Gitlin, Brown, & Jamison, 1990; Fowles, 1993; Lloyd, 1980a, 1980b; Rehm & Tyndall, 1993). A number of studies, both retrospective and prospective, report a relationship between stressful life events and the onset of depression (Brown, Harris, & Hapworth, 1994; Lloyd, 1980a, 1980b; Jacobs, Prusoff, & Paykel, 1974; Kessler, 1997; Monroe, 1990; Monroe & Depue, 1991). Some subsets of depressive patients may be more vulnerable to the effects of stress (Akiskal & McKinney, 1973; Hirschfeld & Cross, 1982). Deaths of loved ones more often precede an episode of depression in women (Brown & Harris, 1978). Similar findings confirm the relationship of stressful events to onset of episodes of bipolar mood disorder (Goodwin & Jamison, 1990; Johnson & Roberts, 1995). Overall, findings support the influence of psychosocial stressors as both formative and precipitative factors in the occurrence of mood disorders. Stressful life situations such as death or loss of loved ones, "fateful" loss events (e.g., natural disasters, job layoffs resulting from workforce reduction), caregiving for demented seniors, preexisting psychiatric disorder, and subtle gender harassment can influence the development of depressive disorders. Also, one class of these stressors, "fateful loss events" (events uncontrolled by the individual), has been found to produce more stress than those that involve some control, as suggested earlier—fateful loss events are present about two-and-one-half times more frequently than usual in persons who later become depressed.

More recent research on stressful life events has considered a much broader range of DSM mental disorders. "There is now little doubt that stressors and chronic strains represent important etiological risk factors for mental health problems" (Avison & Gotlib, 1994, p. 4). Stressful life events can influence the onset, course, and recurrence of mental disorders.

Some evidence (e.g., Monroe & Johnson, 1990) supports the "specificity hypothesis," namely, that specific forms of life stress predispose individuals to specific forms of mental disorder. Finlay-Jones and Brown (1981) offer evidence supporting that severe "loss" events predispose to depression, while severe "danger" events may precede onset of anxiety disorders. Other studies report that negative events that are interpersonal (e.g., death of a spouse) are the ones most likely to trigger a depressed reaction and depressive mental disorder (Bolger, DeLongis, Kessler, & Schilling, 1989; Brown & Harris, 1989; Fowles, 1993).

A recent large scale task force of the American Psychological Society reviewed the available evidence regarding psychosocial stressors and mental disorder. The task force arrived at the following conclusions: (1) Stress can have both transient and permanent effects on the functioning of the human central nervous system; (2) Extensive research on both animals and humans has demonstrated that repeated exposure to stressful experiences can result in persisting changes in brain structure and biochemistry and can reduce the immune response; these changes "may contribute to the negative effects of psychosocial stressors" (1996, p. 13); and (3) Stress is in fact associated with incidence of mental disorder.

Some qualification of the last conclusion may be appropriate. Despite the strong evidence that life events are associated with psychological distress, important reviews report that the magnitude of the association between stressful life events and mental disorders is quite small, with stressful events accounting for less than 10 percent of the variance (Cohen & Edwards, 1989; Rabkin & Struening, 1976; Sarason, de Monchaux, & Hunt, 1975; Tennant, Bebbington, & Hurry, 1981). In short, many persons remain healthy despite exposure to stressors.

This "weak" finding, however, is expected from the literature on person–environment interactions and reflects the essential complexity of the stress process. Important personality, coping, and social support factors all can mediate the effects of stressful events on subsequent occurrence of mental disorder. Among these mediating factors are individuals' adaptive strengths and capacity for resilience, constructive action, and personal growth in the face of challenge.

Social support is one of the most extensively researched of the stress "resistance" or mediating factors. It refers to available interpersonal sources an individual has, persons who can provide emotional, financial, and advisory support. Researchers have emphasized two separate aspects of social support: (a) those that are contributed by larger social networks to which an individual belongs (e.g., church membership, neighborhood groups, larger organizations), and (b) those that come directly from specific persons who act as "a buffer" against a stressor by meeting specific needs (e.g., financial, informational, self-esteem) created by the stressful event.

The predominant orientation to stress and coping research has been the *multiple risk-factor model* (Billings & Moos, 1985; Lazarus & Folkman,

1984; Moos, 1984). In this model, health and illness outcomes are influenced by multiple risk and protective factors in the person and the environment. This perspective clearly moves etiological research away from a preoccupation with single causal factors toward more complex, multicausal and multioutcome models.

Avison and Gotlib (1994) describe an emerging consensus among stress researchers toward adoption of a "stress process paradigm" that targets the manner in which social and psychological sources of stress translate into symptoms and health problems. An extensive body of research has examined the role of personal and social resources in "stress resistance," including the type of coping strategies that help individuals to maintain health functioning when stressors occur (Cohen & McKay, 1984; Cohen & Edwards, 1989; Thoits, 1985). The emerging consensus (Avison & Gotlib, 1994) is that at least three sets of factors mediate the experience of stressors and the experience of symptoms of illness or disorder: (a) social resources–social support, (b) personality or coping resources, and (c) coping responses or behaviors. These factors can both increase an individual's level of vulnerability to disorder, or have "buffering" effects that actually increase an individual's resistance to subsequent disorder.

The evidence is mounting that, just as is the case for physical diseases, mental disorders are influenced by stressful life events. The DSM-IV (American Psychiatric Association, 1994) lists a group of mental disorders that are defined as psychological reactions to moderate and extreme stressful life events. Empirical research has demonstrated that psychosocial stressors have both formative and precipitative influence on certain mental disorders, and likely will be shown to be relevant for a wide range of other mental disorders.

CATEGORIES OF STRESSFUL LIFE EVENTS

A major characteristic of environments is that they can differentially expose people to acute or chronic stress that, in turn, can seriously undermine an individual's physical and mental health, shape-deficient or ineffective coping strategies, and result in poor health habits and infrequent use of health resources (Taylor, Repetti, & Seeman, 1997). For example, environmental factors such as *social class* and *race* are reliably associated with differential exposure to stress and are well-established predictors of all-cause mortality and a variety of specific medical diseases (Adler & Matthews, 1994; Williams & Collins, 1995).

Categories of possible stressful events correspond to the major classes of environments that impinge on human behavior generally. These environmental factors and events have been the focus of study especially of psychology, anthropology, and sociology.

Impersonal Environmental Stressors

By far the most important class of stressors are social or interpersonal. Most, if not all, stress is socially induced as a result of interactions between people (Moss, 1973). Though we can identify exclusively impersonal environmental settings (e.g., being alone in the mountains, in one's home, or fishing on a lake), it is clear that by far the most important environmental influences are those arising from settings in which people are present. The actions of other people in our lives as well as their reactions to us (the interpersonal environment) constitute the major external influences on human behavior and mental disorder (Kiesler, 1996).

However, we need to be careful not to ignore the potential importance of impersonal environmental factors and settings. Ghadirian and Lehmann (1993) remind us that the environment not only includes social and cultural parameters, but also factors such as noise, pollution, starvation, disasters, and tortures. Clearly instances occur in which individuals are exposed to pathogenic influences emanating from physical environmental forces. Research summarized by Ghadirian and Lehmann (1993) supports, for example, that high levels of noise pollution found in our cities is associated with both increased aggression and impaired social behavior as well as higher admissions to mental hospitals. Loud, unpredictable, and uncontrollable noise has been associated with increased stress, which in turn often leads to increased aggressive and antisocial behavior. Air pollution induces symptoms of fatigue, depression, irritability, and insomnia and is associated with increased levels of psychiatric hospital admissions.

Impersonal environmental substances such as neurotoxins (e.g., lead, mercury, and manganese) have long been related to both neurological disease and various forms of "organic" cognitive disorders listed as DSM diagnostic categories—as are head traumas resulting from such accidents as automobile collisions or shootings. DSM-IV also describes a diagnostic category of Seasonal Affective Disorder, an atypical form of depression the onset of which seems tied regularly to winter months in the northern latitudes—periods characterized by short days (with significant reduction of sunlight). The fact that massive doses of fluorescent light successfully treat the condition is consistent with a physical environment etiology.

Within-Culture Stressors

Psychological and sociological analysis place substantial emphasis on the ways in which social structure and established social roles are associated with greater or lesser exposure to stressful life events. Typical sociocultural factors studied by sociologists include phenomena such as *cultural change* (arising from within or without a particular country), *sociocultural disintegration* (especially when societal changes are quick, dramatic, and numerous), *social stratifications* (e.g., belonging to lower versus higher socioeconomic classes), and *deprived minority status* (especially when accompanied by prejudice, discrimination, and abuse from the majority population).

Within-culture stressors can emanate from smaller to larger social–organizational groups: one's family, extended family, peer and friend groups, church and religious group, work group, political group, or cultural group. Stressors can arise from one's neighborhood, town or city, state, country, or hemisphere of the world. Stressors can emerge from one's biographical condition: gender, sexual orientation, race or ethnic identification, socioeconomic level, urban or rural setting.

Social characteristics such as age, place of residence, gender, marital status, family variables (e.g., size, sex, and adoptive status of members), social class, social mobility, religious identity, and ethnicity affect the probabilities that one will experience various stressors (Aneshensel, Rutter, & Lachenbruch, 1991; Dohrenwend et al., 1992; Kessler et al., 1994; Pearlin, 1989). Differential experience of these environmental stressors, in turn, can be related to different rates of occurrence of various mental disorders.

Epidemiological findings provide important evidence regarding the effects of these various demographic and sociocultural stress factors. If social and cultural factors are causative, they should show significant associations with prevalence of particular mental disorders. If a difference in prevalence can be found between different population groups, then the social factors that differentiate the groups may be related to cause. If prevalences, for example, of a particular disorder are different for males versus females, cultural sex roles may play an etiological role.

Cultural Factors and Mental Disorders in the United States

Robins and Regier (1991) reported the findings of a large-scale, Epidemiologic Catchment Area (ECA) study of incidence and prevalence of mental disorders in the United States. The results of this five-site collaborative study provide the best, most authoritative data available to date. Each site sampled 3,000 to 5,000 household residents and 400 to 500 residents of mental hospitals, nursing homes, and prisons. All five sites used standard interviews and DSM-III criteria to determine whether a diagnosis of mental disorder applied and to gather information about demographic characteristics as well as use of health and mental health services. DSM-III diagnoses were generated by computer for various current time intervals or over the respondent's lifetime.

The following results were obtained. Almost 19 percent of Americans were diagnosed with some type of DSM-III mental disorder. The most prominent diagnoses were substance use, phobia, and major depression. Mental disorders were more prevalent in *persons younger than age forty-five* (rates dropped sharply after age 45), in those who were *unmarried*, and in those with *low educational levels*. Persons from *lower socioeconomic levels* generally had higher rates of mental disorder, especially in the case of schizophrenia and cognitive impairment.

Prevalence did not differ between rural and urban settings, except that major depression and substance use disorders occurred more frequently in cities. The overall rate of mental disorder did not differ between men and women. The *genders*, however, differed in prevalence for different disorders. Disorders that predominated in men were antisocial personality disorder and substance abuse; women had higher prevalences of depressive disorders and phobias.

Different *ethnic* (black, white, and Hispanic) prevalences were found for various mental disorders. For example, in the case of schizophrenia and bipolar mood disorder, blacks had the highest rates and hispanics the lowest. Major depression was most prevalent among whites and least among blacks. Among the anxiety disorders, blacks more frequently exhibited phobic disorders, while the prevalences for panic disorder were basically equivalent. Ethnic prevalences for the substance use disorder of alcoholism varied by age for males: in young males, hispanics had the highest rates of alcoholism and blacks the lowest; in older males, blacks had the highest rates and whites the lowest. Overall, blacks were found to have higher prevalence of mental disorders than whites or hispanics.

Most of these ethnic differences, however, could not be interpreted easily since both age and socioeconomic level differed significantly for the three ethnic groups. In some cases, as we just saw, differences in ethnic rates depended on the younger versus older age status of the subjects. Further, as reported above, persons from lower socioeconomic levels generally had higher rates of mental disorder.

In sum, the ECA findings provide the best available estimates of the prevalence of various mental disorders in the U.S. population. ECA findings make it clear that demographic and sociocultural factors have important effects on the incidence and prevalence of mental disorders in our country. Prevalence of mental disorder clearly depends on age, gender, and socioeconomic status. It is also clear that these demographic and other environmental factors often interact with each other in determining prevalence of various mental disorders. These interactions are most clearly evident for ethnic differences, which are saturated with the effects of socioeconomic status, and sometimes with age.

Cross-Cultural Stress Factors

Consistent with anthropological study, it is important to specify stressful events that seem to be peculiar to particular cultures throughout the world. Culture refers to "the nongenetic blueprint for living that is passed from one generation to the next . . . the sum total of habits, beliefs, values, and attitudes and includes such components as language, styles of nonverbal communication, dietary habits, marital and sexual patterns, religious beliefs, art forms, and the acceptable spectrum of occupations" (Prince, 1993, p. 55).

As members of a particular society and participants in a given culture, individuals play certain roles within their groups that are prescribed by norms. Problems can be produced by social conditions and shaped by cultural factors. Individuals can experience mental disorders when their actions are at odds with a society's dominant culture (Triandis & Draguns, 1980).

In the case of mundane human activities, it seems evident that cultural processes routinely shape the content, form, and/or emphasis of these behaviors. Respective cultures (or countries) seem to define desirable and undesirable nonverbal behaviors (e.g., gaze, touch, closeness while standing or seated, or postures), eating patterns, sexual practices (e.g., coital positions, masturbation, paraphinalia, or sexual activity with animals), eliminative processes (e.g., hiding feces or nail clippings, or blowing one's nose using a handkerchief), and conventions for being mourned and buried. We might sensibly expect, then, that cultural factors also can shape various aspects of personality and mental disorder.

Little solid evidence exists that high or low prevalence rates of given mental disorders are associated with one culture as compared to another. The evidence does seem to indicate that mental disorders can be both universal across cultures and also specific or unique to certain cultures. Escobar, in reviewing data from large-scale epidemiologic surveys conducted internationally, found that "there were remarkable similarities in the prevalence of [DSM-IV] psychiatric disorders in different countries and cultures" (1993, p. 64). Another review of sociocultural factors adds, "Several generations of research make it quite clear that however universal broad categories of mental illness may be, the patterns of onset and duration—and even the nature and clustering of specific symptoms—vary widely across cultures" (Basic Behavior Science Task Force of the National Advisory Mental Health Council, 1996, p. 723).

Tseng and Streltzer conclude, "At one extreme are conditions with a predominantly universal core that are essentially free of cultural influence." Examples might be dementia and schizophrenia. "At the other extreme are culture-bound syndromes." For example, *koro*, a disorder that is limited to certain cultural groups, involves the fear that the penis will shrink into the abdomen and the person will die. "Most psychological conditions have both universal and cultural aspects. The cultural influence may sometimes be considered 'core' or etiological. Most commonly, culture has secondary influence affecting the disorder at various levels" (1997, pp. 242–243).

Cultural factors can have complex relationships with development and onset of mental disorders. They can serve as formative, predisposing stressors, or causal factors. Accordingly, they can influence which disorders are to develop, the forms they take, and their courses. They can create stress for an individual subsequently triggering onset of mental disorder (Al-Issa, 1982; Sue & Sue, 1987). They can serve as both risk and protective moderator factors in regard to maladjustment.

IMPORTANT ENVIRONMENTAL STRESSORS: CONCLUSIONS FROM NATIONAL TASK FORCES

The Institute of Medicine's Committee on Prevention of Mental Disorders (Mrazek & Haggerty, 1994) identified major risk and protective factors for a group of five major disorders. An analysis of relevant psychological risk and protective factors included three major important groupings: personal, family, and socioeconomic. (1) Identified *personal factors* included smoking, substance abuse, childhood behavioral problems of poor impulse control, aggression and/or shyness and social withdrawal, educational drop-out, being separated or divorced, good intelligence, and an easy temperament. (2) *Family factors* included disturbed family environment, family communication problems, strong parent–child attachment or bond, and parents who are criminal, alcoholic, or antisocial. Also included were maladjusted parents, erratic and abusive forms of discipline, and marital discord combined with maternal depression. (3) *Socioeconomic factors* included minimal education, low socioeconomic status or downward mobility, neighborhood disorganization, deviant peer-group influence, presence of a supportive adult, poverty and poor housing, living in highly congested urban areas, and having good schools (especially a good high school).

A task force of the National Advisory Mental Health Council (NAMHC) report to the U.S. Congress concluded that "social, cultural, and environmental forces shape who we are and how well we function in the everyday world. The culture we belong to, the neighborhood we live in, the demographic composition of our community, and the opportunities and frustrations of our work environment all profoundly affect our mental health. Other powerful factors include whether we are rich or poor, native-born Americans or immigrants or refugees, and residents of a city or a rural area" (1995, p. 722).

The report summarized important risk factors identified by empirical research. (1) One was being of *minority race and ethnicity* (African and Hispanic Americans), beyond the effects accounted for by lower socioeconomic status. Minority status, especially when accompanied by prejudice and discrimination, can result in chronic levels of stress that have physical and mental health consequences. (2) Among *lower socioeconomic groups* are found the highest rates of mental disorder. "Mental health differences related to age, race, or sex appear modest in comparison with these socioeconomic differences . . . researchers now know that virtually all major psychosocial risk factors for mental illness (including chronic and acute stress, lack of social relationships and supports, and lack of control and mastery) are more prevalent at lower socioeconomic levels . . . many social and personal characteristics and resources may exacerbate or buffer the impacts of stress and other health hazards related to SES" (1995, p. 727). (3) *Conditions nested under lower SES* also are significant risk factors and sources of parental stress that relate to maladaptive modes of interacting with children. These situations include mothers faced with chronic financial problems as well as work that is routine, heavily supervised, and low in complexity leading to a sense of hopelessness and alienation. (4) *Female employment* "per se has few negative effects—and even some beneficial ones—on women, their spouses, and their children. . . . Even among married women with children, employment generally has positive effects on women's psychological well-being." On the other hand, *single parent homes* seem to be a significant risk factor and source of stress: "Research has shown that when single mothers are the only adults in the household, children are at greater risk for maladaptive outcomes than when other adults are present as well." (5) Finally, the NAMHC report states that *instability in people's relationships to communities and organizations* (e.g., resulting from migrancy, immigration, or homelessness) "is often linked to poor physical and mental health" (p. 729).

Finally, a task force of the American Psychological Society (1996) reviewed in detail the empirical literature on stressful events. The task force concluded that four factors have been repeatedly associated with vulnerability for mental disorders. These formative and/or precipitating stressful live events included *low socioeconomic status, family instability, gender,* and *minority ethnic status.*

CONCLUSIONS AND IMPLICATIONS FOR MULTICAUSAL, BIOPSYCHOSOCIAL MODELS

Even though environmental factors are not "sufficient" in themselves to produce mental disorder, they clearly can provide "contributory" and even "necessary" influences. The evidence reviewed in this chapter demonstrates that a central way in which the environment contributes to development and onset of mental disorders is in the form of stressful events that may occur throughout an individual's entire life span.

Stress originates within the external environment and consists of two major processes. Stressful events refer to the external demands, pressures, or forces existing in the external environment that threaten the person's well-being. The strain process denotes the internal physiological and psychological reactions of a person that are triggered in response to the external demands or threats. The term, stress, refers to the overall process.

The bulk of the literature suggests that a stressful event can generate a severe strain process that includes chronic activation of the central and autonomic nervous systems and of the endocrine and catecholamine systems leading to chronic suppression of the immune response. The chronic strain process, in turn, can lead eventually to physical disease or mental disorder. Whether or not it does depends on the meaning the external event has for the stressed person, his or her manner of coping with it, his or her adaptive capacities, and his or her available social support network.

Findings from numerous studies support the conclusion that life stressors of all types place individuals at greater risk for a variety of physical diseases and mental disorders. Psychosocial stressors contribute both formative and precipitative causal influence to occurrence of mental disorders.

The effects of negative life events depend very much on characteristics of the individual person. The important components of external events are the ones subjectively perceived and appraised by the individual. Further, the individual not only shapes and changes the salient external events, but also can transact with them, actually participating in their evocation.

Among these stressful negative events or environments, the most salient class involves other persons—is the *social–interpersonal* environment. The *physical–impersonal* environment also can be clearly stressful in the form of factors such as noise, pollution, starvation, or disasters. A third major class is *subcultural*, including distinctive environmental conditions found within a particular culture or country arising from various societal groupings, demographics, and roles (gender, age, family, church, work, political group, socioeconomic status, or race). A final group of stressful environmental factors are those that emerge *cross-culturally* (from factors that are distinct or unique to a particular culture). These cross-cultural factors can affect the prevalence (development and onset) of mental disorder as well as serve as formative and precipitating stressful events; they can constitute both risk and protective factors for various mental disorders.

The inevitable conclusion from the evidence reviewed by this chapter is that stressful life events serve as important formative and precipitative causes of mental disorders. These stressful life events take the form of various environmental factors: social, physical–impersonal, subcultural, and cross-cultural. Important psychological factors influence the perception, appraisal, and even evocation of psychological stressors and determine whether long-term, harmful, psychopathological effects may occur.

Nurture, then, just as nature, clearly is causative and precipitative of mental disorders. Psychological and social factors, just as biological ones, can serve as "necessary" and/or "contributory" causes of various mental disorders. Accordingly, state-of-the-science explanations of mental disorders must take the form of vulnerability–stress or biopsychosocial models.

In Chapter 8, we concentrate on the description of multicausal theories of psychopathology. However, we need to address a final distinct area of psychopathology research that also demonstrates the need for careful study of an array of biopsychosocial factors. Chapter 7 reviews the evidence that factors across the entire array—biological, psychological, sociocultural—can either *facilitate* development or onset of mental disorders (vulnerability factors), or can *buffer against or prevent* development or onset of mental disorders (protective factors).

REFERENCES

Adler, N. E., & Matthews, K. (1994). Health psychology: Why do some people get sick and some stay healthy? *Annual Review of Psychology, 45,* 229–259.

Adler, R. (1981). Behavioral influences on immune responses. In S. M. Weiss, J. A. Herd, & B. H. Fox (Eds.), *Perspectives on behavioral medicine: Proceedings of the Academy of Behavioral Medicine Research Conference,* Snowbird, Utah, June 3–6, 1979 (pp. 163–182). New York: Academic Press.

Akiskal, H. S., & McKinney, W. T. (1973). Depressive disorders: Toward a unified hypothesis. *Science, 182,* 20–28.

Al-Issa, I. (1982). Does culture make a difference in psychopathology? In I. Al-Issa (Ed.), *Culture and psychopathology.* Baltimore: Unversity Park Press.

American Psychiatric Association. (1980). *Diagnostic and statistical manual of mental disorders* (3d ed., rev.). Washington, DC: Author.

American Psychiatric Association. (1994). *Diagnostic and statistical manual of mental disorders* (4th ed.). Washington, DC: Author.

American Psychological Society. (1996, February 1). Human Capital Initiative (HCI) Report No. 3. *APS Observer* (special issue). Washington, DC: Author.

Andersen, B. L., Kiecolt-Glaser, J. K., & Glaser, R. (1994). A biobehavioral model of cancer stress and disease course. *American Psychologist, 49,* 389–404.

Aneshensel, C. S. (1992). Social stress: Theory and research. *Annual Review of Sociology, 18,* 15–38.

Aneshensel, C. S., Rutter, C., & Lachenbruch, P. (1991). Social structure, stress and mental health: Competing conceptual and analytic models. *American Sociological Review, 56,* 166–178.

Antonini, M. H., Schneiderman, N., Fletcher, M. A., & Goldstein, D. A. (1990). Psychoneuroimmunology and HIV-1. *Journal of Consulting and Clinical Psychology, 58,* 38–49.

Auerbach, S. M., & Gramling, S. E. (1998). *Stress management: Psychological foundations.* Upper Saddle River, NJ: Prentice Hall.

Avison, W. R., & Gotlib, I. H. (1994). Introduction and overview. In W. R. Avison & I. H. Gotlib (Eds.), *Stress and mental health: Contemporary issues and prospects for the future* (pp. 3–12). New York: Plenum.

Avison, W. R., & Turner, R. J. (1988). Stressful life events and depressive symptoms: Disaggregating the effects of chronic strains and eventful stressors. *Journal of Health and Social Behavior, 29,* 253–264.

Barrett, J. E. (Ed.). (1979). *Stress and mental disorder.* New York: Raven Press.

Basic Behavioral Science Task Force of the National Advisory Mental Health Council. (1996). Basic behavioral science research for mental health: Sociocultural and environmental processes. *American Psychologist, 51,* 722–731.

Billings, A. M., & Moos, R. H. (1985). Psychosocial stressors, coping, and depression. In E. Beckham & W. Leber (Eds.), *Handbook of depression: Treatment, assessment, and research* (pp. 940–974). Homewood, IL: Dorsey.

Blaney, P. H. (1985). Stress and depression in adults: A critical review. In T. Field, P. M. Cabe, & N. Schneiderman (Eds.), *Stress and coping* (pp. 263–283). Hillsdale, NJ: Erlbaum.

Bloom, B. L. (1988). *Health psychology: A psychosocial perspective.* Englewood Cliffs, NJ: Prentice Hall.

Bolger, N., DeLongis, A., Kessler, R. C., & Schilling, E. A. (1989). Effects of daily stress on negative mood. *Journal of Personality and Social Psychology, 57,* 808–818.

Borysenko, M., & Borysenko, J. (1982). Stress, behavior, and immunity: Animal models and mediating mechanisms. *General Hospital Psychiatry, 4,* 56–67.

Brown, G. W., & Birley, J. L. T. (1968). Crises and life changes and the onset of schizophrenia. *Journal of Health and Social Behavior, 9,* 203–214.

Brown, G. W., & Harris, T. O. (1978). *The social origins of depression: A study of psychiatric disorder in women.* New York: Free Press.

Brown, G. W., & Harris, T. O. (1989). *Life events and illness.* New York: Guilford.

Brown. G. W., Harris, T. O., & Hepworth, C. (1994). Life events and endogenous depression. *Archives of General Psychiatry, 51,* 525–534.

Cohen, S. (1996). Psychological stress, immunity, and upper respiratory infections. *Current Directions in Psychological Science, 5,* 86–90.

Cohen, S., & Edwards, J. R. (1989). Personality characteristics as moderators of the relationship between stress and disorder. In R.W.J. Neufeld (Ed.), *Advances in the investigation of psychological stress* (pp. 235–283). New York: Wiley.

Cohen, S., & Herbert, T. B. (1996). Psychological factors and physical disease from the perspective of human psychoneuroimmunology. *Annual Review of Psychology, 47,* 113–142.

Cohen, S., & McKay, G. (1984). Social support, stress, and the buffering hypothesis: A theoretical analysis. In A. Baum, J. E. Singer, & S. E. Taylor (Eds.), *Handbook of psychology and health* (Vol. 4, pp. 253–267). Hillsdale, NJ: Erlbaum.

Cohen, S., & Williamson, G. M. (1991). Stress and infectious disease in humans. *Psychological Bulletin, 109,* 5–24.

Cohen, L., Delahanty, D. L., Schmitz, J. B., Jenkins, F. J., & Baum, A. (1993). The effects of stress on natural killer cell activity in healthy men. *Journal of Applied Biobehavioral Research, 1,* 120–132.

Day, R. (1981). Life events and schizophrenia: The triggering hypothesis. *Acta Psychiatrica Scandinavica, 64,* 97–122.

Day, R., Zubin, J., & Steinhauer, S. R. (1987). Psychosocial factors in schizophrenia in light of vulnerability theory. In D. Magnusson & A. Ohman (Eds.), *Psychopathology: An interactional perspective* (pp. 25–39). Orlando, FL: Academic Press.

Dohrenwend, B. P., & Egri, G. (1981). Recent stressful life events and episodes of schizophrenia. *Schizophrenia Bulletin, 7,* 12–23.

Dohrenwend, B. P., Levav, L., Shrout, P. E., Schwartz, S., Naveh, G., Link, B. G., Skodol, A. E., & Stueve, A. (1992). Socioeconomic status and psychiatric disorders: The causation–selection issue. *Science, 255,* 946–952.

Dohrenwend, B. S., & Dohrenwend, B. P. (1981). *Stressful life events and their contexts.* New York: Prodist.

Eckenrode, J. (1984). Impact of chronic and acute stressors on daily reports of moods. *Journal of Personality and Social Psychology, 46,* 907–918.

Ellicott, A., Hammen, C., Gitlin, M., Brown, G., & Jamison, K. (1990). Life events and the course of bipolar disorder. *American Journal of Psychiatry, 147,* 1194–1198.

Elliott, G. R., & Eisdorfer, C. (Eds.). (1982). *Stress and human health.* New York: Springer.

Escobar, J. I. (1993). Psychiatric epidemiology. In A. C. Gaw (Ed.), *Culture, ethnicity and mental illness* (pp. 43–73). Washington, DC: American Psychiatric Press.

Finlay-Jones, R. A., & Brown, G. W. (1981). Types of stressful life event and the onset of anxiety and depressive disorders. *Psychological Medicine, 11,* 803–815.

Fowles, D. C. (1993). Biological variables in psychopathology: A psychobiological perspective. In P. B. Sutker & H. E. Adams (Eds.), *Comprehensive handbook of psychopathology* (2d ed., pp. 57–82). New York: Plenum.

Friedman, H. S., Tucker, J. S., Schwartz, J. E., Tomlinson-Keasey, C., Martin, L. R., Wingard, D. L., & Criqui, M. H. (1995). Psychosocial and behavioral predictors of longevity. *American Psychologist, 50,* 69–78.

Geiser, D. S. (1989). Psychosocial influences on human immunity. *Clinical Psychology Review, 9,* 689–715.

Ghadirian, A-M. A., & Lehmann, H. E. (Eds.). (1993). *Environment and psychopathology.* New York: Springer.

Glaser, R., & Kiecolt-Glaser, J. (Eds.). (1994). *Handbook of human stress and immunity.* New York: Academic Press.

Goodwin, F. K., & Jamison, K. R. (1990). *Manic depressive illness.* New York: Oxford University Press.

Harris, T. O. (1989). Physical illness: An introduction. In G. W. Brown & T. O. Harris (Eds.), *Life events and illness* (pp. 199–212). New York: Guilford.

Herbert, T. B., & Cohen, S. (1993a). Depression and immunity: A meta-analytic review. *Psychological Bulletin, 113,* 472–486.

Herbert, T. B., & Cohen, S. (1993b). Stress and immunity in humans: A meta-analytic review. *Psychosomatic Medicine, 55,* 364–379.

Hirschfeld, R. M., & Cross, C. K. (1982). Epidemiology of affective disorders: Psychosocial risk factors. *Archives of General Psychiatry, 39,* 35–46.

Holmes, T. H., & Rahe, R. H. (1967). The social readjustment rating scale. *Journal of Psychosomatic Research, 11,* 213–218.

Jacobs, S. C., Prusoff, B. A., & Paykel, E. S. (1974). Recent life events in schizophrenia and depression. *Psychological Medicine, 4,* 444–453.

Jahoda, M. (1961). A social–psychological approach to the study of culture. *Human Relations, 14,* 23–30.

Jemmott, J. B., III, & Locke, S. E. (1984). Psychosocial factors, immunologic mediation, and human susceptibility to infectious diseases: How much do we know? *Psychological Bulletin, 95,* 78–108.

Jenkins, C. D. (1978). Behavioral risk factors in coronary artery disease. *Annual Review of Medicine, 29,* 543–562.

Johnson, S. L., & Roberts, J. E. (1995). Life events and bipolar disorder: Implications from biological theories. *Psychological Bulletin, 117,* 434–439.

Kaplan, R. M., Sallis, J. F., Jr., & Patterson, T. L. (1993). *Health and human behavior.* New York: McGraw-Hill.

Kaprio, J., Koskenvuo, M., & Rita, H. (1987). Mortality after bereavement: A prospective study of 95,647 widowed persons. *American Journal of Public Health, 77,* 283–287.

Kessler, R. C. (1997). The effects of stressful life events on depression. *Annual Review of Psychology, 48,* 191–214.

Kessler, R. C., McGonagle, K. A., Zhao, S., Nelson, C. B., Hughes, M., Eshleman, S., Wittchen, H. U., & Kendler, K. S. (1994). Lifetime and 12-month prevalence of DSM-III-R psychiatric disorders in the United States. *Archives of General Psychiatry, 51,* 8–19.

Kiecolt-Glaser, J. K., Fisher, L. D., Ogrocki, P., Stout, J. C., Speicher, C. E., & Glaser, R. (1987). Marital quality, marital disruption, and immune function. *Psychosomatic Medicine, 49,* 13–34.

Kiecolt-Glaser, J. K., & Glaser, R. (1992). Psychoneuroimmunology: Can psychological interventions modulate immunity? *Journal of Consulting and Clinical Psychology, 60,* 569–575.

Kiesler, D. J. (1996). *Contemporary interpersonal theory and research: Personality, psychopathology, and psychotherapy.* New York: Wiley.

Lazarus, R. S., & Folkman, S. (1984). *Stress, appraisal, and coping.* New York: Springer.

Link, B. G., Dohrenwend, B. P., & Skodol, A. (1986). Socio-economic status and schizophrenia: Noisesome occupational characteristics as a risk factor. *American Sociological Review, 52,* 96–112.

Lloyd, C. (1980a). Life events and depressive disorder reviewed: Events as predisposing factors. *Archives of General Psychiatry, 37,* 529–537.

Lloyd, C. (1980b). Life events and depressive disorder reviewed: Events as precipitating factors. *Archives of General Psychiatry, 37,* 541–548.

Lukoff, D., Snyder, K., Ventura, J., & Nuechterlien, K. H. (1984). Life events, familial stress, and coping in the developmental course of schizophrenia. *Schizophrenia Bulletin, 10,* 258–292.

Maier, S. F., Watkins, L. R., & Fleshner, M. (1994). Psychoneuroimmunology: The interface between behavior, brain, and immunity. *American Psychologist, 49,* 1004–1017.

McClelland, D. C., Alexander, C., & Marks, E. (1982). The need for power, stress, immune function, and illness among male prisoners. *Journal of Abnormal Psychology, 91,* 61–70.

McQueen, D., & Siegrist, J. (1982). Sociocultural factors in the etiology of chronic disease. *Social Science Medicine, 16,* 353–367.

Miller, N. E. (1983). Behavioral medicine: Symbiosis between laboratory and clinic. *Annual Review of Psychology, 34,* 1–31.

Miller, T. W. (1989). *Stressful life events.* Madison, CT: International Universities Press.

Mirowsky, J., & Ross, C. E. (1989). *Social causes of psychological distress.* New York: Aldine de Gruyter.

Monroe, S. M. (1990). Psychological factors in anxiety and depression. In J. D. Maser & C. R. Cloninger (Eds.), *Comorbidity of mood and anxiety disorders* (pp. 463–497). Washington, DC: American Psychiatric Press.

Monroe, S. M. (1992). Life events assessment: Current practices, emerging trends. *Clinical Psychology Review, 2,* 435–453.

Monroe, S. M., & Depue, R. A. (1991). Life stress and depression. In J. Becker & A. Kleinman (Eds.), *Psychosocial aspects of depression* (pp. 101–130). Hillsdale, NJ: Erlbaum.

Monroe, S. M., & Johnson, S. L. (1990). The dimensions of life stress and the specificity of the disorder. *Journal of Applied Social Psychology, 20,* 1678–1694.

Moos, R. H. (1984). Context and coping: Toward a unifying conceptual framework. *American Journal of Community Psychology, 12,* 5–25.

Moss, G. E. (1973). *Illness, community, and social interaction.* New York: Wiley.

Mrazek, P. J., & Haggerty, R. J. (Eds.). (1994). *Reducing risk for mental disorders: Frontiers for preventive intervention research.* Washington, DC: National Academy Press.

Murray, H. A. (1938). *Explorations in personality: A clinical and experimental study of fifty men of college age.* New York: Oxford.

National Advisory Mental Health Council. (1995). *Basic behavioral science research for mental health: A national statement.* Washington, DC: U.S. Government Printing Office.

O'Leary, A. (1990). Stress, emotion, and human immune function. *Psychological Bulletin, 108,* 363–382.

Palmblad, J. (1981). Stress and immunocompetence: Studies in man. In R. Adler (Ed.), *Psychoneuroimmunology.* New York: Academic Press.

Paykel, E. S. (1978). Contribution of life events to causation of psychiatric illness. *Psychological Medicine, 8,* 245–253.

Pearlin, L. I. (1989). The sociological study of stress. *Journal of Health and Social Behavior, 30,* 241–256.

Pervin, L. A. (1968). Performance and satisfaction as a function of individual–environment fit. *Psychological Bulletin, 69,* 56–58.

Petersen, D. (1984). *Human-error reduction and safety management.* Deer Park, NY: Aloray.

Prince, R. H. (1993). Culture-bound syndromes: The example of social phobias. In A-M. A. Ghadirian, & H. E. Lehmann (Eds.), *Environment and psychopathology* (pp. 55–72). New York: Springer.

Rabin, B. S., Cohen, S., Ganguli, R., Lysle, D. T., & Cunnick, J. E. (1989). Bidirectional interaction between the central nervous system and the immune system. *Critical Review of Immunology, 9,* 279–312.

Rabkin, J. G. (1980). Stressful life events and schizophrenia: A review of the research literature. *Psychological Bulletin, 87*, 408–425.

Rabkin, J. G., & Struening, E. L. (1976). Life events, stress, and illness. *Science, 194*, 1013–1020.

Rehm, L. P., & Tyndall, C. I. (1993). Mood disorders: Unipolar and bipolar. In P. B. Sutker & H. E. Adams (Eds.), *Comprehensive handbook of psychiatry* (2d ed., pp. 235–261). New York: Plenum.

Riley, V. (1981). Psychneuroendocrine influences on immunocompetence and neoplasia. *Science, 212*, 1100–1109.

Robins, L. N., & Regier, D. A. (Eds.). (1991). *Psychiatric disorders in America.* New York: Free Press.

Rozanski, A., Bairey, C. N., Krantz, D. S., Friedman, J., Resser, K. J., Morell, M., Hilton-Chalfen, S., Hestrin, L., Bietendorf, J., & Berman, D. S. (1988). Mental stress and the induction of silent myocardial ischemia in patients with coronary artery disease. *New England Journal of Medicine, 318*, 1005–1012.

Sarason, I. G., de Monchaux, C., & Hunt, T. (1975). Methodological issues in the assessment of life stress. In L. Levi (Ed.), *Emotions: Their parameters and measurement* (pp. 499–509). New York: Raven.

Sarason, I. G., Johnson, J. H., & Siegel, J. M. (1978). Assessing the impact of life changes: Development of the life experiences survey. *Journal of Consulting and Clinical Psychology, 46*, 932–946.

Sklar, L. S., & Anisman, H. (1981). Stress and cancer. *Psychological Bulletin, 89*, 369–406.

Sue, D., & Sue, S. (1987). Cultural factors in the clinical assessment of Asian Americans. *Journal of Consulting and Clinical Psychology, 55*, 479–487.

Sullivan, H. S. (1953). *Conceptions of modern psychiatry.* New York: Norton.

Taylor, S. E., Repetti, R. L., & Seeman, T. (1997). Health psychology: What is an unhealthy environment and how does it get under the skin? *Annual Review of Psychology, 48*, 411–447.

Tennant, C., Bebbington, P. E., & Hurry, J. (1981). The role of life events in depressive illness: Is there a substantial causal relation? *Psychological Medicine, 11*, 379–389.

Thoits, P. A. (1985). Social support and psychological well-being: Theoretical possibilities. In I. G. Sarason & B. R. Sarason (Eds.), *Social support: Theory, research and applications* (pp. 51–72). The Hague, Netherlands: Nijhoff.

Triandis, H. C., & Draguns, J. G. (Eds.). (1980). *Handbook of cross-cultural psychology: Psychopathology* (Vol. 5). Boston: Allyn & Bacon.

Tseng, W-S., & Streltzer, J. (1997). Integration and conclusions. In W-S. Tseng & J. Streltzer (Eds.), *Culture and psychopathology: A guide to clinical assessment* (pp. 241–252). New York: Brunner/Mazel.

Weisse, C. S. (1992). Depression and immunocompetence: A review of the literature. *Psychological Bulletin, 111*, 475–489.

Williams, D. R., & Collins, C. (1995). U.S. socioeconomic and racial differences in health: Patterns and explanations. *Annual Review of Sociology, 21*, 349–386.

Zegans, L. S. (1982). Stress and the development of somatic disorders. In L. Goldberger & S. Breznitz (Eds.), *Handbook of stress: Theoretical and clinical aspects* (pp. 134–152). New York: Free Press.

Part III

What Causes Mental Disorders? The Multicausal, Biopsychosocial Answer

Chapter 7

Biopsychosocial Risk and Protective Factors in Mental Disorders

Emerging theories of mental disorders have begun to emphasize the complex interactions present among risk (vulnerability) and protective factors, whether the factors be genetic–biomedical, environmental, or psychosocial. The importance of these risk and protective factors has compellingly surfaced from the empirical findings in various subdisciplines of psychopathology, especially developmental psychopathology, epidemiology, and prevention science.

CAUSES OF MENTAL DISORDERS I: RISK OR VULNERABILITY FACTORS

Diathesis–Vulnerability Research

We encounter in Chapter 3 two of the earliest sophisticated theories of schizophrenia—one offered by a clinical psychologist and labeled a diathesis–stress model (Meehl, 1962, 1989, 1990), the other by a psychiatrist and called a stress–vulnerability model (Zubin & Spring, 1977). Both theories were stimulated by the evidence that genetic influence in schizophrenia was strong, yet was not sufficient to explain occurrence of the disorder. Both theorists concluded that what was inherited was a *diathesis, vulnerability*, or *predisposition* toward schizophrenia;

the disorder, in turn, could occur or not depending on the presence of later precipitating stressors in a person's life.

A diathesis is defined as a predisposition or vulnerability toward developing a mental disorder—a potentiality for future occurrence of abnormal behavior. Some people, by virtue of their genetic–biological or social backgrounds, simply are at greater risk than others for a particular mental disorder. People who eventually develop, say, major depressive disorder differ in some predisposing way from those who do not. "Vulnerable" individuals are those who, by virtue of genetic predisposition, chronic illness, hardship, deprivation, or abuse, are more susceptible to life stressors than others.

Earlier uses of the term, diathesis, targeted exclusively some abnormal genetic–biological substrate present within a person that is acted on by stress to produce (or, once established, to exacerbate) a particular mental disorder. Within the biomedical model, the risk factor results from a presumed hereditary predisposition and takes the form of some constitutional biological residue.

Another early usage restricted the term, diathesis, to a factor that is vulnerable to its own unique stressor. The diathesis had to be linked with a specific and distinct real life stressor in order to produce onset of an episode of a particular mental disorder. For example, the schizophrenia diathesis (e.g., a neurointegrative brain deficit) predisposed a person to an inability to cope with its unique set of specific stressors such as too much information, too much time pressure, or too many people (Katschnig, 1991, p. 223).

Current usage of the term diathesis denotes either the biological makeup or the prior environmental (psychological and sociocultural) experience of the person. A diathesis can take the form of biological, psychosocial, or sociocultural factors. When genetically transmitted, a diathesis takes the form of some imbalance or deviation in biological cortical functioning that begins in utero and continues throughout development. But diathesis can also take the form of enduring psychosocial states (e.g., irrational cognitions, rigid personality traits) that result from early childhood interactions with stressful environments (e.g., early parental loss, severe physical or sexual abuse); these enduring states also can predispose a child to subsequent mental disturbances. Vulnerabilities to maladjustment also can emerge from enduring psychological states that result from early childhood encounters with sociocultural factors (e.g., normative suspicion and paranoia in a particular culture, ethnic hatreds and genocides, discriminations and persecutions).

Within diathesis–stress models, vulnerability or risk factors are "necessary" or "contributory" causal variables associated with increased onset, greater severity, and longer duration of particular mental disorders. They are enduring or longstanding life circumstances or conditions that promote maladaptation (Zubin & Spring, 1977).

Developmental Psychopathology

Developmental psychopathology (Achenbach, 1974/1982; Cicchetti, 1984, 1989; Cicchetti & Cohen, 1995a, 1995b; Rutter & Garmezy, 1983) studies various individual pathways or developmental routes to adjustment and maladjustment (Sroufe & Rutter, 1984) through concentration on investigations of high-risk-for-disorder populations. The field adopts a life-span perspective in documenting the impact of biological and psychological changes in the maturing individual.

Prospective longitudinal risk studies were initiated during the 1960s and 1970s (Cicchetti, 1984; Garmezy, 1974a, 1974b; Mednick & McNeil, 1968; Rutter & Garmezy, 1983). Early proponents sought to identify important precursors of schizophrenia and other disorders by prospectively following up at-risk individuals. Known popularly as *high-risk research*, the studies have multiplied and form the heart of the present-day discipline.

The basic research strategy is that children at risk for various childhood and/or adult disorders—as determined by genetic, biological and/ or psychological measures—are followed over the life span to discover distinctive patterns of risk and protective factors that promote (or buffer against) onset of mental disorder. Starting from the finding that mental disorder in a parent constitutes an important risk factor to adult disorder for a child, risk-research most typically studies the offspring of mentally ill parents over varying periods of the child's development. Various at-risk researchers have studied the influence of genetic and environmental factors on subsequent maladjustment in children (e.g., autism, depression, hyperactivity), in adolescents (e.g., conduct disorder, juvenile delinquency), and in adults (e.g., schizophrenia, depression, alcoholism, criminality, personality disorder).

Today, developmental psychopathology has gained recognition as a viable interdisciplinary discipline and perspective, providing an impetus for sustained studies of risk and protective factors in childhood. Together with researchers in epidemiology, children-at-risk psychopathologists have been among the first to discover, invent, classify, and provide empirical support for vulnerability (risk) and protective causal factors in the development of mental disorder. Recent findings are reviewed in Cicchetti (1989); Cicchetti and Cohen (1995a, 1995b); Eisenberg (1987); Essau and Petermann (1998); Grizenko and Fisher (1992); Lewis, Dlugokinski, Caputo, and Griffin (1988); Lewis and

Miller (1990); Luthar, Burack, Cicchetti, and Weisz (1997); Rolf, Masten, Cicchetti, Nuechterlein, and Weintraub (1990); and Werner and Smith (1992). This chapter depends heavily on the concepts and findings of developmental psychopathology.

Epidemiology

Epidemiology studies the prevalence and incidence of mental disorders in the community and corresponding distributions within population subgroups. Mental health epidemiology seeks to identify factors that play a role in the determination and distribution of particular mental disorders. Studies provide data on differential incidence and prevalence of mental disorders in terms of four primary sets of factors: (1) *demographic* (age, gender, educational level, employment status, ethnicity, and socioeconomic level); (2) *environmental* (hazardous conditions, toxic substances, stressful environments, and availability of resources or supports); (3) *psychological* (temperament, personality, attractiveness, and intelligence); and (4) *biological* (genetics, health status, and other biological vulnerability). The major goal of epidemiological research is to clarify how these risk factors contribute to incidence and prevalence of mental disorders—to identify and begin to understand the interaction of causative factors in mental disorder.

The term *risk factor* was coined in the 1960s by cardiovascular epidemiologists after longitudinal community studies had consistently demonstrated that the notion of a single cause for cardiovascular diseases was untenable (Kannel, 1990). However, it was only more recently—for example, the extensive NIMH Epidemiologic Catchment Area Study (Robins & Regier, 1991)—that the field began to identify important risk and protective factors for the various mental disorders. The concept of risk also derived from epidemiology. Mental health epidemiology highlights those individual (innate) and environmental (situational) factors that are expected to increase the probability of developing particular forms of impairment in psychological functioning—factors expected to increase the probability of subsequent mental disorder.

Identification of risk factors is relevant for both medical diseases and mental disorders. For example, in the case of coronary heart disease, epidemiological research has identified a set of risk factors (family history, smoking, inactivity, and elevations of blood pressure and serum cholesterol) that accounts for about half of the variance in incidence of cardiovascular disease (Jenkins, 1988).

Reviews of community surveys and longitudinal epidemiologic studies have emphasized that any particular mental disorder is likely to have multiple risk factors (Gotlib & Avison, 1993; Hawkins, Catalano, & Miller, 1992; Offord, Boyle, & Racine, 1989; Rutter, 1989; Werner & Smith, 1992).

These risk factors have been isolated in a wide range of environmental settings (e.g., home, school, peer group, neighborhood, or work site).

Prevention Science

A long overdue present-day emphasis addresses the prevention of human dysfunction through eliminating or counteracting the causes of mental disorder. Preventive science has as its primary aim the reduction of risk factors for mental disorders and the enhancement of protective factors. Prevention science is a discipline "focused primarily on the systematic study of precursors of dysfunction and health called risk factors and protective factors respectively" (Heller, 1996, p. 1124; see also Mrazek & Haggerty, 1994).

In current mental health preventive models, risk factors are "those characteristics, variables, or hazards that, if present for a given individual, make it more likely that this individual rather than someone selected at random from the general population, will develop a disorder" (Mrazek & Haggerty, 1994, p. 127). To qualify as a risk factor, a variable (a) must be associated with an increased probability of a particular mental disorder, and (b) must antedate (e.g., originate in childhood) the onset of the disorder. "The primary objective of prevention science is to trace the links between *generic* risk factors and specific disorders and to moderate the pervasive effect of risk factors" (Coie et al., 1993, p. 1014). Once research identifies risk factors in various settings, appropriate interventions can be designed to target any or all of them. To construct optimum interventions, it is necessary to identify as many risk and protective factors as possible that impinge on individuals at different stages of development (Steinberg & Silverman, 1987; Mrazek & Haggerty, 1994).

American Psychological Society Report

A task force of the American Psychological Society (APS) recently concluded, "Four factors have been shown time after time to be associated with vulnerability for mental disorder: socioeconomic status, family stability, gender, and ethnicity" (1996, p. 13). *Socioeconomic status* is related to a broad range of disorders in both children and adults. Higher rates of depression, psychosis, adjustment disorders, and anxiety disorders are found among those with low incomes and limited educational backgrounds. Social disadvantage can result from being part of a welfare family, living in subsidized housing, or living in an area that has a high rate of community disorganization.

Research also has shown that *family conflict and family disruption* are linked with increased risk for mental disorder in both parents and children. For example, increased childhood psychopathology is associated with severe marital discord, social disadvantage, overcrowding or large family size, paternal criminality, maternal mental disorder, and even admission into child welfare services (Rutter, 1979). The effects of family discord often are compounded by economic strain and exposure to unsafe neighborhoods.

Pronounced *gender differences* are found in the rates of particular mental disorders. For example, women experience depression, anxiety, and eating disorders at disproportionately high rates. In contrast, male children are at increased risk for autism, conduct disorder, and attention deficit disorder. Male adults experience disproportionately high rates of antisocial, alcohol, and drug problems.

Finally, according to the APS task force, *ethnic minorities* are at increased risk for a variety of mental health problems. This results not only from the increased risk from lower socioeconomic and family discord factors, but also from the stressful effects of being subjected to societal prejudices and discriminations.

Other research has demonstrated that, although some risk factors may be specific to a particular disorder, so far identified risk factors seem to be common to and contribute to the onset of a wide range of mental disorders. With the occasional exception of genetic factors, most risk and protective factors do not seem to be unique to a single disorder. More careful research may eventually be able to find distinctive sets of risk factors for particular mental disorders. It is possible also that future research may isolate universal risk factors that may exert their primary influence at a distinct stage of the developmental cycle.

Research also suggests that the experience of accumulated risk factors is the crucial etiological event—not the occurrence of an individual risk factor. For example, Rutter and Quinton (1977) identified six risk factors within the family environment that were significantly associated with childhood mental disturbances. The set of "adversity factors" included severe marital discord, low social class, large family size, paternal criminality, maternal mental disorder, and foster care placement. Rutter and associates' studies revealed that no single adversity factor increased the risk for mental disorder in children. Rather, *it was the aggregate of adversity factors that led to impaired development.* The presence of two adversity factors resulted in a fourfold increase in risk; the presence of four adversity factors yielded a tenfold increase in risk. Other studies support the notion that aggregated vulnerability factors substantially increase risk for mental disorders.

Vulnerability (risk) variables are factors that predispose an individual to subsequent occurrence of mental disorder. Research shows that risk factors can either reside biologically or psychologically within the in dividual or result from stressors found in the family, community, or larger institutions that surround the individual.

Individuals vary greatly in their exposure to environmental risk factors (Rutter & Rutter, 1993). Further, a variable that serves as a risk factor at one life stage may or may not put an individual at risk at a later stage of development. Though some risk factors may be specific to a particular disorder, so far the research suggests that risk factors are common to multiple mental disorders. Finally, some research supports that the crucial causal contributor is the experience of aggregate risk factors, rather than occurrence of an individual stressor.

CAUSES OF MENTAL DISORDERS II: PROTECTIVE FACTORS

> Human beings differ in their innate capacity for realizing individual talents and buffering against dysfunction.
> —Bronfenbrenner & Ceci, 1994, p. 570.

Resilience

For years, mental health workers singularly studied maladjustment and incompetence by seeking to identify the vulnerability (risk) factors just described (Garmezy, 1983). What psychologists have come to appreciate is that *not everyone encountering risk factors goes on to develop a mental disorder*. Current research seeks to understand why some children appear to be "resilient"—how they come to maturity relatively unscathed by organic and psychosocial insults that seem to handicap other children.

We all have witnessed or experienced examples of this human capacity for turning disadvantage into advantage, for turning adversity into enhanced personal adjustment. Some individuals whose families suffered financial misfortune and privation during the Great Depression found a way to use the trauma as an incentive for enhanced personal success (rather than as an excuse for personal failure). A recent *U.S. News & World Report* article on "Invincible Kids" highlighted other examples: "Most children of teen mothers . . . avoid becoming teen parents themselves. And though the majority of child abusers were themselves abused as children, most abused children do not become abusers. Similarly, children of schizophrenics and children who grew up in refugee camps also tend to defy the odds. And many Iowa youths whose families lost their farms during the 1980s farm crisis became high achievers in school" (Shapiro, Friedman, Meyer, & Loftus, 1996, p. 66).

What came to be called "protective" factors for mental disorder were discovered by the early developmental psychopathologists who studied the offspring of psychiatrically ill parents (Garmezy, 1985; Masten & Garmezy, 1985; Rutter, 1979, 1985, 1987a). The surprising finding was that "high-risk" offspring often did not subsequently develop mental disorder, but rather often turned out surprisingly well.

High-risk studies typically "have noted the marked individual variations in people's responses to stress and adversity; some succumb, and some escape damage" (Rutter, 1990, p. 209). Adaptive high-risk offspring came to be called "resilient" children: those who maintain adaptive functioning in spite of serious risk hazards. Even among children exposed to the most horrible experiences, one can find a group who are unusually resilient, who do not experience later maladjustment. Resilience referred to "a track record of successful adaptation in the individual who has been exposed to biological risk factors or stressful life events [which] also implies an expectation of continued low susceptibility to future stressors" (Werner & Smith, 1992, p. 4). Rutter (1985) defined the closely related notion of protective factors as "those factors that modify, ameliorate or alter a person's response to some environmental hazard that predisposes to a maladaptive outcome" (1985, p. 600).

For these investigators, the intriguing question came to be: "Why do some children survive traumatic childhoods unscathed?" (Shapiro, Friedman, Meyer, & Loftus, 1996, p. 63). Or, as a recent National Institute of Mental Health (NIMH) workshop that focused on psychological "strengths" observed: "The new questions are: 'Who does not become ill, and what are their characteristics?' and 'What are the protective and ameliorating factors that may account for the absence of disorder, despite the presence of risk?'" (Weise, Blehar, Maser, & Akiskal, 1996, pp. 61–62). The slogan for this new way of thinking about mental disorder becomes: "Focus on survivors, not casualties. Don't abandon kids who fail, but learn from those who succeed" (Shapiro, Friedman, Meyer, & Loftus, 1996, p. 64).

Protective factors are not necessarily positive experiences. Sometimes exposure to stressful life events can promote coping. When dealt with successfully, these negative events can promote a sense of self-confidence or self-esteem, thereby serving as a protective factor. This "steeling" or "inoculation" effect is most likely to occur with moderate, rather than mild or severe, stressors (Hetherington, 1991; Rutter, 1987b).

In sum, resilience means the tendency to rebound or recoil, to spring back, or the power to recover (Garmezy, 1981); it means "successful adaptation despite challenging or threatening circumstances." It represents all those means discovered and used by an individual to maintain adjustment through counteracting the otherwise noxious effects imposed by unfortunate life experiences. It can describe three distinct phenomena: good outcomes despite high-risk status, sustained competence under threat, and recovery from trauma (Masten, Best, & Garmezy, 1990, p. 426).

Protective Factors

The first usage of the term *protective factor* targeted the personal and environmental factors that might be shown to characterize "resilient," psychologically "invulnerable" (Anthony, 1974), stress-resistant children. Protective factors were those dispositional attributes, biological predispositions, environmental conditions, and protective events that act to mitigate against early negative experiences (Garmezy, 1981). Protective factors were correlates of resilience signalling that processes had formed and were operating to buffer a child against (ameliorate the effects of) co-occurring or subsequent life adversities. Resilience conveyed the notion that individuals who have experienced protective factors can avoid undesirable outcomes, despite the presence of significant risk factors in their lives.

Like vulnerability (risk) factors, protective factors can reside either biologically or psychologically within the individual and result from interactions with a wide range of environmental factors found within the family, community, or larger societal institutions. Protective factors also tend to be the obverse or reverse of risk or vulnerability factors. Some protective factors (e.g., family cohesion and support) are "polar opposites" to corresponding risk or vulnerability factors (e.g., family discord and neglect). Most generally, protective factors refer to individual or environmental characteristics that predict or correlate with good mental health outcomes for humans at large.

Early theoretical explanations for the phenomenon of resilience (Rutter, 1985; Garmezy, 1983) emphasized the *interaction* of risk and protective factors to explain why some individuals may be spared and others may not. They speculated that protective factors operate in multiple ways to (a) decrease dysfunction directly, (b) prevent initial occurrence of a risk factor, (c) interact with a risk factor by buffering its effects, or (d) disrupt the mediational chain through which the risk factor operates to cause the dysfunction (Wheaton, 1985).

What do we know about the individual, familial, or environmental factors that are able to deflect the trajectory from risk to psychopathology, resulting in adaptive outcomes even in the presence of adversity? In what specific ways are some individuals able to "bounce back" from traumatic experiences while others have grave difficulty doing so?

Reviews of the literature on stress-resistant children (Garmezy, 1983, 1985; Masten & Garmezy, 1985; Rutter, 1979; Samerof & Seifer, 1990; Werner, 1992, 1993) have concluded that three broad sets of variables operate as protective factors: (a) *individual personality features* (e.g., a temperament agreeable to adults, self-esteem, autonomy, or general intellectual skills); (b) *family features* (e.g., family cohesion, absence of discord, or presence of a caring person such as a grandparent); and (c) *availability of external support* (e.g., persons or systems that encourage and support a child's coping efforts; or a social agency, school, or church that offers the child support).

For example, during childhood an important personality characteristic involves a child's being easygoing and responsive, behaviors which apparently call forth the best from parents and from peers, teachers, and other adults. Also, above-average intelligence may allow a child not only to do well in school but to develop problem-solving skills and a sense of psychological differentiation from the family or community; these abilities, in turn, seem to foster growth within the child of the autonomy and independence necessary for optimal adult functioning.

Throughout childhood, adolescence, and adulthood, important buffering effects seem to result from those personality traits that affect a person's ability to cope with stress. Coping is a process that involves cognitive and behavioral efforts to manage the demands on one's resources (Lazarus, 1991). Certain coping strategies seem to serve as protective factors (e.g., active behavioral and cognitive approaches as opposed to emotion-focused or avoidance strategies). Kobasa (1979, 1982) emphasized the personal trait of "hardiness" which renders a person relatively resistant to the stresses, adversities, and turbulence of life changes. Hardiness consists of such characteristics as a sense of commitment to a life goal, positive responses to challenge, and an internal locus of control (a perception that one is in control of one's destiny).

Family factors found likely to be protective include variables such as smaller family structure (e.g., not more than four children with spacing of more than two years between each pair), having a close relationship with a parent who is responsive and accepting, enjoying good sibling relationships, and adequate parental rule-setting.

Examples of protective community factors include intimate and supportive relationships outside the family (e.g., with peers and significant other adults), available external support systems (e.g., church, youth groups, good primary and secondary schools, and recreational activities)—all of which build competence and provide success. Substantial evidence can be found that persons with effective "social support" systems, both individuals and groups, have decreased rates and severity of mental disorder in the face of stressors (Brown & Harris, 1978; Flaherty, Gaviria, Black, Altman, & Mitchell, 1983).

Protective factors may not always consist of positive experiences. Some resilient children seem to develop out of successive mastery of earlier stressful difficulties in living. Exposure to stressful events which a person deals with successfully clearly can promote a sense of self-confidence or self-esteem. Encounters with stressors, even substantial ones, paradoxically can promote coping skills. This "steeling" or "inoculation" effect is most likely to occur with moderate to severe (in contrast to mild or extraordinarily extreme) stressors (Hetherington, 1991; Rutter, 1987b).

One intriguing explanation offered for development of resiliency during childhood takes an interpersonal form (Radke-Yarrow & Sherman, 1990, pp. 112–113). These authors highlighted the *match* or *fit* present between an inborn psychological or physical quality (e.g., health and sturdiness, quiet–happy temperament, or engaging–curious intellect) present in one sibling within a family and a "core need" in one or both parents. The child's quality becomes a source of positive regard and esteem in the child's eyes while simultaneously fulfilling the parent's need. As a result, this special child, in contrast to his or her siblings, receives the maximum social–emotional resources that the parents are capable of providing. Simultaneously, the same qualities in the child so prized by the parents become generalized and accepted outside the family as well.

Protective factors are biological, psychological, or sociocultural conditions or experiences that increase people's resistance to vulnerability factors and/or to subsequent occurrence of mental disorder. Protective factors influence a person's coping responses to environmental stressors, making it less likely that the person will experience the adverse consequences of the stressors (Rolf, Masten, Cicchetti, Nuechterlein, & Weintraub, 1990; Rutter, 1985).

A key characteristic of a person's life is not the absence or avoidance of aversive life events and experiences; stressors, at least to some extent, are inevitable. Rather, the key task in human living involves acquiring the capacity to protect the self through learning to cope with the stressful events in a way that avoids their potentially destructive impacts.

HOW RISK AND PROTECTIVE FACTORS INTERACT

It should be abundantly apparent by now that, in the case of mental disorders, a wide range of vulnerability (risk) and protective factors is operative. These factors do not operate in isolation; rather one finds a dynamic interaction among them that undergoes alteration and change over an individual's life span.

Several models have been proposed to explain how this dynamic interaction might work (Garmezy, Masten, & Tellegen, 1984). In the *compensatory* model, risk factors (including genetic vulnerability and stressful life events) combine additively and potentiate each other. The model emphasizes that what impairs development and promotes mental disorder is the aggregation of risk factors (with varying individual weights), rather than presence of any single factor. One study of intellectual development found that children reared in families with seven or more risk factors scored thirty IQ points below children from families having no risk factors.

In the *challenge* model, a curvilinear relationship exists in which stress as a risk factor (so long as it is not excessive) can actually enhance developmental competence—stress serves an "inoculation" effect. In line with the challenge model, successive (moderately challenging) stressful experiences can strengthen coping capacities.

The *protective* model suggests that the effect of protective factors is to modulate or buffer the impact of risk factors. In contrast to the challenge model, the protective model does not specify an actual enhancement of competence, rather a simple but crucial buffering of any negative impact. The modulation it indicates occurs, for instance, through improvements in coping, adaptation, and competence building.

The *transactional* model (Samerof, 1987) emphasizes ongoing reciprocal interactions between the child and the environment. Interactions of the child's personal attributes with risk and protective factors in the family, school, and community environments are not linear, but are interwoven and bidirectional. For example, infants change the nature of their parents' responses to them, while parents in turn produce impacts on their children; thus continues the interpersonal choreography. Contemporary interpersonal theory (Kiesler, 1996) adds that, as they grow older, children carry the patterns of interaction and expectation learned in the family environment into their relationships with other adults and peers. These interactions mold their adult relationships, and their patterns are molded by them, shaping the developmental trajectory in positive or negative directions.

Other authors observe that the interaction of risk and protective factors reflects a balance between the power of the individual and the power of the social and physical environment. A balance is necessary throughout life, although different factors vary in importance at different developmental stages. For example, constitutional factors are more important during infancy and childhood; social and peer factors are more important during adolescence. Beginning with infancy and continuing throughout life, adaptation appears in large part to be a function of the individual's ability to elicit predominantly satisfactory responses from others in his or her environment.

INTERVENTIONS THAT TARGET RISK AND PROTECTIVE FACTORS: PREVENTION OF MENTAL DISORDER

Use of the Risk Model in Preventive Interventions

Previous chapters have demonstrated that mental disorders have a complex causal chain in which no particular cause is regarded as "sufficient" or as "necessary and sufficient." A particular mental disorder may be preventable at various points throughout childhood and adolescence, indeed at any time before the point of "onset" (the moment when an individual meets full criteria for diagnosis of a particular mental disorder).

Reduction in occurrence (prevention) of new cases of mental disorders needs to be accomplished within the framework of a risk reduction model in which the desired outcomes are a decrease in risk factors and/or an increase in protective factors. Vulnerability factors that have high attributable risk for a specific disorder (or factors having high attributable risk for multiple disorders) are the prime targets for preventive interventions.

A recent NIMH review (National Institute of Mental Health Prevention Research Steering Committee, 1994; National Institute of Mental Health Committee on Prevention Research, 1995; Reiss & Price, 1996), based on a careful review of available developmental research, came to the following conclusions. (1) For many mental disorders, several risk factors are necessary. For example, for drug abuse, risk factors include genetic factors, parenting and other family processes, peer influences, school experiences, and community characteristics. (2) The greater the number of risk factors to which an individual is exposed, the greater is the likelihood the person will develop a more serious mental disorder. (3) Some identifiable risk factors are both general and serious: they have a high likelihood of leading to a number of different mental disorders. For example, marital discord is associated both with conduct disorder in children and with depression in adult women.

Recently, the Committee on Prevention of Mental Disorders of the Institute of Medicine (Mrazek & Haggerty, 1994) reviewed empirical evidence for risk and protective factors for five mental disorders (cf. also Grizenko & Fisher, 1992). The reader can consult the following information for very concrete examples of the kind of "contributory" causes for mental disorders that research is beginning to unveil.

ALZHEIMER'S DISEASE

Biological Risk Factors
1. Genetic vulnerability
2. History of head trauma
3. Medical risk factors, including thyroid disorders
4. Maternal age (unusually young or unusually old) at time of birth

Psychological Risk and Protective Factors
Risk
1. Educational level (less education)
2. Environmental triggers (viruses or environmental toxins)

Protective
1. Educational level (more education)

2. Smoking (inverse correlation: those who smoked more were less likely to have AD)

SCHIZOPHRENIA

Biological Risk Factors

1. Genetic vulnerability
2. Pregnancy (second prenatal trimester insult) and excess obstetrical complications (related to infant anoxia during birth)
3. Winter births
4. Viral exposure
5. Biological "markers": (a) smooth pursuit eye tracking deficits, (b) attentional deficits, (c) neurointegrative defects, (d) electrodermal hyperresponsivity, and (e) increased cerebral ventricular size

Psychological Risk Factors

Risk

1. Low socioeconomic status or downward mobility
2. Disturbed family environment and family communicative problems
3. Serious behavioral and emotional problems in childhood (e.g., poor impulse control and aggression; or social withdrawal or awkwardness and diminished emotional expression)
4. Social dysfunction or incompetence (premorbid level of social incompetence is predictive)
5. Substance abuse (e.g., stimulants, PCP—which mimic schizophrenia)

ALCOHOL ABUSE AND DEPENDENCE

Biological Risk Factors

1. Genetic vulnerability
2. Biological "markers": (a) electrophysiological (low P3 brain wave amplitude, or EEG synchrony), and (b) biochemical (lower stimulated adenylyl cyclase activity, lower MAO activity in type II alcohol abuse cases)
3. Decreased sensitivity to the physiological effects of alcohol
4. Cognitive impairments (lower verbal IQ, reading comprehension, and abstract reasoning)

Psychological Risk and Protective Factors

Risk

1. Initiating frequent use of alcohol in early adolescence
2. Antisocial behavior during childhood

3. Less productivity in high school, greater truancy, and greater incidence of dropping out

4. Children rated as both shy and aggressive

5. High levels of novelty seeking together with low levels of survival dependence and harm avoidance

6. Community use patterns

7. Peer group behavior

8. Low socioeconomic status and neighborhood disorganization

Protective

1. Membership in structured, goal-directed peer groups that do not abuse alcohol (a group norm that does not expect or approve of substance use)

2. Strong attachment or bond between parent (especially father) and adolescent

UNIPOLAR MOOD DISORDERS (MAJOR DEPRESSION)

Biological Risk Factors

1. Genetic vulnerability

2. Preceding medical disorders (e.g., severe infections, tumors, endocrine conditions, metabolic disorders) and use of certain medications (e.g., antihypertensive agents, oral contraceptives, various anticonvulsives)

3. Childhood learning difficulties (especially dyslexia)

Psychological Risk and Protective Factors

Risk

1. Presence of severe and traumatic events in an individual's life (e.g., loss of job; death of a spouse, child, or parent; divorce; child abuse; severe traumatic events: violent crime, natural disaster, sexual assault)

2. A major loss (e.g., of parent) in childhood, especially when it results in loss of care in childhood

3. In adolescent women, an accumulation of stresses at a time of transition (e.g., puberty, new school, breakup of family)

4. Being female

5. Being separated or divorced

6. Not having paid employment or a job with prestige

7. In women especially, absence of a close confiding relationship in adulthood

Protective

1. Presence of close, intimate, supportive relationships

2. Good intelligence

3. Easy temperament

4. Presence of a supportive adult

CONDUCT DISORDER

Biological Risk Factors

1. Genetic vulnerability
2. Physiological abnormalities (e.g., ANS pattern of low heart rate, decreased amplitude and slow recovery of skin conductance, and slow EEG wave activity)—providing a biological basis for the reduced anxiety and impaired passive avoidance following punishment in antisocial individuals
3. Being male
4. Starting off life with a difficult to manage (in contrast to easy) temperament
5. Having as a child attention deficit hyperactivity disorder (ADHD)
6. Low intelligence and language dysfunction (poor language comprehension) combined with impulsivity and aggressiveness
7. As a child, having chronic ill health combined with CNS damage (a functional physical limitation or disability)

Psychological Risk and Protective Factors

Risk

1. Precursor symptoms in a child (e.g., a combination of aggression and shyness; aggressiveness together with peer rejection)
2. Early substance abuse
3. Having criminal and alcoholic parents
4. Maternal antisocial personality
5. Marital discord in family in combination with maternal depression
6. Harsh, erratic, and abusive forms of discipline
7. Socioeconomic disadvantage: poverty, overcrowding, poor housing
8. Living in highly congested urban areas, in neighborhoods having social disintegration, high rates of social problems (e.g., high rates of adult crime, substance abuse, infant mortality, low birthweight, child maltreatment)
9. An accumulation of adverse environmental conditions (the higher the number, the higher the risk)

Protective

1. Shyness without aggression
2. Good intelligence
3. Easy temperament
4. An ability to get along with parents, adults, teachers, and peers
5. Being competent in nonschool skill areas
6. Having a good relationship with one adult (parent or other important adult)
7. A good school, especially high school (Mrazek & Haggerty, 1994, pp. 127–214).

In constructing preventive interventions, one needs to keep in mind that various risk factors may operate differently and be modifiable to varying degrees at different periods or stages in a person's life. In the case where a risk factor has a uniquely important input at one phase of an individual's development (e.g., in infancy or during adolescence), interventions need to be applied during the corresponding time period. The Institute of Medicine's Committee on Prevention of Mental Disorders (Mrazek & Haggerty, 1994) also reviewed preventive interventive strategies designed to be responsive to "developmental tasks" that characterize six stages of the life span. The following provides a summary of these stages and corresponding strategies.

INFANCY

Risk Factors
1. Preventible infections, disease, or injuries that can cause brain damage, neurodevelopmental disorders, or behavioral disorders
2. Problems of parent–infant attachment or parenting
3. Deprivation of cognitive and language stimulation
4. Economic deprivation (unemployment, deteriorating neighborhoods, or increased neighborhood violence)
5. Child maltreatment
6. Developmental impairments (e.g., underweight births)
7. Lack of access to medical care

Protective Factors
1. Robust health
2. "Good-enough" parenting
3. Adequate nutrition and shelter

Preventive Intervention Strategies
1. High-quality prenatal and perinatal care; well-baby health care
2. Childhood immunization
3. Regular home visitation
4. Parenting education
5. Promotion of healthy parent–infant interaction
6. Appropriate cognitive and language stimulation
7. Family support
8. Center-based infant day care

EARLY CHILDHOOD

Examples of Important Developmental Tasks
1. Acquisition of language skills to prepare the child to read and write
2. The development of impulse control

Risk Factors (Related to developmental tasks, as well as to the development of mental and behavior problems)
1. Economic deprivation
2. Poor family management practices
3. Cognitive or developmental delays
4. School failure
5. Early behavioral problems

Protective Factors
(None listed)

Preventive Intervention Strategies
1. Center-based early childhood education (programs designed to enhance social competence and cognitive development)
2. Home visitation to provide a variety of support and educational services
3. Parenting training in caregiving and effective behavior management skills
4. Family survival-focused support services
5. Policy initiatives that address issues of child safety, health, and education

ELEMENTARY SCHOOL AGE (AGES 5–12)

Examples of Important Developmental Tasks
1. Learning to read and perform academic tasks at grade level
2. Develop social competence: learning to interact in ways that gain social approval from peers

Risk Factors
1. Inability to perform academic tasks at grade level
2. Social incompetence
3. Early behavior problems: impulsivity and/or aggressive behavior
4. Poor parenting practices (e.g., lax supervision, an absence of parental demands, lack of parental interest or affection, or inadequate contact)
5. High levels of conflict in the family
6. Low degree of bonding between children and parents

Protective Factors
(None listed)

Preventive Intervention Strategies

1. Enhancement of children's social competence
2. Enhancement of children's academic achievement
3. Crisis intervention services for families whose children are at risk for out-of-home placement
4. Enhancing parenting skills and family functioning

ADOLESCENCE

Examples of Important Developmental Tasks

1. Establishing a satisfying gender identity
2. Developing friendly and intimate relationships with same-sex and opposite-sex peers
3. Initiating discovery of career paths and life plans

Risk Factors

1. Early initiation of delinquent behavior
2. Early initiation of substance use

Protective Factors

(None listed)

Preventive Intervention Strategies

1. Enhancing academic achievement and school behavior
2. Enhancing social competence
3. Providing social influence resistance training and promoting norms against drug use
4. Family-focused training in behavior management and communication skills

ADULTHOOD

Examples of Important Developmental Tasks

1. Establishing and maintaining committed relationships
2. Successful childbearing and effective parenting
3. Assuming and maintaining occupational roles

Risk Factors (Correspond closely to these developmental tasks— especially among those with psychosocial or biological vulnerabilities)

1. Marital conflict and divorce
2. Unsupported childbirth and child rearing
3. Stressful work roles and occupations

4. Involuntary job loss
5. Chronic poverty
6. Racial and other discrimination

Protective Factors

1. Problem-solving skills
2. Availability of responsive social and medical services
3. Social, material, and emotional support from friends, family, and others (work supervisors, health personnel, teachers, or spouses)
4. A variety of social skills: the ability to cope with one's emotions, to control the demands of work and mobilize supportive coworkers, to use job seeking skills, and to nurture spouse and family support

Preventive Intervention Strategies

1. Programs for development, maintenance, and enhancement of marital relationships
2. Programs for coping with separation and divorce
3. Programs aimed at the special stresses of childbearing and child rearing (e.g., enhancing personal development of new mothers)
4. Programs targeting occupational stress, job loss, and reemployment
5. Programs to prevent depressive disorders among adults at risk because of poverty and minority status
6. Programs designed to support adult children who provide care for ill parents

OLD AGE

Examples of Important Developmental Tasks

1. Maintaining meaningful roles and finding new social roles (such as grandparenting, new activities, and interests)
2. Surviving the empty nest
3. Retirement
4. Coping with own and others' illness (especially severe and incapacitating illness) and death
5. Caring

Risk Factors

1. Relationship loss and bereavement
2. Chronic illness and caregiver burden
3. Social isolation
4. Loss of meaningful social roles

Protective Factors

1. Social support in a wide variety of forms: family, peers, informal relation-

ships, more formal support groups, responsive health and social services (e.g., respite care), and opportunities for new productive social roles

Preventive Intervention Strategies

1. Programs to relieve caregiver burden
2. Programs aimed at enhancement of coping with widowhood and bereavement (e.g., mutual-help groups for widowed persons) (Mrazek & Haggerty, 1994, pp. 215–313).

In addition to the absolute prevention of new cases, appropriate interventive aims might be to delay the onset of mental disorder and reduce new cases in the short term. For both mental and physical disorders, the developing abnormal process is reflected in the rate at which individuals cross a variety of "thresholds," including the final threshold that precipitates onset of disorder. These thresholds may be below, or above, a level that would justify diagnosis of the disorder.

At present we do not have good knowledge of the causes that influence either initiation, prolongation, or exacerbation of various mental disorders. Research needs to identify premorbid signs and symptoms (and their age of first occurrence) that are below the criterion level for diagnosis of particular mental disorders. This would permit identification of individuals at heightened risk for developing the full-blown disorder who could become targets of indicated preventive interventions. Even if, despite interventive efforts, individual cases still eventually develop a DSM disorder, the prior preventive intervention may still have the salutary effect of reducing the duration and/or severity of the disorder.

Specific knowledge about the predisposing biopsychosocial risk and protective factors that converge and interact at distinct developmental stages to determine the onset of any mental disorder is critical for decisions about the nature and targets of any preventive intervention strategy. This point is illustrated in detail with the examples previously discussed.

Preventive Interventions for Mental Disorders

The Institute of Medicine's Committee on Prevention of Mental Disorders (Mrazek & Haggerty, 1994) called on the nation to mount a significant program to prevent the highly prevalent mental disorders which affect, sometime during their lives, as many as one-third of our population.

Traditional *therapeutic* interventions for patients diagnosed with a particular mental disorder attempt to alleviate or eliminate an occurrence (episode), or delay recurrence, of that disorder—a disorder, unfortunately, that already has occurred. In contrast, *preventive* interventions seek to thwart, or at least delay, subsequent onset of a mental disorder among persons who are not presently maladjusted. These interventions are developed from knowledge of vulnerability (risk) and protective factors that influence the onset, course, and/or outcome of mental disorders.

Efforts toward prevention of mental disorders result from interdisciplinary applications of psychopathology theory and research. Most current preventive researchers were trained in their primary discipline and then learned their research skills as apprentices on an interdisciplinary preventive research team. In addition to respective parochial curricula, training in preventive intervention research requires additional education and experience in (a) the design of interventions to prevent mental illness, and (b) the analyses of the efficacy and effectiveness of specific preventive interventions. This training most typically requires direct experience at established institutions or centers carrying out prevention studies.

From a mental health perspective, preventive interventions are based on the belief that serious psychological problems can be avoided by timely action *before* the onset of a diagnosable disorder. The original and most popular classification of disease prevention was proposed in 1957 by the Commission on Chronic Illness. *Primary* prevention seeks to decrease the incidence (number of new cases) of a disorder or illness. *Secondary* prevention seeks to lower the prevalence (the number of established cases) of a disorder or illness in the population. *Tertiary* prevention seeks to decrease the amount of disability associated with an existing disorder or illness. Vulnerability and protective factors are relevant to all three types of prevention. Of course, the most salutary potential effects would occur with primary prevention efforts.

In 1994, because of theoretic and practical difficulties that accompanied use of this classification, the Committee on Prevention of Mental Disorders of the Institute of Medicine (Mrazek & Haggerty, 1994) proposed that the term *prevention* be reserved for only those interventions that occur before the initial onset of the disorder. Their system also incorporated an adaptation of Gordon's (1983) tripartite system that was proposed earlier for physical disease prevention. Gordon's system consisted of three categories of preventive measures, all three of which were to be applied to persons not yet disordered or diseased— that is, to pre-onset individuals in the "primary prevention" category of the previous classification. Gordon proposed that prevention research refer only to preventive interventions that could be further classified into "universal," "selective," or "indicated" types.

Universal preventive interventions are desirable for everybody in the eligible population. In this category are those interventions that can be advocated confidently for the general public and for all members of specific eligible groups (e.g., pregnant women, children, or the elderly). Examples include maintenance of an adequate diet, use of seat belts, prevention of smoking, many forms of immunization, and prenatal care. Universal interventions (e.g., childhood immunization, prenatal care, and prevention of smoking) are advantageous when their cost per individual is low, when the intervention is effective and acceptable to the population, and when associated risk is low.

Selective preventive interventions for mental disorders are designed for individuals who are members of a subgroup of the population (e.g., groups different in age, gender, occupation, or family history) whose risk of becoming ill is significantly higher than average. Risk groups may be identified on the basis of biological, psychological, or social risk factors that are known to be associated with the onset of a particular mental disorder (e.g., children of parents with schizophrenia, girls versus boys, or abused children). Examples of selective interventions are home visitation and infant day care for low birthweight children, support groups for elderly widows, annual mammograms for women with a positive family history of breast cancer, and PSA tests for men over fifty-five years of age. Selective interventions are most appropriate when they do not exceed a moderate level of cost and when negative effects are minimal or nonexistent.

Finally, *indicated* preventive interventions for mental disorders are designed for persons who, upon examination (e.g., screening), are found to manifest a risk factor, condition or abnormality that identifies them individually as being at high risk for the future development of a disease. Interventions are targeted to high-risk individuals who are identified as having detectable signs or symptoms foreshadowing mental disorder (e.g., biological or psychological "markers" indicating predisposition for mental disorder), yet who do not meet DSM diagnostic criteria at the current time. Examples are children who score positive for early REM onset during sleep (a potential marker for major depression), or for impaired smooth-pursuit eye movements (schizophrenia); or in the case of medical disorders, young adults who smoke cigarettes (lung cancer), or men with PSA results in the positive range (prostate cancer). Examples of indicated interventions are parent training for children identified at risk for schizophrenia who also show poor premorbid interpersonal histories and have aggressive behavioral problems; or pharmacotherapy for individuals with the risk factor of hypertension. These interventions typically are not inexpensive; they may nevertheless be indicated and justifiable. Indicated preventive interventions put to greatest use whatever evidence is available regarding important vulnerability and protective factors for a particular mental disorder.

All in all, preventive intervention programs can be successfully implemented at all three levels (universal, selective, and indicated)

and can be initiated throughout the life span. All three forms of preventive efforts require validated findings regarding important vulnerability and risk factors. The overall aim of the three types of preventive
intervention is the reduction of the occurrence of new cases.

The Institute of Medicine's Committee of the Prevention of Mental
Disorders concluded, *"The concept of risk reduction, including the strength-
ening of protective factors, should be used as the best available theoretical model
for guiding interventions to prevent the onset of mental disorders"* (Mrazek &
Haggerty, 1994, p. 479; emphasis added). The committee emphasized further that, even if the interventions fail to prevent a disorder, they may
have some effect on reducing the severity or duration of the disorder. For
example, in the case of schizophrenia, delay in treating the early stages of
the disorder can lead to maladaptive coping strategies by families and
patients, the appearance of negative symptoms, refractoriness to drug
therapy, social withdrawal, and greater chronicity. Further, when one
disorder regularly leads to a second, prevention of the first disorder is
a plausible preventive strategy for the second.

The committee also concluded that *priority should be given to research
that illuminates the interaction of biological and psychosocial risk and protective factors, rather than restricting emphasis to either biological or
psychosocial factors.*

MULTICAUSES OF MENTAL DISORDERS:
CONCLUSIONS ABOUT RISK AND PROTECTIVE FACTORS

Though risk factors increase the likelihood of negative psychiatric
outcomes, the potentially adverse influences can be mitigated if certain protective factors are available to the individual and are effectively utilized. *Mental health outcomes depend on the interactions of risk
and protective factors within the child, the family, and the wider environment.*
The nature, timing, severity, and duration of particular risk factors—especially their accumulation as a distinctive set—are key variables in
determining mental health outcomes.

Risk research findings suggest the following conclusions. (1) Particular mental disorders seem to be associated with multiple risk and
protective factors—rather than being identified with a single risk or
protective factor. Risk factors often co-occur, and multiple risk factors
often prove to be more predictive than single risk factors. Therefore,
in seeking to understand particular mental disorders, it makes sense
to study a range of risk factors and their interactions, rather than concentrate solely on individual factors. (2) Risk and protective factors
tend to be generic, in the sense that the same factors seem to influence
development of many different mental disorders. A particular risk or

protective factor rarely is specific to a single disorder, but instead shows influence across a range of mental disorders. (3) Exposure to risk or protective factors tends to have cumulative effects. The presence of multiple vulnerability factors bodes well for the development of disorder; the presence of multiple protective factors reduces its likelihood. (4) Protective or risk factors may not show their effects at all until that time when a person is faced with a stressor. Absent precipitating stressors, a set of risk and protective factors often remains hidden. (5) Some risk and protective factors influence dysfunction only at specific periods of development (at times when specific developmental tasks are indicated); others tend to influence dysfunction continually across long periods of the life span.

Generic risk factors that predispose toward mental disorder in the population at large may lend themselves to "universal" preventive interventions consonant with broad community mental health efforts that focus on public education and social welfare. Risk factors specific to a particular group of people (e.g., children suffering the death of one or both parents) can be addressed in "selective" preventive interventions. Identified individuals with early behavioral symptoms or markers (e.g., children with short latencies to onset of dream-related sleep, in the case of depressive disorders) are potential recipients of "indicated" preventive interventions. Risk reduction and resilience enhancement seem to be highly promising bases for conceptualizing prevention of mental disorders.

CONCLUSION

Research and theory in developmental psychopathology, psychiatric epidemiology, and mental disorder prevention have identified and studied the range of vulnerability (risk) and protective factors that play important effects in the onset, course, and outcome of various mental disorders. What their findings demonstrate is that no valid theory of mental disorder can ignore any of the important genetic–biological, psychological, family, sociocultural, and other environmental factors that can serve both vulnerability or protective influences.

In light of the evidence reviewed in earlier chapters, it is obvious that various vulnerability and protective factors are neither "sufficient" nor "necessary and sufficient" causes of mental disorder. At best they are "necessary," but most typically are "contributory," causes of mental disorders. These important vulnerability and protective factors also are distal causes that initiate their influence at various stages of preadult development ranging from conception, infancy, and childhood, to adolescence.

REFERENCES

Achenbach, T. M. (1974/1982). *Developmental psychopathology.* New York: Wiley.

American Psychological Society. (1996, February 1). Human Capital Initiative (HCI) Report No. 3. *APS Observer* (special issue). Washington, DC: Author.

Anthony, E. J. (1974). The syndrome of the psychologically invulnerable child. In E. J. Anthony & C. Koupernik (Eds.), *The child in his family: Vol. III. Children at psychiatric risk* (pp. 529–544). New York: Wiley.

Bronfenbrenner, U., & Ceci, S. J. (1994). Nature–nurture reconceptualized in developmental perspective: A bioecological model. *Psychological Review, 101,* 568–586.

Brown, G. W., & Harris, T. O. (1978). *The social origins of depression: A study of psychiatric disorder in women.* New York: Free Press.

Cicchetti, D. (Ed.). (1984). Developmental psychopathology (special issue). *Child Development, 55,* 1–314.

Cicchetti, D. (Ed.). (1989). *Rochester symposium on developmental psychopathology: Vol. 1. The emergence of a discipline.* Hillsdale, NJ: Erlbaum.

Cicchetti, D., & Cohen, D. J. (Eds.). (1995a). *Developmental psychopathology: Volume I. Theory and method.* New York: Wiley.

Cicchetti, D., & Cohen, D. J. (Eds.). (1995b). *Developmental psychopathology: Volume II. Risk, disorder, and adaptation.* New York: Wiley.

Coie, J. D., Watt, N. F., West, S. G., Hawkins, J. D., Asarnow, J. R., Markman, H. J., Ramey, S. L., Shure, M. B., & Long, B. (1993). The science of prevention: A conceptual framework and some directions for a national research program. *American Psychologist, 48,* 1013–1022.

Eisenberg, N. (Ed.). (1987). *Contemporary topics in devlopmental psychology.* New York: Wiley.

Essau, C. A., & Petermann, F. (Eds.). (1998). *Developmental psychopathology: Epidemiology, diagnostics, and treatment.* New York: Harwood Academic.

Flaherty, J. A., Gaviria, F. M., Black, E. M., Altman, E., & Mitchell, T. (1983). The role of social support in the functioning of patients with unipolar depression. *American Journal of Psychiatry, 140,* 473–476.

Garmezy, N. (1974a). Children at risk: The search for antecedents of schizophrenia: I. Conceptual models and research methods. *Schizophrenia Bulletin, 8,* 14–90.

Garmezy, N. (1974b). Children at risk: The search for antecedents of schizophrenia: II. Ongoing research programs, issues and interventions. *Schizophrenia Bulletin, 9,* 55–125.

Garmezy, N. (1981). Children under stress: Perspectives on antecedents and correlates of vulnerability and resistance to psychopathology. In A. I. Rabin, J. Aronoff, A. M. Barclay, & R. A. Zucker (Eds.), *Further explorations in personality* (pp. 196–269). New York: Wiley.

Garmezy, N. (1983). Stressors in childhood. In N. Garmezy & M. Rutter (Eds.), *Stress, coping and development in children* (pp. 43–84). New York: McGraw-Hill.

Garmezy, N. (1985). Stress-resistant children: The search for protective factors. In J. E. Stevenson (Ed.), Special series: Recent research in developmental psychopathology (pp. 213–233). *Journal of Child Psychology and Psychiatry, 4,* (Book supplement).

Garmezy, N., Masten, A. S., & Tellegen, A. (1984). The study of stress and competence in children. *Child Development, 55,* 97–111.

Gordon, R. (1983). An operational classification of disease prevention. *Public Health Reports, 98,* 107–109.

Gotlib, I. H., & Avison, W. R. (1993). Children at risk for psychopathology. In C. G. Costello (Ed.), *Basic issues in psychopathology* (pp. 271–319).

Grizenko, N., & Fisher, C. (1992). Review of studies of risk and protective factors for psychopathology in children. *Canadian Journal of Psychiatry, 37,* 711–721.

Hawkins, J. D., Catalano, R. F., & Miller, J. Y. (1992). Risk and protective factors for alcohol and other drug problems in adolescence and early adulthood: Implications for substance abuse prevention. *Psychological Bulletin, 112,* 64–105.

Heller, K. (1996). Coming of age of prevention sciences: Comments on the 1994 National Institute of Mental Health—Institute of Medicine Prevention Reports. *American Psychologist, 51,* 1123–1127.

Hetherington, E. M. (1991). The role of individual differences and family relationships in children's coping with divorce and remarriage. In P. A. Cowan & E. M. Hetherington (Eds.), *Family transitions* (pp. 165–194). Hillsdale, NJ: Erlbaum.

Jenkins, C. D. (1988). Epidemiology of cardiovascular diseases. *Journal of Consulting and Clinical Psychology, 56,* 324–332.

Kannel, W. B. (1990). Contribution of the Framingham study to preventive cardiology. *Journal of the American College of Cardiology, 15,* 206–211.

Katschnig, H. (1991). Vulnerability models for schizophrenia: Discussion. In H. Hafner & W. F. Gattaz (Eds.), *Search for the causes of schizophrenia* (Vol. II, pp. 221–226). New York: Springer-Verlag.

Kiesler, D. J. (1996). *Contemporary interpersonal theory and research: Personality, psychopathology, and psychotherapy.* New York: Wiley.

Kobasa, S. C. (1979). Stressful life events, personality, and health: An inquiry into hardiness. *Journal of Personality and Social Psychology, 37,* 1–11.

Kobasa, S. C. (1982). The hardy personality: Toward a social psychology of stress and health. In G. Sanders & J. Suls (Eds.), *Social psychology of health and illness* (pp. 3–32). Hillsdale, NJ: Erlbaum.

Lazarus, R. S. (1991). Psychological stress in the workplace. *Journal of Social Behavior and Personality, 6,* 1–13.

Lewis, R. J., Dlugokinski, E. L., Caputo, L. M., & Griffin, R. B. (1988). Children at risk for emotional disorder: Risk and resource dimensions. *Clinical Psychology Review, 8,* 417–440.

Lewis, M., & Miller, S. (Eds.). (1990). *Handbook of developmental psychopathology.* New York: Plenum.

Luthar, S. S., Burack, J. A., Cicchetti, D., & Weisz, J. R. (Eds.). (1997). *Developmental psychopathology: Perspectives on adjustment, risk, and disorder.* New York: Cambridge University Press.

Masten, A. S., Best, K., & Garmezy, N. (1990). Resilience and development: Contributions from the study of children who overcome adversity. *Developmental Psychopathology, 2,* 425–444.

Masten, A. S., & Garmezy, N. (1985). Risk, vulnerability, and protective factors in developmental psychopathology. In B. B. Lahey & A. E. Kazdin (Eds.), *Advances in clinical child psychology* (Vol. 8, pp. 1–52). New York: Plenum.

Mednick, S. A., & McNeil, T. F. (1968). Current methodology in research on the etiology of schizophrenia: Serious difficulties which suggest the use of the high-risk group method. *Psychological Bulletin, 70,* 681–693.

Meehl, P. E. (1962). Schizotaxia, schizotypy, schizophrenia. *American Psychologist, 17,* 827–838.

Meehl, P. E. (1989). Schizotaxia revisited. *Archives of General Psychiatry, 46,* 935–944.

Meehl, P. E. (1990). Toward an integrated theory of schizotaxia, schizotypy, and schizophrenia. *Journal of Personality Disorders, 4,* 1–99.

Mrazek, P. J., & Haggerty, R. J. (Eds.). (1994). *Reducing risks for mental disorders: Frontiers for preventive intervention research.* Washington, DC: National Academy Press.

National Institute of Mental Health Committee on Prevention Research. (1995, May 15). *A plan for prevention research for the National Institute of Mental Health.* A report to the National Advisory Mental Health Council. Washington, DC: Author.

National Institute of Mental Health Prevention Research Steering Committee. (1994). *The prevention of mental disorders: A national research agenda.* Washington, DC: Author.

Offord, D. R., Boyle, M. H., & Racine, Y. (1989). Ontario child and health study: Correlates of disorder. *Journal of the American Academy of Child and Adolescent Psychiatry, 28,* 856–860.

Radke-Yarrow, M., & Sherman, T. (1990). Hard growing: Children who survive. In J. Rolf, A. S. Masten, D. Cicchetti, K. H. Nuechterlein, & S. Weintraub (Eds.), *Risk and protective factors in the development of psychopathology* (pp. 77–119). New York: Cambridge University Press.

Reiss, D., & Price, R. H. (1996). National research agenda for prevention research: The National Institute of Mental Health report. *American Psychologist, 51,* 1109–1122.

Robins, L. N., & Regier, D. A. (1991). *Psychiatric disorders in America: The Epidemiologic Catchment Area Study.* New York: Free Press.

Rolf, J., Masten, A. S., Cicchetti, D., Nuechterlein, K. H., & Weintraub, S. (Eds.). (1990). *Risk and protective factors in the development of psychopathology.* New York: Cambridge University Press.

Rutter, M. (1979). Protective factors in children's responses to stress and disadvantage. In M. W. Kent & J. E. Rolf (Eds.), *Primary prevention in psychopathology: Vol. 3. Social competence in children* (pp. 49–74). Hanover, NH: University Press of New England.

Rutter, M. (1985). Resilience in the face of adversity: Protective factors and resistance to psychiatric disorder. *British Journal of Psychiatry, 147,* 598–611.

Rutter, M. (1987a). Psychosocial resilience and protective mechanisms. *American Journal of Orthopsychiatry, 51,* 316–331.

Rutter, M. (1987b). Continuities and discontinuities from infancy. In J. Osofsky (Ed.), *Handbook of infant development* (2d ed., pp. 1256–1296). New York: Wiley.

Rutter, M. (1989). Pathways from childhood to adult life. *Journal of Child Psychology and Psychiatry, 30,* 23–51.

Rutter, M. (1990). Psychosocial resilience and protective mechanisms. In J. Rolf, A. S. Masten, D. Cicchetti, K. H. Nuechterlein, & S. Weintraub (Eds.), *Risk and protective factors in the development of psychopathology* (pp. 181–214). New York: Cambridge University Press.

Rutter, M., & Garmezy, N. (1983). Developmental psychopathology. In E. M. Hetherington (Ed.), *Carmichael's manual of child psychology: Vol. 4. Social and personality development* (pp. 775–911). New York: Wiley.

Rutter, M., & Quinton, D. (1977). Psychiatric disorder: Ecological factors and concepts of causation. In H. McGurk (Ed.), *Ecological factors in human development* (pp. 173–187). Amsterdam: North-Holland Publishing.

Rutter, M. L., & Rutter, M. (1993). *Developing minds: Challenge and continuity across the life span*. New York: Basic Books.

Sameroff, A. J. (1987). The social context of development. In N. Eisenberg (Ed.), *Contemporary topics in devlopmental psychology* (pp. 273–291). New York: Wiley.

Sameroff, A. J., & Seifer, R. (1990). Early contributors to developmental risk. In J. Rolf, A. S. Masten, D. Cicchetti, K. H. Nuechterlein, & S. Weintraub (Eds.), *Risk and protective factors in the development of psychopathology* (pp. 52–66). New York: Cambridge University Press.

Shapiro, J. P., Friedman, D., Meyer, M., & Loftus, M. (1996, November 11). Invincible kids. *U.S. News & World Report, 121*, 62–71.

Sroufe, L. A., & Rutter, M. (1984). The domain of developmental psychopathology. *Child Development, 55*, 17–29.

Steinberg, J. A., & Silverman, M. M. (Eds.). (1987). *Preventing mental disorders: A research perspective* (p. 76). Rockville, MD: Department of Health and Human Services.

Weise, R. E., Blehar, M. C., Maser, J. D., & Akiskal, H. S. (1996). Competence models in adult psychopathology: A report on a National Institute of Mental Health workshop. *Psychotherapy, 33*, 61–67.

Werner, E. E. (1992). The children of Kauai: Resiliency and recovery in adolescence and adulthood. *Journal of Adolescent Health, 13*, 262–268.

Werner, E. E. (1993). Risk, resilience and recovery: Perspectives from the Kauai Longitudinal Study. *Development and Psychopathology, 5*, 503–515.

Werner, E. E., & Smith, R. S. (1992). *Overcoming the odds: High risk children from birth to adulthood*. New York: Cornell University Press.

Wheaton, B. (1985). Models for the stress-buffering functions of coping resources. *Journal of Health and Social Behavior, 26*, 352–364.

Zubin, J., & Spring, B. J. (1977). Vulnerability: A new view of schizophrenia. *Journal of Abnormal Psychology, 86*, 103–126.

Chapter 8

Toward Valid Understanding of Mental Disorders: Multicausal, Biopsychosocial Theories

Neither brainlessness nor mindlessness can be tolerated in psychiatry or medicine.

—Eisenberg, 1986, p. 505.

The undeniable conclusion of our previous analyses is that no single-domain, causal model of mental disorders can provide a scientifically adequate explanation of mental disorders. Mental disorders are not the result of biological abnormalities, be they infectious, biochemical, or neuroanatomical. Mental disorders are not produced by irrational thoughts, erroneous expectations, or rigid and ineffective behavior patterns learned since birth by an individual through interactions with various stressful environmental experiences. Mental disorders do not result from untolerated violations of, or stressful contributions from, role expectations, norms, or values dictated by various human cultures and subcultures.

What the scientific evidence indicates instead is that any particular mental disorder is caused by a particular (probably distinctive) combination of biological, psychological, and sociological developmental influences. No one factor or domain of factors operates in a vacuum; multiple factors interact and seek a balance in various ways and de-

grees. The development of any particular disorder depends on both
the independent and combined effects of multiple causal factors. Valid
scientific explanation of specific mental disorders demand distinctive
biopsychosocial explanatory models. Human behavior is best explained in terms of biological mechanisms, psychological processes,
and social influences (Engel, 1980).

Psychological events, including mental disorders, have complex
causal backgrounds, determined by a multitude of often interacting
causal factors. These causal factors operate throughout the life span of
the individual, and the interactive effects depend on the developmental level, ages, or developmental tasks present at particular moments.

Mental disorders are the result a triad of contributory causes. None
of the three causal domains exerts necessary and sufficient determination. None of the three sets of factors serves as sufficient cause. Future
research may determine—probably in some minority of cases—that
one of the three sets of factors may function as a necessary cause.

An adequate scientific explanation of any particular mental disorder must detail the specific contributory causal (both vulnerability and
protective) factors operative within each domain (biological, psychological, and social), their developmental onsets, and their historical
and current interactions. The percentage of causal influence from each
domain of the triad will unquestionably vary from mental disorder to
mental disorder. The biological contribution or influence is not likely to
exceed half for any given mental condition—it will approach half for major
disorders such as bipolar mood disorder and schizophrenia; for the many
remaining disorders will range to substantially less than half.

Exclusively biological psychiatrists will continue to conduct their
search for the distinctive pattern of biological abnormalities that constitute various mental disorders. Exclusively learning-oriented psychologists will continue their efforts to identify patterns of distinctive
cognitive and behavioral abnormalities. Exclusively culturally oriented
sociologists and anthropologists will continue their analyses of the
societal influences and values that play distinctive contributory roles
for various mental disorders. Invariably, these disciplinary scientists
will, and need to, continue their respective competitive searches. The
field of psychopathology will continue to profit from their competitive perspectives and investments. But, although these widely varied
monocausal approaches to explaining human behavior are all quite
valuable in their own right, they can become even more valuable when
integrated into larger, more comprehensive models.

What biological psychiatrists, learning-oriented psychologists, and
culturally oriented sociologists and anthropologists can no longer
legitimately do is to offer monocausal claims or exclusively single-
domain theoretical explanations. It is no longer valid or useful to view

psychopathology as univariate. The scientific adequacy of present and future theories of any mental disorder is related directly to the extent to which they address and incorporate bio, psycho, and social factors that have been identified as contributory through empirical research. In turn, separate disciplinary research programs cannot help but be influenced by these emerging sophisticated scientific explanations.

A NATIONAL AGENDA FOR PREVENTION OF MENTAL DISORDERS

These basic themes have recently been endorsed strongly by national organizations and federal agencies. Three major national comprehensive reports have arrived at the unanimous conclusion that research and preventive treatment programs in mental health need to operate from a basic premise of biopsychosocial risk and vulnerability factors. Two recent comprehensive reports focused on prevention of mental disorders, with both concluding that preventive interventions must be aimed at reducing biopsychosocial risk factors and promoting biopsychosocial protective factors. The first report was the National Academy of Science's Institute of Medicine Report, "Reducing Risks for Mental Disorders: Frontiers for Preventive Intervention Research" (Mrazek & Haggerty, 1994), which is summarized in detail in Chapter 7. The second was an NIMH report, "The Prevention of Mental Disorders: A National Research Agenda" (NIMH Committee on Prevention Research, 1995; NIMH Prevention Research Steering Committee, 1994; Reiss & Price, 1996). Both reports emphasized the importance of preventive interventions such as helping parents develop better child-rearing skills (a risk factor for both delinquency and substance abuse); enhancing individuals' interpersonal problem-solving skills (protective factors for delinquency and substance abuse); and psychoeducational programs to enhance the emotional quality of the family environment and a family's understanding of mental disorder (a protective factor against relapse in schizophrenia).

A third national report concentrated on recommendations regarding the research agenda for mental health and disorder. Beginning in 1990, more than one hundred researchers from throughout the country and a half dozen federal agencies gathered for the first of several Behavioral Science Summit Meetings. The group was convened under the sponsorship of the American Psychological Society with partial support from NIMH and the U.S. Congress. Summit participants endorsed development of a national research agenda to help policy makers in federal agencies set funding priorities for psychological and related sciences.

Report 3 of this Human Capital Initiative summarized the research on health and behavior and on mental health and proposed a "behavioral science research initiative directed toward reducing the incidence and impact of mental disorders." The major thesis of Report 3 was that "the development of mental disorders is influenced by biological, behavioral, and social factors whose contributions vary for different disorders." The evidence is clear "that acquired and inherited vulnerabilities interact with external stressors in determining mental health outcomes" (American Psychological Society, 1996, p. 15). Research needs to determine how to identify individuals who are at risk: which specific environmental events can trigger the development of the full-blown disorder among those individuals who are vulnerable; and what are the protective factors that might intervene to reduce the occurrence, severity, or frequency of onset and/or relapse of a disorder. In regard to treatment and intervention, "We must increase our ability to specify which clinical interventions are effective for which mental disorders and in which kinds of people" (American Psychological Society, 1996, p. 21; see also Conte, 1997; Kiesler, 1966; Krumboltz, 1966; Paul, 1967). "Answering these important questions will require collaborative investigations that employ a variety of research methods and draw upon the talents of many behavioral scientists" (American Psychological Society, 1996, p. 15).

In sum, the agenda for research and prevention of mental disorders has become clear at the national level and for federal funding agencies. Biopsychosocial risk and protective factors, genetically predisposed and environmentally established, represent the major challenges at hand.

MULTICAUSAL, BIOPSYCHOSOCIAL THEORIES

The current era in medicine began with the growing realization of the limitations of the biological approach to understanding of most of the prevalent current sources of sickness and death (Ahmed, Kolker, & Coelho, 1979). The biomedical view of disease came to be complemented with a more complex model, one that directs attention to interactions among social and psychological as well as biological factors in the etiology, course, and treatment of disease. This emerging view may further represent a general model that applies to all disease, not just to a special subset of diseases (Friedman & DeMatteo, 1979; Jemmott & Locke, 1984).

A Review of Vulnerability–Stress Models

The first multicausal models to appear for mental disorders were the diathesis–stress (vulnerability–stress) models of schizophrenia (Meehl, 1962; Rosenthal, 1970; Zubin & Spring, 1977), reviewed in Chapter 3. The models were based on evidence that what was inherited in schizophrenia was a predisposition or diathesis, not the disorder itself. Zubin and Spring observed that "the primary persistent characteristic of the schizophrenic is his vulnerability, not his disorder" (1997, p. 117). In order for schizophrenia to occur, the individual needs not only to be predisposed, but also must experience cumulative environmental stress that exceeds some threshold level, as a result of which the individual is triggered into an episode of disorder. Other diathesis–stress models of schizophrenia have been offered by Eaton (1980); Eaton, Day, and Kramer (1986); Freeman (1989); Gottesman (1991); Gottesman and Shields (1967, 1982); Mednick (1970); Mednick and Schulsinger (1968); and Nuechterlein and colleagues (1987; Nuechterlein & Dawson, 1984).

In all these models, the causes of schizophrenia are at least two: aberrant *biology* as the genetically transmitted predisposition and aversive *environmental experiences* as the cumulative precipitative stress. The models were offered for schizophrenia, universally regarded as one of the several *most biologically weighted disorders*. Several other models also were offered by highly prestigious psychiatric and genetic researchers.

An unavoidable implication of these models was that neither biology nor the environment alone was "sufficient" explanation—mental disorder was the result of interactions between the biologically predisposed individual and environmental events. A diathesis or predisposition is "a relatively distal necessary or contributory cause, but it is not sufficient to cause the disorder. Instead, there must be a more proximal cause (the stressor) which may also be contributory or necessary but is generally not sufficient by itself to cause the disorder" (Carson, Butcher, & Mineka, 1997, p. 66).

Within appearance of additional models, diatheses or vulnerabilities came to be conceptualized as of two types: inborn and/or acquired. An *inborn* vulnerability is "that which is laid down in the genes and reflected in the internal environment and neurophysiology of the organism;" an *acquired* vulnerability is "due to the influence of traumas, specific diseases, perinatal complications, family experiences, adolescent peer interactions, and other life events that either enhance or inhibit the development of subsequent disorder" (Zubin & Spring, 1977, p. 109).

Increasing numbers of researchers began to develop vulnerability–stress models for other mental disorders. This occurred especially within developmental psychopathology, where most high-risk researchers "view themselves as working within a diathesis–stress framework that acknowledges . . . the potential roles of both heredity and environment in the development of psychopathology" (Richters & Weintraub, 1990, p. 69).

Diathesis–stress models began to appear for depressive disorders. Studies of the effects of stressful life events on depression progressed from a focus on a direct relation between stressors and the onset of depression to more complex diathesis–stress models in which genetic–constitutional, personality, cognitive, interpersonal, and behavioral factors interact with stressors (e.g., parental loss or poor parental care) to produce depression. Recent conceptualizations take four distinct forms (Carson, Butcher, & Mineka, 1997, pp. 220–222). Some propose a *biological* diathesis which, in conjunction with stressful precipitating events, leads to depression (Akiskal & McKinney, 1973, 1975). The second and third types hypothesize a *psychological* diathesis which, in combination with precipitating negative life events, produce a depressive disorder. The first psychological diathesis takes the form of dysfunctional personality traits (e.g., extreme emotionality combined with either extreme extraversion or extreme introversion: Clark & Watson, 1991; Clark, Watson, & Mineka, 1994). The second involves dysfunctional thoughts or cognitions, either irrational beliefs (Beck, 1983, 1987) or biased attributional styles (Abramson, Seligman, & Teasdale, 1978). The fourth depression model proposes a *sociocultural* (environmental) diathesis that results from negative life events occurring during early childhood (e.g., from parental loss through death or permanent separation, Brown & Harris, 1978).

Diathesis–stress models of depression have been offered by Abramson and colleagues (Abramson, Seligman, & Teasdale, 1978; Abramson, Metalsky, & Alloy, 1989; Alloy, Hartlage, & Abramson, 1988); Akiskal and McKinney (1973, 1975); Barnett and Gotlib (1990); Beck (1983, 1987); Clark and colleagues (Clark & Watson, 1991; Clark, Watson, & Mineka, 1994); Dalgleish and Watts (1990); Goplerud and Depue (1985); Hammen and colleagues (Hammen, 1988; Hammen, Elicott, Gitlin, & Jamison, 1989; Gotlib & Hammen, 1992); Kwon and Oel (1992); Monroe and Simons (1991); Nolen-Hoeksema (1987, 1990); and Olinger, Kuiper, and Shaw (1987). Increasing numbers of researchers have concluded that vulnerability–stress models are valid within the entire area of mental disorders.

A Review of Biopsychosocial Models

As we saw in Chapter 3, Engel (1977, 1980) coined the term *biopsychosocial* to assert that the interaction of biological, psychological, and social vulnerability (risk) factors best accounts for the development of mental disorders. Though originated in medical settings, his model has been basic to subsequent developments within psychiatry, psychology, behavioral medicine, and health psychology. Unfortunately, Engel's model continues to serve mostly as an unmet challenge (Fink, 1988) for research and practice.

It is important to note that Engel's model can lead to two separate emphases. It can serve both as a model of etiology and development of disease or disorder and as a model of medical–clinical practice (diagnosis and treatment). Most of the discussion and applications of the model within psychiatry have focused on its usefulness as a guide for clinical practice (Leigh, 1983, 1997a; Leigh & Reiser, 1992). Biopsychosocial clinical models have appeared for psychiatric diagnosis (Leigh, Feinstein, & Reiser, 1980; Wise, 1997); anxiety (Leigh, 1997c); depression (Leigh, 1997d); chronic pain (Streltzer, 1997); Munchausen syndrome (Eisendrath, 1997); childhood asthma (Miller & Wood, 1991, 1994); eating disorders (Conners & Morse, 1993); and psychiatric treatment issues in primary care settings (Leigh, 1997a).

As Leigh observed, at its best Engel's model "embodies an *ideal* of medical practice. A skilled biopsychosocial physician would be somewhat like the old-fashioned family doctor, who knows the patient, his/her family, occupation, subculture, as well as the patient's coping style. He/she would ask the patient about ongoing problems, recent stresses, and the impact of the illness on the family and workplace. The physician would, then, take all these factors into consideration in recommending and implementing state of the art treatment" (1997b, p. vii).

In contrast, one is hard put to find within psychiatry serious attempts at theories that offer distinctive sets of biological, psychological, and sociocultural factors as explanations for the etiology and development of individual mental disorders. Biomedical theories remain abundant, while only a few vulnerability–stress theories have been offered. In fairness, the same critique can be offered of the other mental health disciplines. Fortunately, the picture recently has started to change, with biopsychosocial theories of mental disorders increasingly surfacing.

It is likely that sophisticated applications of the biopsychosocial model to medical and psychiatric practice cannot evolve until more sophisticated, state-of-the-science biopsychosocial etiological theories have been formulated and validated. The practice of biopsychosocial diagnosis and treatment will continue to present challenges to the mental health professions; indeed, it may eventuate in multidisciplinary treatment becoming the treatment of choice in almost all instances. In fact, the combination of chemical and psychological forms of therapy is fast becoming the major thrust of current treatment and treatment research for severe psychopathology (Beitman & Klerman, 1991).

MULTICAUSAL, BIOPSYCHOSOCIAL THEORIES: ESSENTIAL COMPONENTS

Any biopsychosocial (BPS) theory must address the distinctive combination and interaction of person and environmental factors that mold the characteristic pattern of abnormality for a specific mental disorder. A BPS theory details a matrix of (a) hereditarily determined biological and psychological *person* factors, and (b) familial, subcultural, and cultural *environmental* factors, together with (c) how they interact at different *developmental stages* (d) to produce and maintain a particular mental disorder and/or a particular spectrum of mental disorders. Figure 8.1 provides a visual summary of the components of a sophisticated BPS theory of psychopathology.

Person factors involve hereditarily influenced vulnerabilities and resiliencies, or a distinctive pattern of risk and protective factors. Environmental factors involve familial, social, and cultural stressful and protective life events. Hence, both person and environment factors assume distinctive patterns of vulnerable and protective influence.

For example, Ewing (1980) presented a biopsychosocial model in which the probability of an individual's developing a substance abuse problem is given by the conjoint influence of each of four factors: availability (e.g., cost) of the substance, social factors, psychological factors, and constitutional factors (genetic and biochemical variables). Some factors are viewed as protective, such as strong antialcohol religious beliefs or a high cost of the substance; others are thought to place the individual at risk, such as psychological distress or family history of alcoholism.

In multicausal, biopsychosocial theories, an individual's hereditarily predisposed person factors interact with familial, social, and cultural events and experiences throughout the various stages of maturation and development—across the life span extending from prenatal, infancy, early childhood, adolescence, adulthood, and senescence. The consensus is that earlier experiences and events typically have a relatively greater impact and causal influence than do those occurring subsequently in the life span.

The pattern of person and environmental risk and protective factors and their interactions throughout development is distinct for a particular mental disorder. It may also be distinct for a group of associated disorders along a spectrum (Meehl, 1962; Wender, 1977; Davis & Akiskal, 1986; Gunderson & Siever, 1985; Widiger, 1989; Widiger, Frances, & Sweeney, 1988). In the spectrum case, a distinct biological and/or psychological vulnerability or diathesis predisposes an individual to a variety of associated mental disorders, the variant forms being found along the same continuum of severity or chronicity. Along what might be called a schizophrenia spectrum, for example, a particular diathesis may predispose an individual to conditions ranging from a characterological personality disorder (schizotypal personality disorder), to a restricted symptom disorder (schizophreniform disorder or delusional disorder), to a full-blown and severe symptomatic condition (schizophrenia).

The spectrum notion indicates that hereditary influences can predispose an individual to a group of similar disorders, rather than just

Figure 8.1
Adult Mental Disorder: Multicausal Factors

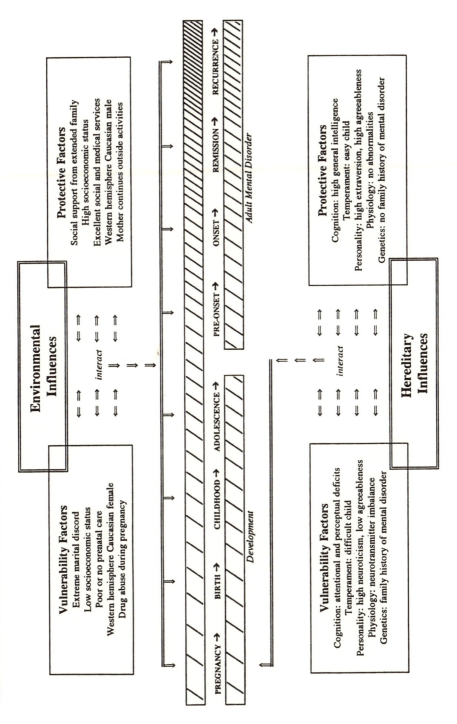

to a single mental disorder. The disorders can range from mild to extreme severity as expressed in symptoms that are similar. The particular disorder (mild, moderate, or extreme) that eventuates is determined by factors such as the given balance of vulnerability and protective factors interacting earlier or later during development with stressful and protective life events.

A spectrum, thus, reflects the notion that a genetic predisposition (genotype) may eventuate in a variety of related specific mental disorders (phenotypes), depending on mixtures of multiple genes and environmental potentiators. BPS spectrum theories, accordingly, need to explain how the associated individual mental disorders respectively occur, including their common mechanisms and distinctive developmental histories.

Postscript

Another contender for the role of an essential component in biopsychosocial models is the notion of a *final common pathway* to disorder. A final common pathway denotes that the heterogeneous causal factors that may operate in a particular disorder all converge on a shared link (physiological and/or psychological) that determines the core symptoms of the disorder. For example, according to Akiskal and McKinney's (1975) "final common pathway" model, any of a variety of psychological or biological events are capable of setting in motion a common final-path, biological process involving dysregulation in the brain limbic system (amygdala, hippocampus, hypothalamus, and related structures), which plays a major role in the regulation of drive and emotion. Once triggered, this dysfunctional brain system is seen as taking on a life of its own, becoming relatively impervious to subsequent psychological input, but having a profound impact on psychological functioning.

MULTICAUSAL, BIOPSYCHOSOCIAL THEORIES: CONTRASTS WITH MONOCAUSAL MODELS

In contrast to the monocausal assumptions of either the biomedical or psychosocial models of mental disorder, BPS models make distinctively important assumptions. (1) Explanations of mental disorders, first and foremost, must rely on multiple causation—on the "doctrine of multiple causality" (Lipowski, 1975, 1978). In contrast, the biomedical and psychosocial models ignore all but their respective monocausal domains. (2) Mental disorders are not biological abnormalities of the body that are sharply separate from the psychological and social processes of the mind. Nor are they singularly unfortunate mixtures of stressful environments and cognitive–behavioral mechanisms acquired totally independently of congenital biology. Rather, mental disorders represent distinct mixtures (reflecting different percentages) of biological, psychological, and sociocultural interacting factors whose interdependence can be pervasive. (3) Much efficacy research indicates that treatments designed to target putative, monocausal abnormal mechanisms instead have more general ameliorative effects. Psychological interventions designed, for example, to remediate irrational cognitive assumptions provide improvements not only in cognitive but also in overt behavioral and physiological activity as well. BPS models, by definition, demand that optimal interventions be multidimensional, targeting the entire set of biological, psychological, and sociocultural abnormalities that constitute the disorder. In addition, the domain components of BPS interventions must be ideally sequenced, either separately in distinct phases and/or simultaneously within phases. A BPS theory must specify, for example, whether an "in vivo" exercise designed to extinguish a specific phobia must be preceded by, accompanied with, or followed by antianxiety medication.

COMPONENTS OF MULTICAUSAL, BIOPSYCHOSOCIAL THEORIES: SOME EXAMPLES

Biological Factors

Biological factors assume a greater theoretical prominence relative to the degree of heritability established by genetic studies. Genetic factors establish causal inputs to disorders most directly in the form of various predispositions or diatheses: inherited biological brain mechanisms, abnormalities, or underpinnings of psychological traits. Evidence of genetic contribution leads biological psychiatrists to isolate and identify these biological underpinnings.

In alcohol abuse research, various researchers have found that alcoholics exhibit a distinctive low amplitude brain-wave pattern and a biologically decreased sensitivity to the effects of alcohol. A BPS theory might integrate the low brain-wave pattern with a corresponding psychological risk factor for alcoholism: for example, that the brain-wave pattern reflects the biological underpinning of the personality trait of high novelty seeking, nonconformity, and intolerance for frustration. The theory may specify further that movement along the pathway to alcohol abuse happens only when the biological–psychological pattern of high novelty seeking co-occurs with a decreased physiological sensitivity to the effects of alcohol within the same individual.

Psychophysiology plays a central role in Nuechterlein and Dawson's (1984) vulnerability–stress model of schizophrenia. In their scheme, hyperactivity of the autonomic nervous system in reaction to aversive (impending harmful) stimuli represents one of several enduring predispositions. They assume, further, that a person's vulnerabilities can interact with environmental factors to generate continuing states within the person, a central aspect of which is autonomic hyperarousal. This enduring physiological condition of the predisposed individual, in turn, progresses into a full-blown psychotic episode when triggered by contemporaneous environmental stressors.

Asberg, Martensson, and Wagner (1987) proposed that low levels of serotonin in the central nervous system may provide a vulnerability factor, possibly under genetic control, for impulsive and self-destructive acts. Given stressful life events conducive to depression and despair, vulnerable persons of this type have an increased likelihood of attempting suicide.

Another BPS model (Paris, 1994) specified two biologically rooted personality traits, impulsivity and affective instability, as necessary but insufficient conditions for the development of borderline personality disorder. Psychological risk factors (e.g., stressful life events such as trauma, loss, or inadequate parenting) cause the traits to become more extreme and maladaptive. Amplification of affective instability results in more extreme emotional lability and dysphoria; attempts to cope with the dysphoria lead to an increase in impulsive behaviors such as substance abuse, disturbance in interpersonal relationships, and promiscuity. In turn, the uncomfortable consequences of these impulsive acts actually heighten the emotional turmoil experienced by the individual, thereby creating a negative feedback loop.

Psychological Factors

Predominant cognitive diathesis–stress models of depression propose that depression results from enduring cognitive predispositions that interact with negative stressors that *match* the vulnerability. For Beck (1987), the cognitive vulnerability is in the form of distinctive dysfunctional attitudes and beliefs; for Abramson, Metalsky, and Alloy (1989), it takes the form of a dysfunctional attributional style in which an individual constantly takes the blame for bad things that happen to him or her. In both theories, the particular vulnerability is triggered by either interpersonal or achievement stressors, but only by the one that matches the relevant cognitive vulnerability. In Beck's system, for example, in the case of a person who has a high need for social interaction and avoidance of disapproval, depression occurs in reaction to perceived interpersonal loss or rejection; in contrast, in the case of a person with a high need for achievement and autonomy, depression occurs only in response to perceived failure or lack of control over the environment.

In their model for antisocial personality disorder, Sher and Trull (1994) specify that the personality traits of impulsivity and disinhibition are crucial in terms of how they interact with poor or inconsistent parenting. Reciprocal interactions are evoked between child and parents that perpetuate negative interactions. Impatient, exasperated, and/or inconsistent parental discipline reinforces and exaggerates the antisocially disposed child's impulsive and difficult behavior. The child's escalated impulsive and uninhibited behaviors then evoke harsher and more erratic parental discipline. Over time, this reciprocal pattern leads to increased parental permissiveness for the child's aggression, self-fulfilling failures in school, and increased rejection by peers and other adults.

Cognitive social learning models of alcohol use hold that a person's cognitions are central. Expectations a person has about the effects of drinking alcohol are developed through exposure to parental, peer, and other persons who drink, the media, and cultural rituals, as well as through personal experience. Before starting to drink, the person has only general expectations from which to predict the effects that his or her drinking may have. After accumulating personal experience, his or her expectancies become more specific. Expectancies, in turn, come to produce the alcohol effects predicted.

Sociocultural Factors

Different cultural patterns of alcohol use have been identified in ethnic groups that exhibit dramatically different patterns of alcohol abuse (Lex, 1985). Within the United States, first-generation Italian and Jewish American families drink heavily exclusively within religious and family settings; offspring of these families show low rates of alcohol problems. Irish Americans, in contrast, drink heavily mostly in settings outside the home such as inns and bars; Irish offspring consistently exhibit higher rates of alcohol problems. Also, regardless of childhood cultural input, once individuals reach adolescence, the behavior and attitudes of peers in regard to alcohol begin to exert an influence that first rivals than surpasses the earlier impact made by parents. Donovan points out that women of all cultures, as well as both male and female orientals, have low rates of alcoholism "in part due to negative social sanction, but these populations tolerate alcohol so poorly physiologically that they also have an 'inborn Antabuse'" (1986, p. 7).

Brown and Harris (1978) identified four vulnerability factors for women that increased the likelihood that they will subsequently incur an episode of depressive disorder: (a) in childhood, loss of mother by death or by separation of at least one year; (b) absence of an intimate confiding relationship with a husband or boyfriend; (c) presence of three or more children in the home; and (d) lack of employment outside the home. They concluded that each vulnerability factor itself is a substantial risk factor for depression; also combinations of the factors, together with various provoking or precipitating events, significantly increased the level of risk. Brown and Harris suggested that each of the four factors led to a woman's lowered self-esteem, the common psychological mediator of subsequent depressive disorder.

It is likely that eating disorders such as bulimia nervosa and anorexia nervosa may have substantial causal input from sociocultural factors. In fact, some have suggested that these disorders in fact are what DSM-IV terms "culture bound disorders," specifically ones that are distinct to Western culture, especially to the United States. Within one BPS model for bulimia nervosa (Johnson & Connors, 1987), an important risk factor is the family environment, which is characterized as disengaged, chaotic, highly conflicted, and neglectful. In addition, family members are deficient in problem-solving skills, nonsupportive of independent behavior, and have a high achievement orientation. The young daughter then experiences significant emotional instability (impulsive behaviors and mood swings) and a lack of control that makes her feel helpless in relation to her bodily experience. Crucially, when certain sociocultural factors are also strongly present—sex role confusion, emphasis on thinness for females, or a stigma against obesity—body-image preoccupations and binges of overeating and purging are further exacerbated.

According to Mason and Chaney, bulimia nervosa is a biopsychosocial disorder in which sociocultural factors provide significant contributions. Contemporary American culture associates thinness with success, beauty, health, and higher socioeconomic success; obesity is linked to unattractiveness, laziness, and lower SES. An increasing discrepancy, however, is found between American women's actual body weight and their ideal body weight, as a result of which a substantial proportion of young women are involved in serious dieting behaviors. Another risk factor is that disproportionately high prevalences of bulimia are found among college females. Also, some undergraduate women are more likely to internalize the sociocultural standard of thinness, as a result being at greater risk for dieting and subsequent eating disorders. They detail a set of three risk factors for bulimia. (1) Personality tendencies to conform to social pressures: Young women who are characterized by personality traits of high public self-consciousness (concern for self-presentation), and low individuation, and who fail to endorse characteristics of the masculine gender role are more likely to conform to social pressures and orient their behavior to comply with these social standards. (2) A particular family environment: Young women who come from "synchronous" families insisting on consensus of ideas, low expression of feeling, and attainment of success (achievement and excellence) are more likely to become bulimic. (3) A particular college environment: Since college sororities emphasize attractiveness, thinness, and appearance and advocate conformity, sorority members are more likely to develop eating disorders. In sum, "because thinness is associated with accomplishment and success and tends to be the standard for women in American society, women who are raised in achieving, conforming families; who demonstrate a conforming personality style; and who are members of groups that focus on appearance, consensus, and achievement are considered more likely than others to adopt the thinness standard" (1996, p. 255).

MULTICAUSAL, BIOPSYCHOSOCIAL RESEARCH: SOME EXAMPLES

The essence of biopsychosocial research is examination, within the same study, of measures from at least two of the biological, psychological, and social domains—preferably all three. Typically this demands a multidisciplinary team that can provide the appropriate expertise; one result typically is a relatively long list of study authors. Only by including biological, psychological, and sociocultural variables in the same study can one determine significant interactions among the triad of measures. Most typically the matrix of variables is examined through some version of statistical multivariate regression analysis.

Russo, Vitaliano, Brewer, Katon, and Becker (1995) identified individuals who either did or did not have a predisposition to develop anxiety disorders and who either were or were not under stress. The individuals who were identified as having a diathesis were those who had suffered from anxiety disorders in the past; individuals who were identified as being under high stress were those who were currently responsible for the care of a spouse who was suffering from Alzheimer's disease. Results showed that the individuals who were most likely to develop an anxiety disorder were those who had the predisposition and who were under high stress, thus offering support for a diathesis–stress explanation.

Kendler, Kessler, Neale, Heath, and Eaves (1993) developed an exploratory causal model to explain major unipolar depression in women, who have much higher prevalences compared to men. In a large group of monozygotic and dizygotic female twins, they examined a set of nine biopsychosocial risk factors they felt would be predictive of depression: predisposing genetic influences, the personality trait of neuroticism, gender, premature parental loss (separation or death), inadequate parental rearing, a history of stressful life events, recent stressful life events, low social support, and a history of previous major depressive episodes. Using a multivariate statistical test (structural equation modeling), they found that the best-fit model explained 50 percent of the variance in liability to major depression. The strongest predictors were stressful life events, genetic factors, previous history of major depression, and neuroticism. Kendler, Kessler, Neale, Heath, and Eaves concluded that major depression is a multifactorial disorder; at least four major and interacting risk factor domains are needed to understand the causes of major depression: stressful life events, genetic factors, temperament–personality, and interpersonal relations.

Bry, McKeon, and Pandina (1982) studied the influence on adolescent substance use of six potential risk factors: grades in school, church affiliation, age at first drug use, the presence of psychological distress, the adolescent's self-esteem, and the adolescent's perception of parental love. Findings revealed that no single risk factor, or any specific combination of risk factors, predicted the extent of drug use. Instead, Bry, McKeon, and Pandina found a linear relationship between extent of drug use and the sheer number of risk factors; the more risk factors present, the more substances were used by adolescents. A similar finding, based on a study of Native American youths, was reported by Moncher, Holden, and Trimble (1990).

Raine, Venables, and Williams (1995) reviewed neurological and obstetric data, collected at birth and after one year, on a large sample of Danish eighteen year olds. They found that those individuals who had both neuromotor deficits in infancy and poverty or family instability during childhood accounted for 70 percent of all the violent crimes committed by the total group of late adolescents. However, those with only one of the risk factors (neuromotor or social) exhibited significantly less criminal conduct. In sum, the combination of biological and psychological factors offered the best prediction of subsequent antisocial conduct and violent behavior.

Lewis, Pincus, Lovely, Spitzer, & Moy (1987) compared thirty-one incarcerated delinquents with thirty-one nondelinquents matched for age, sex, ethnicity, and race. A constellation of variables including abuse–family violence, severe psychiatric symptomatology, cognitive impairment, minor neurological signs, and psychomotor symptoms correctly predicted group membership 84 percent of the time. The constellation also distinguished more aggressive from less aggressive subjects within each group. The authors concluded the existence of a syndrome that is characteristic of recurrently violent individuals.

Silverton (1988) studied the relationship between schizophrenia and antisocial behavior among 207 Danish children with schizophrenic mothers (high risk) and 104 Danish children with normal mothers (low risk). The variables found to distinguish criminal versus noncriminal behavior among the high risk children-turned-adults included the following: irritability and shortened attention span in infancy, paternal absence during ages fifteen to seventeen, lower Weschler Adult Intelligence Scale Verbal IQ, an impoverished neighborhood, family discord, and negative attitudes toward father. Shortened attention spans were found to precede both criminal behavior and schizophrenia.

Parker, Smarr, Walker, and Hagglund (1991) evaluated the applicability of a biopsychosocial model for estimating disease activity in rheumatoid arthritis by examining a group of patients at baseline, three months, and six months. Peripheral blood immunophenotypic subsets, demographic characteristics, and psychological measures were obtained and entered into hierarchical regression analyses, with disease activity (joint counts) as the dependent variable. Immunophenotypic subsets were predictive of disease activity at all three time points. At baseline and three months, psychological variables (i.e., helplessness and depression) were significantly related to joint counts, and the full model was highly significant.

Other examples of multivariate biopsychosocial studies include the following: Barnett and Gotlib (1990); Clark, Beck, and Brown (1992); Goldstein (1988); Hunsley (1989); Kirkpatrick-Smith, Rich, Bonner, and Jans (1991–1992); Lewis, Moy, Jackson, Aaronson, Restifo, Serra, and Simos (1985); Mednick, Cudeck, Griffith, Talovic, and Schulsinger (1984); Metalsky, Halberstadt, and Abramson (1987); Metalsky and Joiner (1992); O'Hara, Schlechte, Lewis, and Varner (1991); Peyrot and McMurry (1985); Resnick, Kilpatrick, Best, and Kramer (1992); Rich and Bonner (1987); Robins and Block (1989); Schall, Kemeny, and Maltzman (1992); Schotte, Cools, and Payvar (1990); Segal, Shaw, Vella, and Katz (1992); Silverton (1988); Spangler, Simons, Monroe, and Thase (1996); Stuart, Hammond, and Pett (1987); Temoshok, Sagebiel, Blois, Heller, Sweet, DiClemente, and Gold (1985); and Weiner, Thaler, Reiser, and Mirsky (1957).

Hopefully, interdisciplinary research teams increasingly will combine their distinctive viewpoints and methods in cooperative, combined studies. BPS models at some point require for their validation *multivariate* studies and methods that begin to tease out the relevant risk and protective factors in each of the tripartite domains. Incorporation of respective state-of-the-art variables and measures most typically requires input from experts in each of the three domains. As Galizio and Maisto note in regard to the research in substance abuse, "We suspect that it will become increasingly common to include blood assays, urinalyses, and indexes of brain function along with personality tests, demographic data, and experimental analysis of response to drugs" (1985, p. 427). In general, the most useful research will be multivariate and interdisciplinary. Kendler and colleagues add that multivariate methods "permit a more definitive resolution of the structure of the genetic and environmental risk factors for a range of psychiatric disorders"; moreover, multivariate methods "can be powerfully applied in twin studies" (1995, pp. 374–375).

Schwartz argued that the ultimate challenge facing behavioral medicine is an empirical test of the biopsychosocial model. He added, "Implicit in the biopsychosocial approach to behavioral medicine is that a team approach to diagnosis and treatment is necessary to ensure that appropriate biological, psychological, and social data are collected, integrated, and interpreted comprehensively" (1982, p. 1050).

Carson and Sanislow (1993) note that it is unfortunate and counterproductive that biological and psychological research are often conceived as mutually antagonistic and that they rarely make contact with each other. Carson, Butcher, and Mineka add that impediments to progress within a biopsychosocial perspective stem "from difficulties mental health professionals with the different orientations have in communicating with one another because of lack of knowledge and understanding of other approaches. . . . Many of the problems stem from the fact that many of these mental health professionals are simply entrenched in their beliefs about the superiority of one approach relative to the other. Yet there is hope that this situation may change. Today, there are more interdisciplinary research teams consisting of people trained in all of these perspectives than there ever [have] been in the past" (1997, p. 196).

If the field of psychopathology is to progress, twenty-first-century researchers, whatever their particular scientific discipline, need to keep the biopsychosocial template constantly on the "fore burners," or at least the "back burners," of their research applications.

MULTICAUSAL, BIOPSYCHOSOCIAL THEORIES: EMERGING STRENGTHS AND PROBLEMS

It seems easy to articulate the advantages of BPS theories of mental disorder. Since they are more complex and incorporate multifaceted dimensions that contribute to disorder, they are more credible—they seem to address a more comprehensive and unique array of human reality. Since they not only are multifaceted but also incorporate systems and transactional components, they encourage a holistic perspective of the patient from which to conceptualize etiology and treatment. Their complexity also leads to specification of novel and comprehensive treatment packages that can routinely be evaluated in comparative efficacy and effectiveness studies.

At present, available, relatively primitive BPS theories reveal weaknesses and problems. "At the present time such models can only identify factors or variables that can be demonstrated to be protective or to increase risk, but the relative variance accounted for by these various factors is largely unknown. . . . [In given instances] it is not at all clear which variables account for the greatest amount of variance and which may be trivial in the particular case" (Galizio & Maisto, 1985, p. 427).

Some early BPS models simply present an atheoretical additive list of known risk and protective factors, while offering little help in designating the variables that are most important and relevant to a particular disorder. Peterson (1996, 1997) cautions us that "attempts to apply [the biopsychosocial] perspective have often been little more than successive comments using the language of the different models (e.g., Vasile et al., 1987). A true integration of biological, psychological, and social factors is just now beginning to occur" (Peterson, 1996, p. 92). He continues, echoing Fink's (1988) earlier characterization, that so often the biopsychosocial model "remains simply a slogan until the details are filled in" (Peterson, 1996, p. 347). In short, what is needed is a comprehensive, cross-theoretical integration of the specific set of contributory causal factors. This deficiency highlights the need for additional and more comprehensive research to fill in the many blanks in our knowledge.

Also, one can find isolated and disconnected BPS models that may address in detail a particular mental disorder and yet fail to consider or explain similarities and differences with other different but associated (comorbid) mental disorders.

RECOMMENDATIONS FOR MORE VALID MULTICAUSAL, BIOPSYCHOSOCIAL THEORIES

Mental disorders fall on a continuum according to the degree of relative contributions from psychosocial and biological influences. The relative contributions of the tripartite factors vary from disorder to disorder.

BPS theories, then, should provide different weights (reflecting corresponding relative influence and importance) to the biological, psychological, and social factors specified to explain a particular mental disorder. Good theories will explicitly evaluate and incorporate the importance of the different variables and will explicitly reflect percentages of influence from factors varying along the biological–psychological continuum.

The closer to the biological end of the continuum, the more likely biological factors may be "necessary" (though not sufficient) conditions for mental disorder, and not merely contributory. Some disorders may have operative biological casual factors, while others may not. A biological diathesis can show up especially in differences in temperament and personality traits. Specific personality traits, in turn, may be necessary but not sufficient for development of a particular mental disorder. In this sense, biological underpinnings of personality traits can serve as a limiting factor on the type of disorder than may develop.

Causal factors may vary in their significance depending on the age or developmental stage at which they have their primary influence. The potency of specific risk and protective factors for development varies according to the specific developmental stage or period during which they occur (Bell, 1968). For example, family factors typically exert substantial influence in early childhood, but less in adolescence and adulthood; in contrast, peer influences are not as pertinent in early childhood, but are highly relevant during adolescence. Also, with alcohol and drug abuse, it may be that cultural features exert their greatest influences on the initial decision to experiment with a particular substance; biological factors (e.g., individual differences in tolerance, drug sensitivity and metabolism, or reinforcing strength of substances) may be more important in determining continuation of use and in the transition from use to abuse; and psychosocial and environmental factors may be most crucial for cessation and relapse.

The same causal factor may function differently depending on the context in which it occurs. For example, a specific vulnerability factor, such as loss of job by a parent, can have different meaning and effect depending on whether it occurs in a low versus higher SES family.

BPS theories vary in the extent to which they incorporate personality trait factors as contributing substantially to development of disorder. Any specification of personality trait factors should be based in, or triangulated with, the robustly established Big Five factors of personality (see Chapter 5).

Reciprocity (transactionism) prevails throughout interactions among the multiple causal factors. Personality factors may lead an individual to use drugs. Use of drugs may alter a person's personality, which then may increase the likelihood of further substance use and abuse (causality in both directions). Similarly, development of substance use may be a joint result of influence on a person from drug abuse peers and his or her original selection of peers who have similar drug using tendencies (persons choose situations).

Some BPS models are stronger in dealing with etiology, but brief in discussing maintenance mechanisms or treatment; others may concentrate on management or treatment with limited discussion of etiology. Optimal treatment or preventive interventions must be designed to address each tripartite causal factor or condition, in some optimal sequence. It is likely that some risk factors (biological, psychological, or sociocultural) are modifiable, while others are not.

The major evaluative criterion for BPS models is the same as that for any scientific theory: namely the extent to which it is based in supportive empirical research. A good BPS theory is one that incorporates risk and protective factors and other mechanisms that, based on specific research findings, have been established as influential factors for a particular mental disorder.

Recent advances in the conceptualization and measurement of life stress indicate that investigators need to become much more precise about the particular stressful circumstances (or categories of stressful events) hypothesized to interact with diatheses (Monroe & Simons, 1991).

Stressful life events can precipitate onset of an episode of disorder and can cause normal personality traits to become more extreme, rigid, and maladaptive—to move methodically in the direction of personality disorder. Rigid and extreme personality traits, in turn, can predispose one to episodes of other mental disorders as well as to increased frequency and intensity of stressful life events.

REFERENCES

Abramson, L. Y., Seligman, M. E. P., & Teasdale, J. D. (1978). Learned helplessness in humans: Critique and reformulation. *Journal of Abnormal Psychology, 87*, 49–74.

Abramson, L. Y., Metalsky, G. I., & Alloy, L. B. (1989). Hopelessness depression: A theory-based subtype of depression. *Psychological Review, 96*, 358–372.

Ahmed, P. I., Kolker, A., & Coelho, G. V. (1979). Toward a new definition of health: An overview. In P. I. Ahmed & G. V. Coelho (Eds.), *Toward a new definition of health: Psychosocial dimensions* (pp. 7–22). New York: Plenum.

Akiskal, H. S., & McKinney, W. T. (1973). Depressive disorders: Toward a unified hypothesis. *Science, 182*, 20–29.

Akiskal, H. S., & McKinney, W. T. (1975). Overview of recent research in depression: Integration of ten conceptual models into a comprehensive clinical frame. *Archives of General Psychiatry, 32*, 285–305.

Alloy, L. B., Hartlage, S., & Abramson, L. Y. (1988). Testing the cognitive diathesis–stress theories of depression: Issues of research design, conceptualization, and assessment. In L. B. Alloy (Ed.), *Cognitive processes in depression* (pp. 31–73). New York: Guilford.

American Psychological Society. (1996, February 1). Human Capital Inititiative (HCI) Report No. 3. *APS Observer* (special issue). Washington, DC: Author.

Asberg, M., Martensson, B., & Wagner, A. (1987). Psychobiological aspects of suicidal behavior. In D. Magnusson & A. Ohman (Eds.), *Psychopathology: An interactional perspective* (pp. 81–94). Orlando, FL: Academic Press.

Barnett, P. A., & Gotlib, I. H. (1990). Cognitive vulnerability to depressive symptoms among men and women. *Cognitive Therapy and Research, 14*, 47–61.

Beck, A. T. (1983). Cognitive therapy for depression: New perspectives. In P. J. Clayton & J. E. Barrett (Eds.), *Treatment of depression: Old controversies and new approaches* (pp. 265–290). New York: Raven.

Beck, A. T. (1987). Cognitive models of depression. *Journal of Cognitive Psychotherapy: An International Quarterly, 1*, 5–37.

Beitman, B. D., & Klerman, G. L. (Eds.). (1991). *Integrating pharmacotherapy and psychotherapy.* Washington, DC: American Psychiatric Press.

Bell, R. Q. (1968). A reinterpretation of the direction of effects in studies of socialization. *Psychological Review, 75,* 81–95.

Brown, G. W., & Harris, T. (1978). *The social origins of depression: A study of psychiatric disorder in women.* London: Tavistock.

Bry, B. H., McKeon, P., & Pandina, R. J. (1982). Extent of drug use as a function of number of risk factors. *Journal of Abnormal Psychology, 91,* 272–279.

Carson, R. C., Butcher, J. N., & Mineka, S. (1997). *Abnormal psychology and modern life* (10th ed.). New York: HarperCollins.

Carson, R. C., & Sanislow, C. A. (1993). The schizophrenias. In P. B. Sutker & H. E. Adams (Eds.), *Comprehensive handbook of psychopathology* (2d ed., pp. 295–333). New York: Plenum.

Clark, D. A., Beck, A. T., & Brown, G. K. (1992). Sociotropy, autonomy, and life event perceptions in dysphoric and nondysphoric individuals. *Cognitive Therapy and Research, 16,* 635–652.

Clark, D. A., & Watson, D. (1991). Tripartite model of anxiety and depression: Psychometric evidence and taxonomic implications. *Journal of Abnormal Psychology, 100,* 316–336.

Clark, D. A., Watson, D., & Mineka, S. (1994). Temperament, personality, and the mood and anxiety disorders. *Journal of Abnormal Psychology, 103,* 103–116.

Conners, M., & Morse, W. (1993). Sexual abuse and eating disorders: A review. *International Journal of Eating Disorders, 13,* 1–11.

Conte, H. R. (1997). The evolving nature of psychotherapy outcome research. *American Journal of Psychotherapy, 5,* 445–448.

Dalgleish, T., & Watts, F. N. (1990). Biases of attention and memory in disorders of anxiety and depression. *Clinical Psychology Review, 10,* 589–604.

Davis, G., & Akiskal, H. (1986). Descriptive, biological, and theoretical aspects of borderline personality disorder. *Hospital and Community Psychiatry, 17,* 685–692.

Donovan, J. A. (1986). An etiologic model of alcoholism. *American Journal of Psychiatry, 143,* 1–11.

Eaton, W. W. (1980). A formal theory of selection for schizophrenia. *American Journal of Sociology, 86,* 149–157.

Eaton, W. W., Day, R., & Kramer, M. (1986). A formal theory of selection for schizophrenia. In M. Tsuang & J. Simpson (Eds.), *Handbook of schizophrenia* (Vol. 4). Amsterdam: Elsevier.

Eisenberg, L. (1986). Mindlessness and brainlessness in psychiatry. *British Journal of Psychiatry, 148,* 497–508.

Eisendrath, S. J. (1997). Factitious physical disorders in the managed care setting. In H. Leigh (Ed.), *Biopsychosocial approaches in primary care: State of the art and challenges for the 21st century* (pp. 65–80). New York: Plenum.

Engel, G. L. (1977). The need for a new medical model: A challenge to biomedicine. *Science, 196,* 129–136.

Engel, G. L. (1980). The clinical application of the biopsychosocial model. *American Journal of Psychiatry, 137,* 535–544.

Ewing, J. A. (1980). Biopsychosocial approaches to drinking and alcoholism. In W. E. Fann, I. Karacan, A. D. Polorny, & R. L. Williams (Eds.), *Phenomenology and treatment of alcoholism.* New York: Spectrum.

Fink, P. J. (1988). Response to the presidential address: Is "biopsychosocial" the psychiatric shibboleth? *Ametican Journal of Psychiatry, 145*, 1061–1067.

Freeman, H. (1989). Relationship of schizophrenia to the environment. *British Journal of Psychiatry, 155* (Supplement 5), 90–99.

Friedman, H. S., & DeMatteo, M. R. (1979). Health care as an interpersonal process. *Journal of Social Issues, 35*, 1–11.

Galizio, M., & Maisto, S. A. (1985). Toward a biopsychosocial theory of substance abuse. In M. Galizio & S. A. Maisto (Eds.), *Determinants of substance abuse: Biological, psychological, and environmental factors* (pp. 425–429). New York: Plenum.

Goldstein, M. J. (1988). The family and psychopathology. *Annual Review of Psychology, 39*, 283–299.

Goplerud, E., & Depue, R. (1985). Behavioral response to naturally-occurring stress in cyclothymes, dysthymes, and controls. *Journal of Abnormal Psychology, 94*, 128–139.

Gotlib, I. H., & Hammen, C. L. (1992). *Psychological aspects of depression: Toward a cognitive–interpersonal integration.* New York: Wiley.

Gottesman, I. I. (1991). *Schizophrenia genesis: The origins of madness.* New York: Freeman.

Gottesman, I. I., & Shields, J. (1967). A polygenic theory of schizophrenia. *Proceedings of the National Academy of Sciences, United States of America, 58*, 199–205.

Gottesman, I. I., & Shields, J. (1982). *Schizophrenia: The epigenetic puzzle.* New York: Cambridge University Press.

Gunderson, J., & Siever, L. (1985). Relatedness of schizotypal to schizophrenic disorders: Editors' introduction. *Schizophrenia Bulletin, 11*, 532–537.

Hammen, C. L. (1988). Self-cognitions, stressful events, and the prediction of depression in children of depressed mothers. *Journal of Abnormal Child Psychology, 16*, 347–360.

Hammen, C. L., Ellicott, A., Gitlin, M. J., & Jamison, K. R. (1989). Sociotropy/ autonomy and vulnerability to specific life events in unipolar and bipolar patients. *Journal of Abnormal Psychology, 98*, 154–160.

Hunsley, J. (1989). Vulnerability to depressive mood: An examination of the temporal consistency of the reformulated learned helplessness model. *Cognitive Therapy and Research, 13*, 599–608.

Jemmott, J. B., & Locke, S. E. (1984). Psychosocial factors, immunological mediation, and human susceptibility to infectious disease: How much do we know? *Psychological Bulletin, 95*, 78–108.

Johnson, C., & Connors, M. E. (1987). *The etiology and treatment of bulimia nervosa: A biopsychosocial perspective.* New York: Basic Books.

Kendler, K. S., Kessler, R. C., Neale, M. C., Heath, A. C., & Eaves, L. J. (1993). The prediction of major depression in women: Toward an integrated etiological model. *American Journal of Psychiatry, 150*, 1139–1148.

Kendler, K. S., Walters, E. E., Neale, M. C., Kessler, R. C., Heath, A. C., & Eaves, L. J. (1995). The structure of the genetic and environmental risk factors for six major psychiatric disorders in women: Phobia, generalized anxiety disorder, panic disorder, bulimia, major depression, and alcoholism. *Archives of General Psychiatry, 52*, 374–383.

Kiesler, D. J. (1966). Some myths of psychotherapy research and the search for a paradigm. *Psychological Bulletin, 65*, 110–136.

Kirkpatrick-Smith, J., Rich, A. R., Bonner, R., & Jans, F. (1991–1992). Psychological vulnerability and substance abuse as predictors of suicide ideation among adolescents. *Omega Journal of Death and Dying, 24,* 21–33.

Krumboltz, J. D. (1966). *Resolution in counseling: Impacts of behavioral science.* Boston: Houghton Mifflin.

Kwon, S., & Oel, T. P. S. (1992). Differential causal roles of dysfunctional attitudes and automatic thoughts in depression. *Cognitive Therapy and Research, 16,* 309–328.

Leigh, H. (1983). The clinical applications of the biopsychosocial model. In A. J. Krakowski & C. P. Kimball (Eds.), *Psychosomatic medicine* (pp. 541–549). New York: Plenum.

Leigh, H. (Ed.). (1997a). *Biopsychosocial approaches in primary care: State of the art and challenges for the 21st century.* New York: Plenum.

Leigh, H. (1997b). Preface. In H. Leigh (Ed.), *Biopsychosocial approaches in primary care: State of the art and challenges for the 21st century* (pp. vii–viii). New York: Plenum.

Leigh, H. (1997c). Biopsychosocial approaches to anxiety in primary care. In H. Leigh (Ed.), *Biopsychosocial approaches in primary care: State of the art and challenges for the 21st century* (pp. 19–27). New York: Plenum.

Leigh, H. (1997d). Biopsychosocial approaches to depression. In H. Leigh (Ed.), *Biopsychosocial approaches in primary care: State of the art and challenges for the 21st century* (pp. 29–43). New York: Plenum.

Leigh, H., Feinstein, A. R., & Reiser, M. F. (1980). The Patient Evaluation Grid: A systematic approach to comprehensive care. *General Hospital Psychiatry, 2,* 3–9.

Leigh, H., & Reiser, M. F. (1992). *The patient: Biological, psychological, and social dimensions of medical practice* (3d ed.). New York: Plenum.

Lewis, D. O., Moy, E., Jackson, L. D., Aaronson, R., Restifo, N., Serra, S., & Simos, A. (1985). Biopsychosocial characteristics of children who later murder: A prospective study. *American Journal of Psychiatry, 142,* 1161–1167.

Lewis, D. O., Pincus, J. H., Lovely, R., Spitzer, E., & Moy, E. (1987). Biopsychosocial characteristics of matched samples of delinquents and nondelinquents. *Journal of the American Academy of Child and Adolescent Psychiatry, 26,* 744–752.

Lex, B. W. (1985). Alcohol problems in special populations. In J. H. Mendelson & N. K. Mello (Eds.), *The diagnosis and treatment of alcoholism* (2d ed., pp. 89–187). New York: McGraw-Hill.

Lipowski, Z. J. (1975). Psychiatry of somatic diseases: Epidemiology, pathogenesis, classification. *Comprehensive Psychiatry, 16,* 105–124.

Lipowski, Z. J. (1978). Organic brain syndrome: A reformulation. *Comprehensive Psychiatry, 19,* 309–322.

Mason, N. S., & Chaney, J. M. (1996). Bulimia nervosa in undergraduate women: Factors associated with internalization of the sociocultural standard of thinness. *Applied & Preventive Psychology, 5,* 249–259.

Mednick, S. A. (1970). Breakdown in individuals at high risk for schizophrenia: Possible predispositional perinatal factors. *Mental Hygiene, 54,* 50–61.

Mednick, S. A., Cudeck, R., Griffith, J. J., Talovic, S. A., & Schulsinger, F. A. (1984). The Danish High-Risk Project: Recent methods and findings. In

N. F. Watt, E. J. Anthony, L. C. Wynne, & J. E. Rolf (Eds.), *Children at risk for schizophrenia*. Cambridge, England: Cambridge University Press.

Mednick, S. A., & Schulsinger, F. (1968). Some premorbid characteristics related to breakdown in children with schizophrenic mothers. In D. Rosenthal & S. Kety (Eds.), *The transmission of schizophrenia*. Oxford, England: Pergamon.

Meehl, P. E. (1962). Schizotaxia, schizotypy, schizophrenia. *American Psychologist, 17*, 827–838.

Metalsky, G. I., Halberstadt, L. J., & Abramson, L. Y. (1987). Vulnerability to depressive mood reactions: Toward a more powerful test of the diathesis–stress and causal mediation components of the reformulated theory of depression. *Journal of Personality and Social Psychology, 52*, 386–393.

Metalsky, G. I., & Joiner, T. E. (1992). Vulnerability to depressive symptomatology: A prospective test of the diathesis–stress and causal mediation components of the hopelessness theory of depression. *Journal of Personality and Social Psychology, 63*, 667–675.

Miller, B., & Wood, B. (1991). Childhood asthma in interaction with family, school, and peer systems: A developmental model for primary care. *Journal of Asthma, 28*, 405–414.

Miller, B., & Wood, B. (1994). Psychophysiologic reactivity in asthmatic children: A cholinergically mediated confluence of pathways. *Journal of the American Academy of Child and Adolescent Psychiatry, 33*, 1236–1245.

Moncher, M., Holden, G., & Trimble, J. (1990). Substance abuse among Native American youth. *Journal of Consulting and Clinical Psychology, 58*, 408–415.

Monroe, S. M., & Simons, A. D. (1991). Diathesis–stress theories in the context of life stress research: Implications for the depressive disorders. *Psychological Bulletin, 119*, 406–425.

Mrazek, P. J., & Haggerty, R. J. (Eds.). (1994). *Reducing risks for mental disorders: Frontiers for preventive intervention research*. Washington, DC: National Academy Press.

National Advisory Mental Health Council. (1995). *Basic behavioral science research for mental health: A national investment*. Washington, DC: U.S. Government Printing Office.

NIMH Committee on Prevention Research. (1995, May 15). *A plan for prevention research for the National Institute of Mental Health*, a report to the National Advisory Mental Health Council. Washington, DC: Author.

NIMH Prevention Research Steering Committee. (1994). *The prevention of mental disorders: A national research agenda*. Washington, DC: Author.

Nolen-Hoeksema, S. (1987). Sex differences in unipolar depression: Evidence and theory. *Psychological Bulletin, 101*, 259–282.

Nolen-Hoeksema, S. (1990). *Sex differences in depression*. Stanford, CA: Stanford Press.

Nuechterlien, K. H. (1987). Vulnerability models for schizophrenia: State of the art. In H. Hafner, W. F. Gattax, & W. Janzarik (Eds.), *Search for the causes of schizophrenia* (pp. 297–316). New York: Springer-Verlag.

Nuechterlien, K. H., & Dawson, M. E. (1984). A heuristic vulnerability–stress model of schizophrenia episodes. *Schizophrenia Bulletin, 10*, 300–312.

O'Hara, M. W., Schlechte, J. A., Lewis, D. A., & Varner, M. W. (1991). Controlled prospective study of postpartum mood disorders: Psychological, environmental, and hormonal variables. *Journal of Abnormal Psychology, 100,* 63–73.

Olinger, L. J., Kuiper, N. A., & Shaw, B. F. (1987). Dysfunctional attitudes and stressful life events: An interactive model of depression. *Cognitive Therapy and Research, 11,* 25–40.

Paris, J. (1994). *Borderline personality disorder: A multidimensional approach.* Washington, DC: American Psychiatric Press.

Parker, J. C., Smarr, K. L., Walker, S. E., & Hagglund, K. J. (1991). Biopsychosocial parameters of disease activity in rheumatoid arthritis. *Arthritis Care and Research, 4,* 73–80.

Paul, G. (1967). Strategy in outcome research in psychotherapy. *Journal of Consulting Psychology, 31,* 109–118.

Peterson, C. (1996). *The psychology of abnormality.* Fort Worth, TX: Harcourt Brace.

Peterson, C. (1997). *Psychology: A biopsychosocial approach* (2d ed.). New York: Longman.

Peyrot, M, & McMurry, J. F. (1985). Psychosocial factors in diabetes control: Adjustment of insulin-treated adults. *Psychosomatic Medicine, 47,* 542–557.

Raine, A., Venables, P. H., & Williams, M. (1995). High autonomic arousal and electrodermal orienting at age 15 years as protective factors against criminal behavior at age 29 years. *American Journal of Psychiatry, 152,* 1595–1600.

Reiss, D., & Price, R. H. (1996). National research agenda for prevention research: The National Institute of Mental Health report. *American Psychologist, 51,* 1109–1122.

Resnick, H. S., Kilpatrick, D. G., Best, C. L., & Kramer, T. L. (1992). Vulnerability–stress factors in development of posttraumatic stress disorder. *Journal of Nervous and Mental Disease, 180,* 424–430.

Rich, A. R., & Bonner, R. L. (1987). Concurrent validity of a stress–vulnerability model of suicidal ideation and behavior: A follow-up study. *Suicide and Life Threatening Behavior, 17,* 265–270.

Richters, J., & Weintraub, S. (1990). Beyond diathesis: Toward an understanding of high-risk environments. In J. Rolf, A. S. Masten, D. Cicchetti, K. N. Nuechterlein, & S. Weintraub (Eds.), *Risk and protective factors in the development of psychopathology* (pp. 67–96). New York: Cambridge University Press.

Robins, C. J., & Block, P. (1989). Cognitive theories of depression viewed from a diathesis–stress perspective: Evaluations of the models of Beck and of Abramson, Seligman, and Teasdale. *Cognitive Therapy and Research, 13,* 297–313.

Rosenthal, D. (1970). *Genetic theory and abnormal behavior.* New York: McGraw-Hill.

Russo, J., Vitaliano, P. P., Brewer, D. D., Katon, W., & Becker, J. (1995). Psychiatric disorders in spouse caregivers of care recipients with Alzheimer's disease and matched controls: A diathesis–stress model of psychopathology. *Journal of Abnormal Psychology, 104,* 197–204.

Schall, M., Kemeny, A., & Maltzman, I. (1992). Factors associated with alcohol use in university students. *Journal of Studies on Alcohol, 53,* 122–136.

Schotte, D. E., Cools, J., & Payvar, S. (1990). Problem-solving deficits in suicidal patients: Trait vulnerability or state phenomenon? *Journal of Consulting and Clinical Psychology, 58,* 562–564.

Schwartz, G. E. (1982). Testing the biopsychosocial model: The ultimate challenge facing behavioral medicine. *Journal of Consulting and Clinical Psychology, 50,* 1040–1053.

Segal, Z. V., Shaw, B. F., Vella, D. D., & Katz, R. (1992). Cognitive and life stress predictors of relapse in remitted unipolar depressed patients: A test of the congruency hypothesis. *Journal of Abnormal Psychology, 101,* 26–36.

Sher, K. J., & Trull, T. J. (1994). Personality and disinhibitory psychopathology: Alcoholism and antisocial personality disorder. *Journal of Abnormal Psychology, 103,* 92–102.

Silverton, L. (1988). Crime and the schizophrenia spectrum: A diathesis–stress model. *Acta Psychiatrica Scandinavica, 78,* 72–81.

Spangler, D. L., Simons, A. D., Monroe, S. M., & Thase, M. E. (1996). Gender differences in cognitive diathesis–stress domain match: Implications for different pathways to depression. *Journal of Abnormal Psychology, 105,* 653–657.

Streltzer, J. (1997). Chronic pain. In H. Leigh (Ed.), *Biopsychosocial approaches in primary care: State of the art and challenges for the 21st century* (pp. 81–91). New York: Plenum.

Stuart, F. M., Hammond, D. C., & Pett, M. A. (1987). Inhibited sexual desire in women. *Archives of Sexual Behavior, 16,* 91–106.

Temoshok, L., Sagebiel, R. W., Blois, M. S., Heller, B. W., Sweet, D. M., DiClemente, R. J., & Gold, M. L. (1985). The relationship of psychosocial factors to prognostic indicators in cutaneous malignant melonoma. *Journal of Psychosomatic Research, 29,* 139–153.

Vasile, R. G., Samson, J. A., Bemporad, J., Bloomingdale, K. L., Creasey, D., Fenton, B. T., Gudeman, J. E., & Schildkraut, J. S. (1987). A biopsychosocial approach to treating patients with affective disorders. *American Journal of Psychiatry, 144,* 341–344.

Weiner, H., Thaler, M., Reiser, M. F., & Mirsky, I. A. (1957). Etiology of duodenal ulcer: 1. Relation of specific psychological characteristics to rate of gastric secretion. *Psychosomatic Medicine, 17,* 1–10.

Wender, P. L. (1977). The scope and validity of the schizophrenic spectrum concept. In V. R. Rakoff, H. C. Stancer, & H. B. Kedward (Eds.), *Psychiatric diagnosis.* New York: Brunner/Mazel.

Widiger, T. A. (1989). *Personality disorder dimensional models for DSM-IV.* Unpublished manuscript, Cornell University Medical College, Payne Whitney Psychiatric Clinic, New York.

Widiger, T. A., Frances, A. J., & Sweeney, M. (1988). Schizophrenia spectrum disorders. *Current Opinion in Psychiatry, 1,* 13–18.

Wise, T. N. (1997). Psychiatric diagnosis in primary care. In H. Leigh (Ed.), *Biopsychosocial approaches in primary care: State of the art and challenges for the 21st century* (pp. 9–18). New York: Plenum.

Zubin, J., & Spring, B. J. (1977). Vulnerability: A new view of schizophrenia. *Journal of Abnormal Psychology, 86,* 103–126.

Chapter 9

Implications of Multicausal Theories for the Science and Disciplines of Psychopathology

The scientific study and understanding of mental disorders could not enjoy a more opportune and promising moment. Biopsychosocial currents are flowing through every area and discipline within psychopathology. It behooves all serious scientists and laypersons who seek understanding of mental disorders to follow these currents to whatever beaches may appear on the horizon.

Disciplinary researchers within psychopathology—psychiatrists, psychologists, anthropologists, and sociologists—need to, and will undoubtedly, continue their separate monocausal empirical efforts. In the past, these divergent emphases have provided creative causal insights and findings. These respective findings, in turn, have stimulated constructive controversies and sparked reciprocal challenges from all concerned, advancing psychopathology in a manner not otherwise possible.

In light of this, what now does the scientific multicausal biopsychosocial perspective demand? First, *all educated lay persons and scientists of psychopathology must quit professing, or tolerating others who advocate or imply, single causes of mental disorders*. We have to stop acquiescing to pontifications that mental disorders are brain diseases—we need to insist that the necessary psychosocial stressors be added. We have to stop blaming individuals' psychological dispositions (thoughts and coping strategies) for mental disorders—unless biological and socio-cultural elaboration occurs. We must quit blaming sick societies, sub-cultures, or organizations for mental disorders—unless we specify also relevant biological and psychological factors. Perhaps, most of all we all need to invent new language, whenever necessary, to describe the now undeniable multicausal complexity of mental disorders.

Second, *researchers in the various biopsychosocial disciplines of psycho-pathology must stop remaining only casually aware of each other's research; instead, they need to master each other's latest theories and findings.* Up-to-date expert knowledge in each of the biopsychosocial domains needs constantly to inform and add sophistication to investigations con-ducted in the other tripartite domains. For example, knowledge about cognitive mechanisms (e.g., cognitive slippage in attentional and per-ceptual processes) demonstrated for a particular mental disorder can-not help but provide leads and checks on studies of the corresponding brain areas and functions.

Third, *increased instances of biopsychosocially driven, multidisciplinary research projects are direly needed.* Larger-scale cooperative projects that incorporate experts from various disciplines (bringing together state-of-the-science biological, psychological, and sociocultural variables and measures) are indispensable to teasing out the relative contributions, and important interactions, among these multiple causative factors. Fortunately, the field has available sophisticated multivariate designs and statistics that permit robust answers to emerge from these com-plex sets of biopsychosocial data.

Fourth, *the most vital arena for introduction of a vigorous biopsychosocial perspective is within the various training programs of the mental health dis-ciplines and sciences.* A basic precondition for this occurrence is that the textbooks of psychopathology and abnormal psychology published within the separate disciplines need to show substantial changes. Chap-ters devoted to each of the mental disorders must converge on com-prehensive presentation of theories constructed to integrate available multicausal scientific findings: biological, psychological, and socio-cultural. The upshot would be that textbooks found within such areas as psychiatry, clinical psychology, social work, and psychiatric nurs-ing would all begin to look the same, except for differential coverage and emphasis for each discipline's traditional specialty.

In hopes of facilitating the latter outcome, the following list offers what I call "The Universal Outine of Psychopathology." Directly re-flecting the multicausal, biopsychosocial framework of this book, this outline specifies for textbooks of psychopathology the minimal cover-age each chapter on a particular mental disorder should provide, re-gardless of scientific discipline.

A. Defining the disorder
1. Classification criteria (DSM-IV and others)
2. Evidence of reliability and validity of diagnosis
3. Incidence and prevalence of the disorder (epidemiological evidence)
4. Relationship of diagnosis to other forms of pathology: comorbidity with other mental disorders
5. Central features of differential diagnosis

B. Course of disorder
1. Age and nature of onset
2. Duration and course of episode(s)
3. Nature and course of recovery

C. Approaches and methods of diagnostic assessment
1. Structured diagnostic interviews
2. Biological tests and robust biological markers
3. Psychological tests and robust psychological markers
4. Epidemiological tests and robust sociocultural markers

D. Developmental antecedents of the disorder
1. Biopsychosocial risk and protective factors: high-risk and other developmental psychopathology research
2. Formative environmental stressors: unshared and shared family environmental factors
3. Critical developmental stages
4. Precipitating major and chronic stressors

E. Etiological factors and evidence
1. Contributory biological factors
   a. Genetic evidence
   b. Biochemical and other biological dysfunctions
2. Contributory psychological factors
   a. Psychological cognitive and dispositional dysfunctions
   b. Family interactional and communicational dysfunctions
3. Contributory sociocultural factors
   a. Demographic correlates: epidemiologic evidence
   b. Cultural correlates: within-cultural and cross-cultural evidence
4. Major multicausal (diathesis–stress and biopsychosocial) theories

F. Prevention and intervention approaches
1. Biological: psychopharmacological and other
2. Psychological: individual, group, and family
3. Sociocultural: neighborhood, community, national and international
4. Biopsychosocial preventions and interventions
5. Evidence of efficacy and cost-effectiveness

Fifth, *all scientists of psychopathology need to stay knowledgeable of existing multicausal, biopsychosocial models that have been offered for the various mental disorders*. Psychiatrists, psychologists, sociologists, and others also need to contribute to development of new multicausal, biopsychosocial theories.

In sum, *any valid explanatory attempt has to deal with biological, psychological, and sociocultural formative and precipitating factors. Any multicausal, diathesis–stress theory has to specify relevant diathesis and stress factors from each of the tripartite domains. Research efforts and programs may remain monocausal, but attempts at valid theoretical explanations may not be anything other than multicausal.*

The Appendix presents a summary (undoubtedly incomplete) of all the multicasual (diathesis–stress and biopsychosocial) theories of psychopathology I could locate. The lists details only *etiological* theories of mental disorders; it does not include exclusive discussions and/or conceptualizations of biopsychosocial *treatments or care strategies* for the mental disorders. It seems plausible that sophisticated biopsychosocial treatment models necessarily require prior existence of advanced etiological formulations.

Development of treatment models based on specific biopsychosocial etiological theories should constitute an exciting and creative challenge. Distinctive treatment components will need to target specifically the biological, psychological, and sociocultural vulnerability and protective factors identified by a particular theory. Effort also will be required to target the tripartite components in a manner reflecting their relative etiological contribution and in a sequence reflecting specific conceptualization of their successive interactions.

A new era of combining biological and psychosocial treatments has begun to arrive (Robinson, Berman, & Neimeyer, 1990). Increasing evidence suggests, for example, that in the case of depressive disorders, antidepressant medications combined with psychological therapies are superior to either by itself (Karasu, 1990; Lazarus, 1992; Perry, 1990). It is plausible that similar combinations may become the preferred means of treating depressive disorders.

Until more validated etiological theories become established, it is likely that design of biopsychosocial treatment packages will remain primarily an art based substantially on creative hunches. On the other hand, validation of biopsychosocial treatment packages for a particular disorder, through efficacy and effectiveness studies, can confirm and suggest modification of existing biopsychosocial etiological notions.

Regardless, anyone seriously interested in understanding a particular mental disorder needs first to touch base seriously with the initial multicausal (biopsychosocial and vulnerability–stress) theoretical offerings listed in the Appendix. These references can serve as springboards to increasingly more heuristic future theory, research, and practice in psychopathology.

REFERENCES

Karasu, T. B. (1990). Toward a clinical model of psychotherapy for depression: I. Systematic comparison of three psychotherapies. *American Journal of Psychiatry, 147,* 133–147.

Lazarus, A. A. (1992). The multimodal approach to the treatment of minor depression. *American Journal of Psychotherapy, 46,* 50–57.

Perry, S. W. (1990). Combining antidepressants and psychotherapy: Rationale and strategies. *Journal of Clinical Psychiatry, 51,* 16–20.

Robinson, L. A., Berman, J. S., & Neimeyer, R. A. (1990). Psychotherapy for the treatment of depression: A comprehensive review of controlled outcome research. *Psychological Bulletin, 108,* 30–49.

Appendix

Multicausal (Diathesis–Stress and Other Biopsychosocial) Theories of Mental Disorders

References are arranged alphabetically for individual DSM disorders; accompanying "disorders" listed within parentheses are the DSM-IV Major Categories under which the individual disorders are classified.

ADJUSTMENT DISORDERS ("ADJUSTMENT DISORDERS")

Frankenhaeuser, M. (1989). A biopsychosocial approach to work life issues. *International Journal of Health Services, 19,* 747–758.

ALCOHOL-RELATED DISORDERS ("SUBSTANCE-RELATED DISORDERS")

Alonso-Fernandez, F. (1987). El metodo de los modelos en la representacion de los tipos alcoholicos. *Psicopathologia, 7,* 9–18.

Cox, W. M., & Klinger, E. (1988). A motivational model of alcohol use. *Journal of Abnormal Psychology, 97,* 168–180.

Cox, W. M., & Klinger, E. (1990). Inventive motivation, affective change, and alcohol use: A model. In W. M. Cox & E. Klinger (Eds.), *Why people drink: Parameters of alcohol as a reinforcer.* New York: Gardner.

Donovan, J. A. (1986). An etiologic model of alcoholism. *American Journal of Psychiatry, 143,* 1–11.

Ewing, J. A. (1980). Biopsychosocial approaches to drinking and alcoholism. In W. E. Fann, I. Karacan, A. D. Pokorny, & R. L. Williams (Eds.), *Phenomenology and treatment of alcoholism.* New York: Spectrum.

Kissin, B., & Hanson, M. (1982). The bio-psycho-social perspective in alcoholism. In J. Solomon (Ed.), *Alcoholism and clinical psychiatry* (pp. 1–19). New York: Plenum.

Levin, J. D. (1989). *Alcoholism: A bio-psycho-social approach.* New York: Hemisphere.

McCord, J. (1988). Alcoholism: Toward understanding genetic and social factors. *Psychiatry, 51,* 131–141.

Miller, W. R. (1993). Alcoholism: Toward a better disease model. *Psychology of Addictive Behaviors, 7,* 129–136.

Nathan, P. E. (1990). Integration of biological and psychosocial research on alcoholism. *Alcoholism: Clinical and Experimental Research, 14,* 368–374.

Nathan, P. E., & Hay, W. M. (1984). Alcoholism: Psychopathology, etiology, and treatment. In H. E. Adams & P. B. Sutker (Eds.), *Comprehensive handbook of psychopathology* (pp. 549–583). New York: Plenum.

National Institute on Alcohol Abuse and Alcoholism (NIAAA). (1997, April 2–3). *A Symposium. Genes and the environment in complex diseases: A focus on alcoholism.* Washington, DC: NIH Natcher Conference Center.

Newcomb, M., & Earleywine, M. (1996). Intrapersonal contributors to drug use: The willing host. *American Behavioral Scientist, 39,* 823–837.

Potvin, R. H., & Lee, C. (1980). Multistage path models of adolescent alcohol and drug use. *Journal of Studies on Alcohol, 41,* 531–542.

Searles, J. S. (1991). The genetics of alcoholism: Impact on family and sociological models of addiction. *Family Dynamics of Addiction Quarterly, 1,* 8–21.

Tarter, R. E., & Edwards, K. L. (1987). Vulnerability to alcohol and drug abuse: A behavior–genetic view. *Journal of Drug Issues, 17,* 67–81.

Tarter, R. E., & Edwards, K. L. (1988). Vulnerability to alcohol and drug abuse: A behavior–genetic view. In S. Peele (Ed.), *Visions of addiction: Major contemporary perspective on addiction and alcoholism* (pp. 67–84). Lexington, MA: Lexington Books.

Van Dijk, W. K. (1979). Alcoholism, a many-sided problem. In J. Mendlewicz & H. M. van Praag (Eds.), *Alcoholism: A multidisciplinary approach* (pp. 2–10). Basel, Switzerland: Kargel.

Wallace, J. (1989). A biopsychosocial model of alcoholism. *Social Casework, 70,* 325–332.

Zucker, R. A., & Linsansky-Gomberg, E. S. (1986). Etiology of alcoholism reconsidered: The case for a biopsychosocial process. *American Psychologist, 41,* 783–793.

ANOREXIA NERVOSA & BULIMIA NERVOSA ("EATING DISORDERS")

Bemis-Vitousek, K., & Orimoto, L. (1993). Cognitive–behavioral models of anorexia nervosa, bulimia nervosa, and obesity. In K. S. Dobson & P. C. Kendall (Eds.), *Psychopathology and cognition.* San Diego, CA: Academic Press.

Garfinkel, P. E., & Garner, D. M. (1982). *Anorexia nervosa: A multidimensional perspective.* New York: Brunner/Mazel.

Garfinkel, P. E., Garner, D. M., & Goldbloom, D. S. (1987). Eating disorders: Implications for the 1990's. *Canadian Journal of Psychiatry, 32,* 624–629.

Garner, D. M., & Garfinkel, P. E. (1980). Socio-cultural factors in the development of anorexia nervosa. *Psychological Medicine, 10,* 647–656.

Johnson, C., & Connors, M. W. (1987). *The etiology and treatment of bulimia nervosa: A biopsychosocial perspective.* New York: Basic Books.

Nagel, K. L., & Jones, K. H. (1992a). Predisposition factors in anorexia nervosa. *Adolescence, 27,* 381–386.

Nagel, K. L., & Jones, K. H. (1992b). Sociological factors in the development of eating disorders. *Adolescence, 27,* 107–113.

Rodin, J., Striegel-Moore, R. H., & Silberstein, L. R. (1990). Vulnerability and resilience in the age of eating disorders: Risk and protective factors for bulimia nervosa. In J. Rolf, A. S. Masten, D. Cicchetti, K. H. Nuechterlein, & S. Weintraub (Eds.), *Risk and protective factors in the development of psychopathology* (pp. 361–383). New York: Cambridge University Press.

Slade, P. D. (1982). Towards a functional analysis of anorexia nervosa and bulimia nervosa. *British Journal of Clinical Psychology, 21,* 167–179.

Stice, E. (1994). Review of the evidence for a sociocultural model of bulimia nervosa and an exploration of the mechanisms of action. *Clinical Psychology Review, 14,* 633–661.

ANTISOCIAL PERSONALITY DISORDER
("PERSONALITY DISORDERS")

Cadoret, R. J., & Cain, C. (1981). Environmental and genetic factors in predicting adolescent antisocial behavior in adoptees. *Psychiatric Journal of the University of Ottawa, 6,* 220–225.

Cadoret, R. J., Troughton, E., Bagford, J., & Woodworth, G. (1990). Genetic and environmental factors in adoptee antisocial personality. *European Archives of Psychiatry and Neurological Sciences, 239,* 231–240.

Cadoret, R. J., Yates, W. R., Troughton, E., Woodworth, G., & Stewart, M. A. (1995). Genetic–environmental interaction in the genesis of aggressivity and conduct disorders. *Archives of General Psychiatry, 52,* 916–924.

Cloninger, C. R., Reich, T., & Guze, S. B. (1978). Genetic–environmental interactions and antisocial behavior. In R. D. Hare & D. Schalling (Eds.), *Psychopathic behavior: Approaches to research.* New York: Wiley.

Cortes, J. B. (1972). *Delinquency and crime: A biopsychosocial approach. Empirical, theoretical, and practical aspects of criminal behavior.* New York: Seminar.

Paris, J. (1996). Antisocial personality disorder: A biopsychosocial model. *Canadian Journal of Psychiatry, 41,* 75–80.

Sher, K. J., & Trull, T. J. (1994). Personality and disinhibitory psychopathology: Alcoholism and antisocial personality disorder. *Journal of Abnormal Psychology, 103,* 92–102.

ANXIETY DISORDERS ("ANXIETY DISORDERS")

Barlow, D. H. (1988). *Anxiety and its disorders: The nature and treatment of anxiety and panic.* New York: Guilford.

Eysenck, M. W. (1997). *Anxiety and cognition: A unified theory.* Hove, England: Psychology Press.

Russo, J., Vitaliano, P. P., Brewer, D. D., Katon, W., & Becker, J. (1995). Psychiatric disorders in spouse caregivers of care recipients with Alzheimer's disease and matched controls: A diathesis–stress model of psychopathology. *Journal of Abnormal Psychology, 104,* 197–204.

BIPOLAR DISORDERS ("MOOD DISORDERS")

Akiskal, H. S., & McKinney, W. T. (1975). Overview of recent research in depression: Integration of ten conceptual models into a comprehensive clinical frame. *Archives of General Psychiatry, 32,* 285–305.

Glassner, B. (1978). Sociological origins of manic–depression among working-class women. Paper presented at the annual meeting of the Society for the Study of Social Problems.

Glassner, B., & Light, D., Jr. (1979). Manic depression and the biopsychosocial dynamics of role loss. Paper presented at the annual meeting of the Southern Sociological Society.

BORDERLINE PERSONALITY DISORDER ("PERSONALITY DISORDERS")

Davis, G. C., & Akiskal, H. S. (1986). Descriptive, biological, and theoretical aspects of borderline personality disorder. *Hospital and Community Psychiatry, 37,* 685–692.

Linehan, M. M., & Kehrer, C. A. (1993). Borderline personality disorder. In D. H. Barlow (Ed.), *Clinical handbook of psychological disorders* (2d ed., pp. 396–441). New York: Guilford.

Linehan, M. M., & Koerner, K. (1992). A behavioral theory of borderline personality disorder. In J. Paris (Ed.), *Borderline personality disorder: Etiology and treatment* (pp. 103–121). Washington, DC: American Psychiatric Press.

Paris, J. (1994a). *Borderline personality disorder: A multidimensional approach.* Washington, DC: American Psychiatric Press.

Paris, J. (1994b). The etiology of borderline personality disorder: A biopsychosocial approach. *Psychiatry, 57,* 316–325.

Siever, L. J. (1984). A vulnerability model of borderline personality disorder. *Integrative Psychiatry, 2,* 187–188.

DELIRIUM, DEMENTIA, & AMNESTIC AND OTHER COGNITIVE DISORDERS

Lipowski, Z. J. (1975). Psychiatry of somatic diseases: Epidemiology, pathogenesis, classification. *Comprehensive Psychiatry, 16,* 105–124.

Lipowski, Z. J. (1978). Organic brain syndrome: A reformulation. *Comprehensive Psychiatry, 19,* 309–322.

Lipowski, Z. J. (1980). Delirium updated. *Comprehensive Psychiatry, 21,* 190–196.

DEMENTIA ("DELIRIUM, DEMENTIA, & AMNESTIC AND OTHER COGNITIVE DISORDERS")

Amaducci, L. A., Fratiglioni, L., Rocca, W. A., Fieschi, C., Livrea, P., Pedone, D., Bracco, L., Lippi, A., Gandolfo, C., & Bino, G. (1986). Risk factors for clinically diagnosed Alzheimer's disease. *Neurology, 36,* 922–931.

DEPRESSIVE DISORDERS: MAJOR DEPRESSIVE DISORDER & DYSTHYMIC DISORDER ("MOOD DISORDERS")

Abramson, L. Y., Alloy, L. B., & Metalsky, G. I. (1988). The cognitive diathesis–stress theories of depression: Toward an adequate evaluation of the theories' validities. In L. B. Alloy (Ed.), *Cognitive processes in depression* (pp. 3–30). New York: Guilford.

Abramson, L. Y., Metalsky, G. I., & Alloy, L. B. (1989). Hopelessness depression: A theory-based subtype of depression. *Psychological Review, 96,* 358–372.

Akiskal, H. S. (1985). Interaction of biologic and psychologic factors in the origin of depressive disorder. *Acta Psychiatrica Scandinavica, 71,* 131–139.

Akiskal, H. S., & McKinney, W. T. (1973). Depressive disorders: Toward a unified hypothesis. *Science, 182,* 20–29.

Akiskal, H. S., & McKinney, W. T. (1975). Overview of recent research in depression: Integration of ten conceptual models into a comprehensive clinical frame. *Archives of General Psychiatry, 32,* 285–305.

Anthony, J. C., & Petronis, K. R. (1991). Suspected risk factors for depression among adults 18–44 years old. *Epidemiology, 2,* 123–132.

Alloy, L. B., Hartlage, S., & Abramson, L. Y. (1988). Testing the cognitive diathesis–stress theories of depression: Issues of research design, conceptualization, and assessment. In L. B. Alloy (Ed.), *Cognitive processes in depression* (pp. 31–73). New York: Guilford.

Beck, A. T. (1983). Cognitive therapy for depression: New perspectives. In P. J. Clayton & J. E. Barrett (Eds.), *Treatment of depression: Old controversies and new approaches* (pp. 265–290). New York: Raven.

Beck, A. T. (1987). Cognitive models of depression. *Journal of Cognitive Psychotherapy: An International Quarterly, 1,* 5–37.

Billings, A. G., & Moos, R. H. (1986). Psychosocial theory and research on depression: An integrative framework and review. In J. C. Coyne (Ed.), *Essential papers on depression* (pp. 331–365). New York: New York University Press.

Brown, G. W. (1986). A three-factor causal model of depression. In J. C. Coyne (Ed.), *Essential papers on depression* (pp. 390–402). New York: New York University Press.

Brown, G. W. (1989). Depression: A radical social perspective. In K. R. Herbst & E. S. Paykel (Eds.), *Depression: An integrative approach.* London: Heinemann Medical Books.

Clark, D. A., & Watson, D. (1991). Tripartite model of anxiety and depression: Psychometric evidence and taxonomic implications. *Journal of Abnormal Psychology, 100,* 316–336.

Clark, D. A., Watson, D., & Mineka, S. (1994). Temperament, personality, and the mood and anxiety disorders. *Journal of Abnormal Psychology, 103,* 103–116.

Dalgleish, T., & Watts, F. N. (1990). Biases of attention and memory in disorders of anxiety and depression. *Clinical Psychology Review, 10,* 589–604.

Ehlers, C. L., Frank, E., & Kupfer, D. J. (1988). Social zeitgebers and biological rhythms: A unified approach to understanding the etiology of depression. *Archives of General Psychiatry, 45,* 948–952.

Free, M. L., & Oei, T. P. S. (1989). Biological and psychological processes in the treatment and maintenance of depression. *Clinical Psychology Review, 9,* 653–688.

Goplerud, E., & Depue, R. (1985). Behavioral response to naturally-occurring stress in cyclothymes, dysthymes, and controls. *Journal of Abnormal Psychology, 94*, 128–139.

Gotlib, I. H., & Hammen, C. L. (1992). *Psychological aspects of depression: Toward a cognitive–interpersonal integration.* New York: Wiley.

Hammen, C. L. (1988). Self-cognitions, stressful events, and the prediction of depression in children of depressed mothers. *Journal of Abnormal Child Psychology, 16*, 347–360.

Hammen, C. L. (1992). Cognitive, life stress, and interpersonal approaches to a developmental psychopathology model of depression. *Development and Psychopathology, 4*, 189–206.

Hollon, S. D. (1992). Cognitive models of depression from a biopsychosocial perspective. *Psychological Inquiry, 3*, 249–253.

Kendler, K. S., Kessler, R. C., Neale, M. C., Heath, A. C., & Eaves, L. J. (1993). The prediction of major depression in women: Toward an integrated etiological model. *American Journal of Psychiatry, 150*, 1139–1148.

Kwon, S., & Oel, T. P. S. (1992). Differential causal roles of dysfunctional attitudes and automatic thoughts in depression. *Cognitive Therapy and Research, 16*, 309–328.

Lewinsohn, P. M., Hoberman, H., Teri, L., & Hautzinger, M. (1985). An integrative theory of depression. In S. Reiss & R. R. Bootzin (Eds.), *Theoretical issues in behavior therapy* (pp. 331–353). New York: Academic Press.

Monroe, S. M., & Simons, A. D. (1991). Diathesis–stress theories in the context of life stress research: Implications for the depressive disorders. *Psychological Bulletin, 119*, 406–425.

Nolen-Hoeksema, S. (1987). Sex differences in unipolar depression: Evidence and theory. *Psychological Bulletin, 101*, 259–282.

Nolen-Hoeksema, S. (1990). *Sex differences in depression.* Stanford, CA: Stanford Press.

Olinger, L. J., Kuiper, N. A., & Shaw, B. F. (1987). Dysfunctional attitudes and stressful life events: An interactive model of depression. *Cognitive Therapy and Research, 11*, 25–40.

Peterson, C., & Seligman, M. E. P. (1984). Causal explanations as a risk factor for depression: Theory and evidence. *Psychological Review, 91*, 347–374.

Shelton, R. C., Hollon, S. D., Purdon, S. E., & Loosen, P. T. (1991). Biological and psychological aspects of depression. *Behavior Therapy, 22*, 201–228.

Zisook, S. (Ed.). (1987). *Biopsychosocial aspects of bereavement.* Washington, DC: American Psychiatric Press.

Zuroff, D. C., & Mongrain, M. (1987). Dependency and self-criticism: Vulnerability factors for depressive affective states. *Journal of Abnormal Psychology, 96*, 14–22.

DISORDERS USUALLY FIRST DIAGNOSED IN INFANCY, CHILDHOOD, OR ADOLESCENCE ("DISORDERS USUALLY FIRST DIAGNOSED IN INFANCY, CHILDHOOD, OR ADOLESCENCE")

Baumeister, A. A., Kupstas, F. D., & Klindworth, L. M. (1991). The new morbidity: A national plan of action [mild mental retardation]. *American Behavioral Scientist, 34*, 468–500.

Capaldi, D. M., & Patterson, G. R. (1994). Interrelated influences of contextual factors on antisocial behavior in childhood and adolescence for males. In D. C. Fowles, P. Sutker, & S. H. Goodman (Eds.), *Progress in experimental personality and psychopathology research*. New York: Springer.

Cicchetti, D., & Schneider-Rosen, K. (1984). Toward a transactional model of childhood depression. In D. Cicchetti & K. Schneider-Rosen (Eds.), *Childhood depression*. San Francisco: Jossey-Bass.

Connors, M., & Morse, W. (1993). Sexual abuse and eating disorders: A review. *International Journal of Eating Disorders, 13*, 1–11.

Cole, D. A., & Turner, J. E. (1993). Models of cognitive mediation and moderation in child depression. *Journal of Abnormal Psychology, 102*, 271–281.

Hinshaw, S. P. (1992). Externalizing behavior problems and academic underachievement in childhood and adolescence: Causal relationships and underlying mechanisms [Attention Deficit Hyperactivity Disorder]. *Psychological Bulletin, 111*, 127–155.

Hinshaw, S. P. (1994). Conduct disorder in childhood: Conceptualization, diagnosis, comorbidity, and risk status for antisocial functioning in adulthood. In D. C. Fowles, P. Sutker, & S. A. Goodman (Eds.), *Progress in experimental personality and psychopathology research*. New York: Springer.

Jacobvitz, D., & Sroufe, L. A. (1987). The early caregiver–child relationship and attention-deficit disorder with hyperactivity in kindergarten: A prospective study. *Child Development, 58*, 1488–1495.

Rapoport, J. L., & Quinn, P. O. (1975). Minor physical anomalies (stigmata) and early developmental deviation: Major biologic subgroups of "hyperactive children." *International Journal of Mental Health, 4*, 29–44.

Sameroff, A. J. (1993). Models of development and developmental risk. In C. H. Zeanah (Ed.), *Handbook of infant mental health* (pp. 3–13). New York: Guilford.

Sameroff, A. J. (1995). General systems theories of developmental psychopathology. In D. Cicchetti & D. J. Cohen (Eds.), *Developmental psychopathology: Volume 1. Theory and methods* (pp. 659–695). New York: Wiley.

Weiner, J. M., & Hendren, R. L. (1983). Childhood depression. *Journal of Developmental and Behavioral Pediatrics, 4*, 43–49.

DISSOCIATIVE IDENTITY DISORDER
("DISSOCIATIVE DISORDERS")

Braun, B. G., & Sachs, R. G. (1985). The development of multiple personality disorder: Predisposing, precipitating, and perpetuating factors. In R. P. Kluft (Ed.), *Childhood antecedents of multiple personality* (pp. 37–64). Washington, DC: American Psychiatric Press.

FETISHISM: PARAPHILIAS
("SEXUAL & GENDER IDENTITY DISORDERS")

Wise, T. N. (1985). Fetishism—Etiology and treatment: A review from multiple perspectives. *Comprehensive Psychiatry, 26*, 249–257.

HYPOACTIVE SEXUAL DESIRE DISORDER: SEXUAL DYSFUNCTION ("SEXUAL & GENDER IDENTITY DISORDERS")

Beck, J. G. (1995). Hypoactive sexual desire disorder: An overview. *Journal of Consulting and Clinical Psychology, 63,* 919–927.

MALE ERECTILE DISORDER: SEXUAL DYSFUNCTION ("SEXUAL & GENDER IDENTITY DISORDERS")

Carey, M. P., Wincze, J. P., & Meisler, A. W. (1993). Sexual dysfunction: Male erectile disorder. In D. H. Barlow (Ed.), *Clinical handbook of psychological disorders* (2d ed., pp. 442–480). New York: Guilford.

Meisler, A. W., & Carey, M. P. (1990). A critical reevaluation of nocturnal penile tumescence monitoring in the diagnosis of erectile dysfunction. *Journal of Nervous and Mental Disease, 178,* 78–89.

Wincze, J. P., & Carey, M. P. (1991). *Sexual dysfunction: A guide for assessment and treatment.* New York: Guilford.

OBSESSIVE–COMPULSIVE DISORDER ("ANXIETY DISORDERS")

Turner, S. M., Beidel, D. C., & Nathan, R. S. (1985). Biological factors in obsessive–compulsive disorders. *Psychological Bulletin, 97,* 430–450.

PAIN DISORDER ("SOMATOFORM DISORDERS")

Dworkin, S. F., Von Korff, M. R., & LeResche, L. (1992). Epidemiologic studies of chronic pain: A dynamic–ecologic perspective. *Annals of Behavioral Medicine, 14,* 3–11.

Melzack, R., & Wall, P. (1965). Pain mechanisms: A new theory. *Science, 50,* 971–979.

Turk, D. C., & Holzman, A. D. (1986). Chronic pain: Interfaces among physical, psychological, and social parameters. In A. D. Holzman & D. C. Turk (Eds.), *Pain management: A handbook of psychological treatment approaches* (pp. 1–9). Elmsford, NY: Pergamon.

PANIC DISORDER ("ANXIETY DISORDERS")

Barlow, D. H. (1988). *Anxiety and its disorders: The nature and treatment of anxiety and panic.* New York: Guilford.

PEDOPHILIA: PARAPHILIAS ("SEXUAL & GENDER IDENTITY DISORDERS")

Finkelhor, D., & Araji, S. (1986). Explanation of pedophilia: A four factor model. *The Journal of Sex Research, 22,* 145–161.

PERSONALITY DISORDERS ("PERSONALITY DISORDERS")

Endler, S., & Edwards, J. M. (1988). Personality disorders from an interactional perspective. *Journal of Personality Disorders, 2,* 326–333.

Millon, T. (1983). An integrative theory of personality and psychopathology. In T. Millon (Ed.), *Theories of personality and psychopathology*. New York: Holt, Rinehart & Winston.

Paris, J. (1993). Personality disorders: A biopsychosocial model. *Journal of Personality Disorders, 7*, 255–264.

Siever, L. J., & Davis, K. L. (1991). A psychobiological perspective on the personality disorders. *American Journal of Psychiatry, 148*, 1647–1658.

POST-TRAUMATIC STRESS DISORDER: PTSD ("ANXIETY DISORDERS")

Brewin, C. R., Dalgleish, T., & Joseph, S. (1996). A dual representation theory of posttraumatic stress disorder. *Psychological Review, 103*, 670–686.

Foy, D. W., Osato, S. S., Houskamp, B. M., & Neumann, D. A. (1991). PTSD etiology. In P.A. Saigh (Ed.), *Post-traumatic stress disorder: A behavioral approach to assessment and treatment*. New York: Elsevier Science.

Jones, J. C., & Barlow, D. H. (1990). The etiology of posttraumatic stress disorder. *Clinical Psychology Review, 10*, 299–328.

Jones, J. C., & Barlow, D. H. (1992). A new model of posttraumatic stress disorder: Implications for the future. In P. A. Saigh (Ed.), *Posttraumatic stress disorder* (pp. 147–165). New York: Macmillan.

Van Der Kolk, B. A. (1984). *Post-traumatic stress disorder: Psychological and biological sequelae*. Washington, DC: American Psychiatric Press.

Van Der Kolk, B. A., Greenberg, M. S., Boyd, H., & Krystal, J. (1985). Inescapable shock, neurotransmitters, and addiction to trauma: Toward a psychobiology of post-traumatic stress. *Biological Psychiatry, 20*, 314–325.

PREMATURE EJACULATION–ORGASMIC DISORDER: SEXUAL DYSFUNCTIONS ("SEXUAL & GENDER IDENTITY DISORDERS")

Strassberg, D. S., Kelly, M. P., Carroll, C., & Kircher, J. C. (1987). The psychophysiological nature of premature ejaculation. *Archives of Sexual Behavior, 16*, 327–336.

PSYCHOLOGICAL FACTORS AFFECTING PHYSICAL CONDITION ("OTHER CONDITIONS THAT MAY BE A FOCUS OF CLINICAL ATTENTION")

Andersen, B. L., Kiecolt-Glaser, J. K., & Glaser, R. (1994). A biobehavioral model of cancer stress and disease course. *American Psychologist, 49*, 389–404.

Barglow, P., Berndt, D. J., Burns, W. J., & Hatcher, R. (1986). Neuroendocrine and psychological factors in childhood diabetes mellitus. *Journal of the American Academy of Child Psychiatry, 25*, 785–793.

Dumont, S., Deshaies, G., & Dube, C. (1992). Vers une compréhension bio-psycho-sociale du developpement de la maladie coronarienne et de son evolution suite à l'infarctus. *Canadian Journal of Counselling, 26*, 41–56.

Miller, B., & Wood, B. (1991). Childhood asthma in interaction with family, school, and peer systems: A developmental model for primary care. *Journal of Asthma, 28*, 405–414.

Miller, B., & Wood, B. (1994). Psychophysiologic reactivity in asthmatic children: A cholinergically mediated confluence of pathways. *Journal of the American Academy of Child and Adolescent Psychiatry, 33,* 1236–1245.

Schoenfeld-Smith, K., Petroski, G. F., Hewett, J. E., Johnson, J. C., Wright, G. E., Smarr, K. L., Walker, S. E., & Parker, J. C. (1996). A biopsychosocial model of disability in rheumatoid arthritis. *Arthritis Care Research, 9,* 368–375.

Smith, T. W. (1992). Hostility and health: Current status of a psychosomatic hypothesis. *Health Psychology, 11,* 139–150.

Smith, T. W. (1995). Assessment and modification of coronary-prone behavior: A transactional view of the person in social context. In A. J. Goreczny (Ed.), *Handbook of health and rehabilitation psychology* (pp. 197–217). New York: Plenum.

Steptoe, A. (1991). The links between stress and illness. *Journal of Psychosomatic Research, 35,* 633–644.

Temoshok, L. (1990). On attempting to articulate the biopsychosocial model: Psychological–psychophysiological homeostasis. In H. Friedman (Ed.), *Personality and disease* (pp. 38–64). New York: Wiley.

Vandvik, I. H., Fagertun, H., & Hoyeraal, H. M. (1991). Prediction of short term prognosis by biopsychosocial variables in patients with juvenile rheumatic diseases. *Journal of Rheumatology, 18,* 125–132.

Vandvik, I. H., & Eckblad, G. (1991). Mothers of children with recent onset of rheumatic disease: Associations between maternal distress, psychosocial variables, and the disease of the children. *Developmental Behavioral Pediatrics, 12,* 84–91.

Vandvik, I. H., & Hoyeraal, H. M. (1993). Juvenile chronic arthritis: A biobehavioral disease; some unsolved questions. *Clinical and Experimental Rheumatology, 11,* 669–680.

Weiner, H. (1991). From simplicity to complexity (1950–1990): The case of peptic ulceration: 1. Human studies. *Psychosomatic Medicine, 53,* 467–490.

Wood, B. L. (1996). A developmental biopsychosocial approach to the treatment of chronic illness in children and adolescents. In R. H. Mikesell, D. Lusterman, & S. H. McDaniel (Eds.), *Integrating family therapy: Handbook of family psychology and systems theory* (pp. 437–458). Washington, DC: American Psychological Association.

SCHIZOAFFECTIVE DISORDER
("SCHIZOPHRENIA & OTHER PSYCHOTIC DISORDERS")

Braden, W. (1984). Vulnerability and schizoaffective psychosis: A two-factor model. *Schizophrenia Bulletin, 10,* 71–86.

SCHIZOPHRENIA
("SCHIZOPHRENIA & OTHER PSYCHOTIC DISORDERS")

Asarnow, R. F., Asarnow, J. R., & Strandburg, R. (1989). Schizophrenia: A developmental perspective. In D. Cicchetti (Ed.), *Rochester Symposium on Developmental Psychopathology: Vol. 1. The emergence of a discipline* (pp. 189–220). Hillsdale, NJ: Erlbaum.

Brenner, H. D., Roder, V., Hodel, B., Kienzle, N., Reed, D., & Liberman, R. P. (1994). *Integrated psychological therapy for schizophrenic patients (IPI).* Gottinger, Germany: Hogrefe & Huber.

Dawson, M. E., & Nuechterlein, K. H. (1987). The role of autonomic dysfunctions within a vulnerability–stress model of schizophrenic disorders. In D. Magnusson & A. Ohman (Eds.), *Psychopathology: An interactional perspective* (pp. 41–57). Orlando, FL: Academic Press.

Eaton, W. W. (1980). A formal theory of selection for schizophrenia. *American Journal of Sociology, 86,* 149–157.

Eaton, W. W., Day, R., & Kramer, M. (1986). A formal theory of selection for schizophrneia. In M. Tsuang & J. Simpson (Eds.), *Handbook of schizophrenia* (Vol. 4). Amsterdam: Elsevier.

Fowles, D. C. (1992). Schizophrenia: Diathesis–stress revisited. *Annual Review of Psychology, 43,* 303–336.

Gottesman, I. I. (1991). *Schizophrenia genesis: The origins of madness.* New York: Freeman.

Gottesman, I. I., & Shields, J. (1967). A polygenic theory of schizophrenia. *Proceedings of the National Academy of Sciences, United States of America, 58,* 199–205.

Gottesman, I. I., & Shields, J. (1971). Schizophrenia: Geneticism and environmentalism. *Human Heredity, 21,* 517–522.

Grinker, R. R., & Harrow, M. (Eds.). (1987). *Clinical research in schizophrenia: A multidimensional approach.* Springfield, IL: Thomas.

Katschnig, H. (1991). Vulnerability models for schizophrenia: Discussion. In H. Hafner & W. F. Gattaz (Eds.), *Search for the causes of schizophrenia* (Vol. II, pp. 221–226). New York: Springer-Verlag.

Kavanagh, D. J. (1992). Recent developments in expressed emotion and schizophrenia. *British Journal of Psychiatry, 160,* 601–620.

Leff, J. (1987). A model of schizophrenic vulnerability to environmental factors. In H. Hafner, W. F. Gattaz, & W. Janzarik (Eds.), *Search for the causes of schizophrenia* (pp. 317–330). New York: Springer-Verlag.

Mednick, S. A. (1970). Breakdown in individuals at high risk for schizophrenia: Possible predispositional perinatal factors. *Mental Hygiene, 54,* 50–61.

Mednick, S. A., & Schulsinger, F. (1968). Some premorbid characteristics related to breakdown in children with schizophrenic mothers. In D. Rosenthal & S. Kety (Eds.), *The transmission of schizophrenia.* Oxford, England: Pergamon.

Meehl, P. E. (1962). Schizotaxia, schizotypy, schizophrenia. *American Psychologist, 17,* 827–838.

Meehl, P. E. (1989). Schizotaxia revisited. *Archives of General Psychiatry, 46,* 935–944.

Meehl, P. E. (1990). Toward an integrated theory of schizotaxia, schizotypy, and schizophrenia. *Journal of Personality Disorders, 4,* 1–99.

Mirsky, A. F., & Duncan, C. C. (1986). Etiology and expression of schizophrenia: Neurobiological and psychosocial factors. *Annual Review of Psychology, 37,* 291–319.

Neuchterlein, K. H. (1987). Vulnerability models for schizophrenia: State of the art. In H. Hafner, W. F. Gattax, & W. Janzarik (Eds.), *Search for the causes of schizophrenia* (pp. 297–316). New York: Springer.

Neuchterlein, K. H., & Dawson, M. E. (1984). A heuristic vulnerability–stress model of schizophrenia episodes. *Schizophrenia Bulletin, 10,* 300–312.

Waltzer, H. (1982). The biopsychosocial model for brief inpatient treatment of the schizophrenic syndrome. *Psychiatric Quarterly, 54,* 97–108.

Zubin, J., & Spring, B. J. (1977). Vulnerability: A new view of schizophrenia. *Journal of Abnormal Psychology, 86,* 103–126.

Zubin, J. (1986). Models for the aetiology of schizophrenia. In G. D. Burrows, T. R. Norman, & F. Rubinstein (Eds.), *Handbook of studies on schizophrenia, Part 1* (pp. 97–104). Amsterdam: Elsevier.

SOMATIZATION DISORDER ("SOMATOFORM DISORDERS")

Kellner, R. (1985). Functional somatic symptoms and hypochondriasis. *Archives of General Psychiatry, 42,* 821–833.

Kellner, R. (1990). Somatization: Theories and research. *Journal of Nervous and Mental Disease, 178,* 150–160.

Kirmayer, L. J., Robbins, J. M., & Paris, J. (1994). Somatoform disorders: Personality and the social matrix of somatic distress. *Journal of Abnormal Psychology, 103,* 125–136.

Miller, L. (1984). Neuropsychological concepts of somatoform disorders. *International Journal of Psychiatry in Medicine, 14,* 31–46.

SUBSTANCE-RELATED DISORDERS
("SUBSTANCE-RELATED DISORDERS")

Chiauzzi, E. J. (1991). *Preventing relapse in the addictions: A biopsychosocial approach.* Elmsford, NY: Pergamon.

Donovan, D. M. (1988). Assessment of addictive behaviors: Implications of an emerging biopsychosocial model. In D. M. Donovan & G. A. Marlatt (Eds.), *Assessment of addictive behaviors* (pp. 3–48). New York: Guilford.

Donovan, J. A. (1986). An etiological model of alcoholism. *American Journal of Psychiatry, 143,* 1–11.

Ewing, J. A. (1980). Biopsychosocial approaches to drinking and alcoholism. In W. E. Fann, I. Karacan, A. D. Pokorny, & R. L. Williams (Eds.), *Phenomenology and treatment of alcoholism.* New York: Spectrum.

Galizio, M., & Maisto, S. A. (1985b). Toward a biopsychosocial theory of substance abuse. In M. Galizio & S. A. Maisto (Eds.), *Determinants of substance abuse: Biological, psychological, and environmental factors* (pp. 425–429). New York: Plenum.

Hawkins, J. D., Catalano, R. F., & Miller, J. Y. (1992). Risk and protective factors for alcohol and other drug problems in adolescence and early adulthood: Implications for substance abuse prevention. *Psychological Bulletin, 112,* 64–105.

Kumpfer, K. L. (1987). Special populations: Etiology and prevention of vulnerability to chemical dependency in children of substance abusers. In B. S. Brown & A. R. Mills (Eds.), *Youth at high risk for substance abuse.* National Institute on Drug Abuse, DHHS Publication No. (ADM) 87-1537. Washington, DC: U.S. Government Printing Office.

Marlatt, G. A., Baer, J. S., Donovan, D. M., & Kivlahan, D. R. (1988). Addictive behaviors: Etiology and treatment. *Annual Review of Psychology, 39,* 223–252.

McKirnan, D. J., & Peterson, P. L. (1988). Stress, expectancies, and vulnerability to substance abuse: A test of a model among homosexual men. *Journal of Abnormal Psychology, 97,* 461–466.

Moos, R. H., & Finney, J. W. (1983). The expanding scope of alcoholism treatment evaluation. *American Psychologist, 38,* 1036–1044.

Newcomb, M. D., Bentler, P. M., & Fahy, B. (1987). Cocaine use and psychopathology: Associations among young adults. *International Journal of the Addictions, 22,* 1167–1188.

Newcomb, M. D., & Earleywine, M. (1996). Intrapersonal contributors to drug use: The willing host. *American Behavioral Scientist, 39,* 823–837.

Pihl, R. O., & Peterson, J. B. (1992). Etiology. *Annual review of addictions research and treatment.* New York: Pergamon.

Sutker, P. B., & Allain, A. N. (1988). Issues in personality conceptualizations of addictive behaviors. *Journal of Consulting and Clinical Psychology, 56,* 172–188.

Tarter, R. E. (1988). The high-risk paradigm in alcohol and drug abuse research. In R. W. Pickens & D. S. Svikis (Eds.), *Biological vulnerability to drug abuse* (pp. 73–86). Rockville, MD: National Institute on Drug Abuse.

Tarter, R. E., & Edwards, K. L. (1988). Vulnerability to alcohol and drug abuse: A behavior–genetic view. In S. Peele (Ed.), *Visions of addiction: Major contemporary perspective on addiction and alcoholism* (pp. 67–84). Lexington, MA: Lexington Books.

MISCELLANEOUS PSYCHOPATHOLOGICAL CONDITIONS

Asberg, M., Martensson, B., & Wagner, A. (1987). Psychobiological aspects of suicidal behavior. In D. Magnusson & A. Ohman (Eds.), *Psychopathology: An interactional perspective* (pp. 81–94). Orlando, FL: Academic Press.

Berman, M. E. (1997). Biopsychosocial approaches to understanding human aggression: The first 30 years. *Clinical Psychology Review, 17,* 585–588.

Bjorntorp, P., & Brodoff, B. (Eds.). (1992). *Obesity.* Philadelphia: Lippincott.

Bonner, R. L., & Rich, A. R. (1987). Toward a predictive model of suicidal ideation and behavior: Some preliminary data in college students. *Suicide and Life Threatening Behavior, 17,* 50–63.

Brownell, K. D., & Wadden, T. A. (1992). Etiology and treatment of obesity: Understanding a serious, prevalent, and refractory disorder. *Journal of Consulting and Clinical Psychology, 60,* 505–517.

Cadoret, R., & Cain, C. (1981). Environmental and genetic factors in predicting adolescent antisocial behavior in adoptees. *Psychiatric Journal of the University of Ottawa, 6,* 220–225.

Cadoret, R. J., Yates, W. R., Troughton, E., Woodworth, G., & Stewart, M. A. (1995). Genetic–environmental interaction in the genesis of aggressivity and conduct disorders. *Archives of General Psychiatry, 52,* 916–924.

Chermack, S. T., & Giancola, P. R. (1997). The relation between alcohol and aggression: An integrated biopsychosocial conceptualization. *Clinical Psychology Review, 17,* 621–649.

Ellis, L. (1991). A synthesized (biosocial) theory of rape. *Journal of Consulting and Clinical Psychology, 59,* 631–642.

Raine, A., Venables, P. H., & Williams, M. (1995). High autonomic arousal and electrodermal orienting at age 15 years as protective factors against criminal behavior at age 29 years. *American Journal of Psychiatry, 152,* 1595–1600.

Schotte, D. E., & Clum, G. A. (1987). Problem-solving skills in suicidal psychiatric patients. *Journal of Consulting and Clinical Psychology, 55,* 49–54.

Name Index

Subject Index

ABOUT THE AUTHOR

DONALD J. KIESLER is Professor and former Director of the doctoral program in clinical psychology at Virginia Commonwealth University in Richmond, Virginia.

ISBN 0-275-96570-8